freaks in the world of writers, since almost all of the other ink-stained wretches in that world reveal a lot about themselves to readers. We call these revelations, accidental and intentional, elements of style.

These revelations tell us as readers what sort of person it is with whom we are spending time. Does the writer sound ignorant or informed, stupid or bright, crooked or honest, humorless or playful —? And on and on.

Why should you examine your writing style with the idea of improving it? Do so as a mark of respect for your readers, whatever you're writing. If you scribble your thoughts any which way, your readers will surely feel that you care nothing about them. They will mark you down as an egomaniac or a chowderhead — or, worse, they will stop reading you.

The most damning revelation you can make about yourself is that you do not know what is interesting and what is not. Don't you yourself like or dislike writers

the girl next door will do.

2. Do not ramble, though

I won't ramble on about that.

3. Keep it simple

As for your use of language: Remember that two great masters of language, William Shakespeare and James Joyce, wrote sentences which were almost childlike when their subjects were most profound. "To be or not to be?" asks Shakespeare's Hamlet. The longest word is three letters long. Joyce, when he was frisky, could put together a sentence as intricate and as glittering as a necklace for Cleopatra, but my favorite sentence in his short story "Eveline" is this one: "She was tired." At that point in the story, no other words could break the heart of a reader as those three words do.

English was the novelist Joseph Conrad's third language, and much that seems piquant in his use of English was no doubt colored by his first language, which was Polish. And lucky indeed is the writer who has grown up in Ireland, for the English spoken there is so amusing and musical. I myself grew up in Indianapolis, where common speech sounds like a band saw cutting galvanized tin,

To be or not to be?

Should I act upon the urgings that I feel, or remain passive and thus cease to exist?

"Keep it simple. Shakespeare did, with Hamlet's famous soliloquy.

PITY
THE
READER

Kurt Vonnegut, Barnstable Bay, Massachusetts, 1969.
Photo: Suzanne McConnell.

Kurt Vonnegut
AND SUZANNE McCONNELL

PITY
THE
READER

ON WRITING
WITH STYLE

New York • Oakland • London

SEVEN STORIES PRESS
140 Watts Street
New York, NY 10013
www.sevenstories.com

College professors and high school and middle school teachers may
order free examination copies of Seven Stories Press titles.
To order, visit www.sevenstories.com
or send a fax on school letterhead to (212) 226-1411.

Library of Congress Cataloging–in–Publication Data
Names: Vonnegut, Kurt, author. | McConnell, Suzanne, author.
Title: Pity the reader : on writing with style /
Kurt Vonnegut, Suzanne McConnell.
Description: Seven Stories Press first edition. | New York : Seven Stories Press, 2019.
| Includes bibliographical references.
Identifiers: LCCN 2019023380 | ISBN 9781609809621 (hardcover)
Subjects: LCSH: Vonnegut, Kurt--Technique. | Vonnegut, Kurt--Anecdotes. |
Vonnegut, Kurt--Criticism and interpretation. | Fiction--Authorship.
Classification: LCC PS3572.O5 A6 2019 | DDC 813/.54--dc23
LC record available at https://lccn.loc.gov/2019023380

Book design by Stewart Cauley

Printed in the USA.

9 8 7 6 5 4 3 2 1

FOR ALL MY STUDENTS, PAST AND FUTURE,
AND FOR ALL OF KURT'S.

"Write like a human being. Write like a writer."

KURT VONNEGUT JR.
to his students at Iowa Writers' Workshop, 1966

CONTENTS

INTRODUCTION

Here we go again with real life and opinions made to look like one big, preposterous animal not unlike an invention by Dr. Seuss, the great writer and illustrator of children's books, like an oobleck or a grinch or a lorax, or like a sneech perhaps.
—KURT VONNEGUT, *Fates Worse than Death*

I was a student of Kurt Vonnegut Jr.'s at the University of Iowa Writers' Workshop in the late '60s, and we remained friends from those years until his death. I gained a great deal of wisdom from him as a writer, as a teacher, and as a human being. This book is intended to be the story of Vonnegut's advice for *all* writers, teachers, readers, and everyone else.

Vonnegut was not famous when he started teaching at the Iowa Writers' Workshop. He'd published four novels. He was working on *Slaughterhouse-Five*. He was forty-two years old.

The first time I saw him (and I didn't know who he was), he struck my funny bone. He stood in front of a lecture hall with the other writers who were to be our teachers. He was tall, with curving shoulders (a man shaped like a banana, as he once described himself), and he was smoking a cigarette in a long black cigarette holder, tilting his head and exhaling smoke, with a clear awareness of the absurdity and affectedness of it: in other words, he had—as Oscar Wilde said is the first duty in life—assumed a pose.

He was, I learned later, seriously trying to reduce the effects of smoking by using the cigarette holder.

The Iowa MFA was a two-year program, long enough so that students eventually gravitated, as if by osmosis, to teachers with whom they had an affinity. I found my way to Vonnegut's workshop classes by my second year.

Meanwhile I read *Cat's Cradle* and *Mother Night*, the two books he'd most recently published. So I became acquainted with him as a writer through those novels at the same time as I was getting to know him as a teacher and a person.

I lived next door to the Vonnegut family my first year, in a place inhabited by grad students called Black's Gaslight Village. Our geography continued to be adjacent. I visited Kurt in Barnstable, saw him in Michigan when I first taught and he lectured there, moved to New York City about the same time he did, and for the last thirty-five years have spent summers an hour from where he lived for two decades on Cape Cod. Kurt and I had lunch occasionally, wrote letters, spoke on the phone, ran into each other at events. He sent a lovely blown-glass vase as a wedding present. We never lost touch.

You probably met Vonnegut also through reading his books, assigned in high school or college or read independently, depending on your age. If you read *Slaughterhouse-Five*, the most well known, you also know the experience that drove him to write that book because he introduces it in the opening chapter: as a twenty-year-old American of German ancestry in World War II, he was captured by the Germans and taken to Dresden, which was then firebombed by the British and Americans. He and his fellow prisoners, taken to an underground slaughterhouse, survived. Not many other people, animals, or vegetation did.

That event, and others, fueled his writing and shaped his views. (It did not, however, as is often assumed, initiate it. He was already headed in the direction of being a writer when he enlisted.) I intend to guide you through the maze of his advice like a director-puppeteer, relating experiences from his life when they shed light on how he obtained the wisdom he imparts; specifying, insofar as possible, from what point in his life a piece of advice derived—as a beginner, mid-career, or a mature writer; and telling anecdotes about him and from my own life, when relevant.

I was asked to write this book at the behest of the Vonnegut Trust. Dan Wakefield was supposed to do it. But exhausted from compiling two other marvelous books of Vonnegut work, *Letters*, an annotated selection of letters, and *If This Isn't Nice, What Is?*, an anthology of speeches, and yearning to return to his own fiction, he phoned me. "You're the perfect person to do this book," he said, persuasively. "You've been a teacher of writing, you're a fiction writer yourself, you were his student, and you knew him. It's a great fit."

About 60 percent of it had to be the words of Kurt Vonnegut. Otherwise, how it was composed would be entirely up to me.

All I had to do, Dan said, was write an introductory proposal, and send it and the profiles I had published on Vonnegut in the *Brooklyn Rail* and *Writer's Digest*, as evidence of my capability and writing style, to the head of the Vonnegut Trust, Vonnegut's friend and lawyer Don Farber, and the e-book publisher Arthur

Klebanoff, head of RosettaBooks. Dan Wakefield had already told them about me.

A month later, while volunteering at the Kurt Vonnegut Museum and Library table at the Brooklyn Book Fair, the library's director, Julia Whitehead, introduced me to Dan Simon, the founder of Seven Stories Press, who had published the final two books by Vonnegut, and knew him well. I explained this project. Simon murmured, "I'd love to publish that book." The result was a new contract between the Vonnegut Trust, RosettaBooks, Seven Stories Press, and myself. Voilà. Whatever form you're reading this in, we've got you covered.

Wilfred Sheed said of Vonnegut, "He won't be trussed up by an ism, even a good one." He preferred to "play his politics, and even his pacifism, by ear."[1] Vonnegut was prone to seeing the other side of the coin, ambiguity, and contradiction.

He had, after all, been captured, imprisoned, and forced into labor carting corpses by an enemy regime rotten with idolatry, decayed by a people's desire for easy, authoritarian solutions.

He would appreciate this palindrome by Swiss artist André Thomkins: "DOGMA I AM GOD."

For my part, I want to avert, as much as possible, my own and the reader's impulse to make dogma out of Kurt Vonnegut's advice. One way I hope to accomplish that is by adopting the concept of "endarkenment."

It's borrowed from *Profound Simplicity* by Will Schutz, published in 1979, "the one book that gives meaning to the Human Potential Movement," according to the cover. Schutz, a leading psychiatrist in that movement, lists his credentials early on: he'd explored every mind-, body-, and soul-expanding avenue the movement had yielded up. He'd also led innumerable seminars at Esalon Institute. It's a concise, down-to-earth, truly helpful book (presently out of print). But the part that has stuck with me for forty years is his final chapter, "Endarkenment." It begins, "Sometimes my striving toward growth becomes the object of amusement to the part of me that is watching me." He tired, occasionally, of that striving and rebelled.

So he devised a workshop called "Endarkenment." In it the participants were encouraged to be devious, superficial, and to wallow in their self-made misery. They drank hard, smoked like chimneys, stuffed themselves with junk food, and blamed everybody else for their problems, starting with the other workshop members all the way up to Almighty God. In teaching sessions, each person divulged their worst trait and explained how the others could acquire it. One man said he never finished things. He promised he'd teach the group how to do that the following Wednesday. When Wednesday came, he had dropped out of the workshop.

The results of the Endarkenment workshops were startling. They were as effective as regular workshops in raising people's awareness of the human comedy, and in realizing that they themselves chose what they did and that therefore they could make other choices.

I've adapted the word "endarkenment" and redefined it to use as a guiding principle. When alternatives, ironies, warnings about, or contradictions to previous advice or ideas pop up, the concept of endarkenment is at work. (Originally the word in bold marked those places, but these intrusions bit the dust in the editing process). This term and methodology, I hope, will trigger the notions that truth (not the same as facts) can be many sided, and that Vonnegut was a human being, not a dogma god.[2]

Right after I was offered this project, Julia Whitehead turned me on to artist Tim Youd, who had just been doing a performance at the Kurt Vonnegut Museum and Library. His art? Retyping novels, using the typewriter model that the writer used, in the same place where the writer worked or the novel takes place. He types the entire novel using the same page over and over, with a cushioning sheet beneath, reading aloud, "sort of in a mumble," to keep his place and stay engaged. The page rips. He applies masking tape and continues. The accidental punctures and tears create the tangible work of art: at the end, he separates the top and bottom sheets and frames each.

At the Kurt Vonnegut Museum and Library, Tim Youd typed *Breakfast of Champions* one week and *Slapstick* the second, using an electric Smith Corona Coronamatic 2200.

Tim Youd, Kurt Vonnegut's *Breakfast of Champions*, 2013, typewriter ink on paper. 303 pages typed on a Smith Corona Coronamatic 2200, Kurt Vonnegut Museum and Library, Indianapolis, Indiana, September 2013.

"The experience of immersing myself for two solid weeks gave me an appreciation of Vonnegut's genius. And especially of his bleakness," Youd said.

One of Youd's purposes is to focus people's attention on the writer's work. "We've come to the point where we're more interested in looking at the scrolls of Kerouac than reading Kerouac. The same with Hemingway's home in Key West." Fetishism of famous writers, he suggested, occurs because "it's such heavy-lifting to actually read books."

Swag proliferates around Vonnegut: mugs, greeting cards, bookmarks, note cards, mouse pads, T-shirts. Indianapolis sports a mural of him on a downtown wall. His phrases name coffee shops, bars, bands. People tattoo his quotes on themselves.

Whether these artifacts honor or defile, act as talisman or kitsch, only God and the individual can know.

Tim Youd acknowledges that his own performances may contribute to fetishism. I fear contributing as well. Because I've taken Vonnegut's marvelous words out of context. I've shifted, shortened, somersaulted, and squished them into molds for the purposes of this book.

It's like the quotes of Vonnegut's that appear frequently online. They're out of context, like anyone's quotes, and sometimes misleading. For example, his rules for writing the short story, listed in the short story collection *Bagombo Snuff Box*, aren't intended to apply to the novel. But they pop up as rules for writing all fiction.

A person could read *Pity the Reader* without ever reading Vonnegut's fiction. But his words within these pages belong first in their proper homes, where they were born.

When Dan Wakefield published his first best-selling novel in the '50s, his publisher, who was also Vonnegut's, asked Vonnegut if he would be Wakefield's editor. That editorial work, Dan says, "consisted of a two-page letter to me with seven suggestions for improving my novel. I carried out four of the seven, and my novel was better for it. Most important of all was his advice that I should not follow any of his suggestions 'just because I suggested them.' He emphasized that I should only carry out those suggestions 'that ring a bell with you.' He said I should not write or change anything simply because he (or any other editor or writer) suggested it *unless* the suggestions fit my own intention and vision for the book." Wakefield says it was "one of the most valuable editorial lessons I ever learned."

Looking back at Vonnegut's assignments at the Writers' Workshop now, I see that more importantly than the craft of writing, they were designed to teach us to do our own thinking, to find out who we were, what we loved, abhorred, what set off our trip wires, what tripped up our hearts.

It's my ambition that Vonnegut's words in this book will provoke similar effects for readers.

Kurt Vonnegut said:

> When I write, I feel like an armless, legless man with a crayon in his mouth.[3]

Is this advice? It is for me. It says: You can do it. Every writer feels inept. Even Kurt Vonnegut. Just stick to your chair and keep on typing.

What's more, though, and uniquely Vonnegut-esque, is that it's outrageously comic and demands perspective. Because I'm fortunate. I'm not armless or legless, and I have more than a crayon. Don't most of you?

And so it goes as good advice for teachers who despair of teaching, for readers who don't understand a difficult text, for anybody tackling anything and feeling inadequate to the task. That just about takes in all of us. Carry on! Cheer up! Have a good laugh! We're all inadequate to our tasks!

———

Vonnegut was fueled as a writer by humanitarian issues he wanted to bring to the attention of others. Those of us who were his students were fortunate. But his readers are his largest, most important student body.

As a teacher at the Writers' Workshop, Vonnegut was passionate, indignant. He wheezed with laughter. He was considerate, sharp, witty, entertaining, and smart. In other words, he was similar to the author of his books. Though not without protective poses, he was very much himself—the same funny, earnest, truth-seeking, plainspoken Hoosier—whenever he spoke and in whatever he wrote.

Kurt Vonnegut was always teaching. He was always learning and passing on what he learned.

I have assigned Vonnegut's stories, novels, and essays to a wide spectrum of students. His work crosses borders of age, ethnicity, and time. Two of the best assignments and liveliest, most effective classes I've ever taught were inspired by *Cat's Cradle*—one in an Introduction to Literature class in the late '60s at Delta Community College, and the other in a Literature of the '60s class shortly after September 11 in 2001 at Hunter College—thirty years apart.

What I hope we will be doing here, to quote Vonnegut on the pleasure of reading stories, is "eavesdropping on a fascinating conversation" that he was having with his readers.

I am reminded of the way one begins a letter to an anonymous but responsible and hopefully responsive person: "To Whom It May Concern." This phrase may sound formal and removed to some, since that's how it's usually used. But please take it literally and as it's meant here, as a warm welcome: TO ALL WHOM IT MAY CONCERN.

CHAPTER 1
ADVICE FOR EVERYONE ON WRITING ANYTHING

> **When I teach—and I've taught at the Iowa Writers' Workshop for a couple of years, at City College, Harvard—I'm not looking for people who want to be writers. I'm looking for people who are passionate, who care terribly about something.**
> —KURT VONNEGUT, *Like Shaking Hands with God*

In 1980, the International Paper Company sponsored an advice series in the *New York Times*. Each two-page piece was composed by a well-known expert. Each featured the principal points in headline bold, with illustrations and further explanation beneath. They included "How to Make a Speech" by George Plimpton, "... Write a Resume" by Jerrold Simon of Harvard Business School, "... Enjoy Poetry" by James Dickey, and so on.

"In view of the fact that I had nearly flunked chemistry, mechanical engineering, and anthropology, and had never taken a course in literature or composition, I was elected to write about literary style," Kurt Vonnegut said of his contribution.[4]

I spotted Vonnegut's "How to Write with Style" in the *Times* when it was first published, and handed out copies of it every semester after to my writing students at Hunter College. That's the Vonnegut format I'll follow to begin with here. It offers general advice directed to everyone, about writing anything, including seven numbered "rules."

There is a five-paragraph introduction. Then Vonnegut offers this first, most important, suggestion: **"Find a subject you care about."**

Notice *how* he writes that. He assumes that, since you're a human being, you care about something. All you have to do is search around in the storehouse of yourself and locate it. Beneath the bold headline, though, his complete sentence is more complex:

> Find a subject you care about *and which you in your heart feel others should care about* [italics mine]. It is this genuine caring, and not your games with language, which will be the most compelling and seductive element in your style.
>
> I am not urging you to write a novel, by the way— although I would not be sorry if you wrote one, provided you genuinely cared about something. A petition to the mayor about a pothole in front of your house or a love letter to the girl next door will do.[5]

The following anecdote will illustrate his complete sincerity in what he says about these comparatively humble forms. Discussing his six children in *Palm Sunday*, he talks about interests and artistic proclivities he feels he bequeathed them, in woodworking, drawing, music, and chess. At that time, his son Mark had published his first book, and his daughter Edie had illustrated a published book. He praises those achievements, along with the artistic and general productivity of his other children, but saves his highest praise for a letter his daughter Nanette wrote to a complete stranger.

> What is my favorite among all the works of art my children

have so far produced? It is perhaps a letter written by my youngest daughter Nanette. It is so *organic*! She wrote it to "Mr. X," an irascible customer at a Cape Cod restaurant where she worked as a waitress in the summer of 1978. The customer was so mad about the service he had received one evening, you see, that he had complained in writing to the management. The management posted the letter on the kitchen bulletin board.

Nanette's reply went like this:

Dear Mr. X,

As a newly trained waitress I feel that I must respond to the letter of complaint which you recently wrote to the ABC Inn. Your letter has caused more suffering to an innocent young woman this summer than the inconvenience you experienced in not receiving your soup on time and having your bread taken away prematurely and so on.

I believe that you did in fact receive poor service from this new waitress. I recall her as being very flustered and upset that evening, but she hoped that her errors, clumsy as they were, would be understood sympathetically as inexperience. I myself have made mistakes in serving. Fortunately, the customers were humorous and compassionate. I have learned so much from these mistakes, and through the support and understanding of other waitresses and customers in the span of only one week, that I feel confident now about what I am doing, and seldom make mistakes.

There is no doubt in my mind that Katharine is on her way to becoming a competent waitress. You must understand that learning how to waitress is very much the same as learning how to juggle. It is difficult to find the correct balance and timing. Once these are found, though, waitressing becomes a solid and unshakable skill.

There must be room for error even in such a finely tuned establishment as the ABC Inn. There must be allowance for waitresses being human. Maybe you did not realize that in naming this young woman you made it necessary for the management to fire her. Katharine is now without a summer job on Cape Cod, and school is ahead.

Can you imagine how difficult it is to find jobs here now? Do you know how hard it is for many young students to make ends meet these days? I feel it is my duty as a human being to ask you to think twice about what is of importance in life. I hope that in all fairness you will think about what I have said, and that in the future you will be more thoughtful and humane in your actions.

Sincerely,
Nanette Vonnegut.[6]

I myself have uncommon sympathy for the contents of Nanette's letter. My first published story was from the point of view of a dishwasher in a restaurant who exacts revenge upon an oppressive boss.[7] I waitressed my way through college. Later I discovered it paid as well as adjunct teaching. As the poet Jane Hershfield quips, many writers have been in "the food trades."[8]

At any rate, Nanette's letter fulfills her father's primary criteria. She cares enough about her subject to write the letter and she thinks others should care: specifically, her boss, the man who complained, the waitress in question, and presumably the other employees at the restaurant.

Nanny's letter is quite serious. But you can write about a serious subject in a playful way. God knows, Kurt Vonnegut did.

Thirty-one years earlier, at the age of twenty-five, Kurt wrote a contract for himself and his wife Jane to observe. They were newly married and expecting their first child.

CONTRACT between KURT VONNEGUT, JR. and
JANE C. VONNEGUT, effective as of Saturday, January
26, 1947

I, Kurt Vonnegut, Jr., that is, do hereby swear that I will
be faithful to the commitments hereunder listed:

I. With the agreement that my wife will not nag, heckle,
and otherwise disturb me on the subject, I promise to scrub
the bathroom and kitchen floors once a week, on a day and
hour of my own choosing. Not only that, but I will do a
good and thorough job, and by that she means that I will get
under the bathtub, *behind* the toilet, *under* the sink, *under* the
icebox, *into* the corners; and I will pick up and put in some
other location whatever moveable objects happen to be on
said floors at the time so as to get under them too, and not
just around them. Furthermore, while I am undertaking
these tasks I will refrain from indulging in such remarks as
"Shit," "Goddamn sonofabitch," and similar vulgarities, as
such language is nervewracking to have around the house
when nothing more drastic is taking place than the facing
of Necessity. *If I do not live up to this agreement,* my wife is to
feel free to nag, heckle and otherwise disturb me until I am
driven to scrub the floors anyway—*no matter how busy I am.*

II. I furthermore swear that I will observe the following
minor amenities:

I will hang up my clothes and put my shoes in the closet
when I am not wearing them;

I will not track dirt into the house needlessly, by such
means as not wiping my feet on the mat outside, and by
wearing my bedroom slippers to take out the garbage, and
other things;

I will throw such things as used up match folders, empty cigarette packages, the piece of cardboard that comes in shirt collars, etc., into a wastebasket instead of leaving them around on chairs and the floor;

After shaving I will put my shaving equipment back in the medicine closet;

In case I should be the direct cause of a ring around the bathtub after taking a bath, I will, with the aid of Swift's Cleanser and a brush, *not* my washcloth, remove said ring;

With the agreement that my wife collects the laundry, places it in a laundry bag, and leaves the laundry bag in plain sight in the hall, I will take said laundry to the Laundry not more than three days after said laundry has made an appearance in the hall; I will furthermore bring the *clean* laundry back from the Laundry within two weeks after I have taken it, dirty that is;

When smoking I will make every effort to keep the ashtray which I am using at the time upon a surface that does not slant, sag, slope, dip, wrinkle, or give way upon the slightest provocation; such surfaces may be understood to include stacks of books precariously mounted on the edge of a chair, the arms of the chair that has arms, and my own knees;

I will not put out cigarettes upon the sides of, or throw ashes into either the red leather waste-basket, or the stamp waste-basket which my loving wife made me for Christmas, 1945, as such practice noticeably impairs the beauty, and the ultimate practicability of said waste-baskets;

In the event that my wife makes a request of me, and that request cannot be regarded as other than reasonable and wholly within the province of a man's work (when his wife is pregnant, that is), I will comply with said request within three days after my wife has presented it: It is understood that my wife will make no reference to the subject, other than saying thank you, of course, *within these three days*; if, however, I fail to comply with said request after a more substantial length of time has elapsed, my wife shall be completely justified in nagging, heckling and otherwise disturbing me, until I am driven to do that which I should have done;

An exception to the above three-day time limit is the taking out of the garbage, which, as any fool knows, had better not wait that long; I will take out the garbage within three *hours* after the need for disposal has been pointed out to me by my wife. It would be nice, however, if, upon observing the need for disposal with my own two eyes, I should perform this particular task upon my own initiative, and thus not make it necessary for my wife to bring up a subject which is moderately distasteful to her;

It is understood that, should I find these commitments in any way unreasonable or too binding upon my freedom, I will take steps to amend them by counter-proposals, constitutionally presented and politely discussed, instead of unlawfully terminating my obligations with a simple burst of obscenity, or something like that, and the subsequent persistent neglect of said obligations;

The terms of this contract are understood to be binding up until that time after the arrival of our child, (to be specified by the doctor,) when my wife will once again be in full possession of all her faculties, and able to undertake more arduous pursuits than are now advisable.[9]

Imagine being the recipient, dear wives, of such a letter. (Especially if you were a wife in the '50s when housework was unquestionably your job.) At the least, you'd know your husband had heard your complaints. You'd know he regarded them as worthy of his attention. You'd be assured he cared enough about those complaints, about you, your marriage, and your daily getting along together, to set all this down on paper. And you'd adore him, wouldn't you? You might even forgive him the next time you emptied his overflowing ashtray.

———

Let's imagine that both of these epistles, the letter to the ABC Inn customer and the commitments contract, made a difference. Whether the inefficient waitress got her job back or not, she certainly must have felt defended. The customer and boss were invited to be more empathetic and may have become so. (I myself was fired from my first waitressing job at the age of sixteen, and I felt terrible, as if I couldn't do anything right. My niece was once left a napkin, instead of a tip, at the restaurant where she worked, upon which the customer had printed, "Please don't breed." A letter written on behalf of either of us would have been greatly appreciated.) Kurt and Jane must've gained peace from the disputes that obviously precipitated Kurt's contract.

———

The point is, writing well, even an ordinary letter or a well-considered e-mail, demands the generosity of your time, effort, and thought. You have to care enough that it's worth your energy, weighing that cost against the cost of not doing it.

———

Sometimes a subject finds you. It is not a matter of seeking what you care about. Something happens right in your face that you end up caring about so fiercely that it becomes integral to your being.

Circumstances dictated that Kurt Vonnegut Jr. write a letter home, when he was at last again on Allied territory, after being a prisoner of war. For all his relatives in Indianapolis knew, he was dead. He had been missing. He had to let them know what had happened.

FROM: Pfc. K. Vonnegut, Jr.
12102964 U.S. Army.

TO:
Kurt Vonnegut,
Williams Creek,
Indianapolis, Indiana

Dear people:

I'm told that you were probably never informed that I was anything other than "missing in action." Chances are that you also failed to receive any of the letters I wrote from Germany. That leaves me a lot of explaining to do—in precis:

I've been a prisoner of war since December 19th, 1944, when our division was cut to ribbons by Hitler's last desperate thrust through Luxemburg and Belgium. Seven Fanatical Panzer Divisions hit us and cut us off from the rest of Hodges' First Army. The other American Divisions on our flanks managed to pull out: We were obliged to stay and fight. Bayonets aren't much good against tanks: Our ammunition, food and medical supplies gave out and our casualties out-numbered those who could still fight - so we gave up. The 106th got a Presidential Citation and some British Decoration from Montgomery for it, I'm told, but I'll be damned if it was worth it. I was one of the few who weren't wounded. For that much thank God.

Well, the supermen marched us, without food, water or sleep to Limberg, a distance of about sixty miles, I think, where we were loaded and locked up, sixty men to each small, unventilated, unheated box car. There were no sanitary accommodations -- the floors were covered with fresh cow dung. There wasn't room for all of us to lie down. Half slept while the other half stood. We spent several days, including Christmas, on that Limberg siding. On Christmas Eve the Royal Air Force bombed and strafed our unmarked train. They killed about one-hundred-and-fifty of us.

We got a little water Christmas Day and moved slowly across Germany to a large P.O.W. Camp in Muhlburg, South of Berlin. We were released from the box cars on New Year's Day. The Germans herded us through scalding delousing showers. Many men died from shock in the showers after ten days of starvation, thirst and exposure. But I didn't.

Under the Geneva Convention, Officers and Non-commissioned Officers are not obliged to work when taken prisoner. I am, as you know, a Private. One-hundred-and-fifty such minor beings were shipped to a Dresden work camp on January 10th. I was their leader by virtue of the little German I spoke. It was our misfortune to have sadistic and fanatical guards. We were refused medical attention and clothing: We were given long hours at extremely hard labor. Our food ration was two-hundred-and-fifty grams of black bread and one pint of unseasoned potato soup each day. After desperately trying to improve our situation for two months and having been met with bland smiles I told the guards just what I was going to do to them when the Russians came. They beat me up a little. I was fired as group leader. Beatings were very small time: one boy starved to death and the SS Troops shot two for stealing food.

On about February 14th the Americans came over, followed by the R.A.F. their combined labors killed 250,000 people in twenty-four hours and destroyed all of Dresden—possibly the world's most beautiful city. But not me.

After that we were put to work carrying corpses from Air-Raid shelters; women, children, old men; dead from concussion, fire or suffocation. Civilians cursed us and threw rocks as we carried bodies to huge funeral pyres in the city.

When General Patton took Leipzig we were evacuated on foot to ('the Saxony-Czechoslovakian border'?). There we remained until the war ended. Our guards deserted us. On that happy day the Russians were intent on mopping up isolated outlaw resistance in our sector. Their planes (P-39's) strafed and bombed us, killing fourteen, but not me.

Eight of us stole a team and wagon. We traveled and looted our way through Sudetenland and Saxony for eight days, living like kings. The Russians are crazy about Americans. The Russians picked us up in Dresden. We rode from there to the American lines at Halle in Lend-Lease Ford trucks. We've since been flown to Le Havre.

I'm writing from a Red Cross Club in the Le Havre P.O.W. Repatriation Camp. I'm being wonderfully well fed and entertained. The state-bound ships are jammed, naturally, so I'll have to be patient. I hope to be home in a month. Once home I'll be given twenty-one days recuperation at Atterbury, about $600 back pay and—get this—sixty (60) days furlough.

I've too damned much to say, the rest will have to wait, I can't receive mail here so don't write.

May 29, 1945
Love,
Kurt—Jr.

This letter was first published posthumously in 2008, in *Armageddon in Retrospect*.[10] What is astounding about it, retrospectively, as will be apparent to all Vonnegut readers, is that in it lay the seeds of Kurt Vonnegut's style, especially in *Slaughterhouse-Five*, as well as the experience that fueled it and affected him and all his work for the rest of his life. That style is inseparable from the content of the letter.

The letter makes Kurt's own superb point about style resulting from your caring. He did not sit down and think, "Now how shall I write this with style?" or "Now, how can I write this to impress future readers?"

He was twenty-two years old. He wrote out of his deep need to communicate to his family what had happened to him. He wrote out of his amazed bewilderment at his own survival. He wrote also, perhaps, out of a consciousness of himself as one of a handful of singular witnesses to a cataclysmic event, one with enormous political and cultural implications, a "fancy" experience, as he would describe it later.

It is this genuine caring, and not your games with language, which will be the most compelling and seductive element in your style.[11]

"Form follows function," as architect Louis Sullivan famously said.

"I do feel evolution is being controlled by some sort of divine engineer," Kurt Vonnegut would tell Jon Stewart on *The Daily Show* in September 2005. "I can't help thinking that. And this engineer knows exactly what he or she is doing, and why and where evolution is headed." He paused. Stewart waited. "And that's why we've got giraffes and hippopotami and the clap."[12]

Though the divine engineer's evolutionary plan may be up for grabs, as Kurt jokes, his citing these astonishingly diverse life-forms provokes our wonder at the engineer's sense of individual design: each creature is superbly well formed for its own function and survival. Sullivan's architectural dictate is in accord.

Follow suit: Write according to your purpose.

Vonnegut had worked on his high school and college newspapers. Both were excellent. That training must have had bearing on the style of his letter home. He was reporting. He had ambitions to be a journalist. He'd taken a typewriter with him to basic training. I believe that there is something in ourselves that wants to grow in a certain direction, something fated. That's my own experience of becoming a writer. Young Kurt Vonnegut Jr. must certainly have known that this would be a seminal event in his life—one that would haunt him with the question of why he escaped injury and death when others didn't, among other things—and the letter was a document of all that as well.

The second suggestion Vonnegut makes in "How to Write with Style" is **"Do not ramble."** I won't, as he said he wouldn't, "ramble on about that."

The third is **"Keep it simple."** Some of the most profound lines in all of literature, he points out, are the simplest: "'To be or not to be?' asks Shakespeare's Hamlet."

A cartoon in the *Times* piece shows Shakespeare, finger to forehead, a billowing thought cloud above him: "Should I act upon the urgings that I feel, or remain passive and thus cease to exist?"

Vonnegut continues,

> Simplicity of language is not only reputable, but perhaps even sacred. The Bible opens with a sentence well within the writing skills of a lively fourteen-year-old: "In the beginning God created the heaven and the earth."[13]

A notion abounds that difficult writing—archaic, convoluted, or chock-full of esoteric words—is somehow elevated, more intelligent than plainspoken language. If you can't understand it, it must be really superior. Vonnegut based more than one novel on the absurdity of such premises.

Some reviewers dismissed Kurt Vonnegut's writing for being too simple. John Irving criticized Vonnegut's critics. They think,

Irving wrote, that "if the work is tortured and a ghastly effort to read, it must be serious," whereas "if the work is lucid and sharp and the narrative flows like water, we should suspect the work of being simplistic, and as light and as lacking in seriousness as fluff. This is simplistic criticism, of course; it is easy criticism too.

"Why is 'readable' such a bad thing to be these days?" Some people "are gratified by the struggle to make sense of what they read . . . I am more often gratified by a writer who has accepted the enormous effort necessary to make writing clear."[14]

Vonnegut criticized lit critics too. They wrote "rococo argle-bargle," he once said.[15]

How do you keep from rambling? How do you "keep it simple"? Take Vonnegut's fourth piece of advice: **"Have the guts to cut."**

> It may be that you, too, are capable of making necklaces for Cleopatra, so to speak. But your eloquence should be the servant of the ideas in your head. Your rule might be this: If a sentence, no matter how excellent, does not illuminate your subject in some new and useful way, scratch it out.[16]

If you have a tendency to blather or croon or lavish on the detail, one way to handle those impulses is to go right ahead—prattle, garnish and glitter.

Rather than strangle the inclinations, curbing the flow and squelching the possibility of unearthing the diamonds that might result, scratch out the excess *after* your first draft's wanderings and flourishes.

A piece of advice I myself would give anyone about writing anything is to separate the composing process from the editing process.

First write full tilt, without examining what you're writing. Let it alone for a period of time. Then read it with fresh eyes, edit and revise it. Repeat this process, ad infinitum if necessary, until you're satisfied that it's finished.

This method has become a truism among teachers of writing. "Freewriting" is a common expression.[17] Elementary school kids know it. It implies another kind of writing, a kind that is not free: it implies the constraint of editing.

Years ago, no one ever heard of freewriting. We diagrammed sentences. Doing it was a tedious but delightful game. We learned the structure of language that way. It made beautiful, geometrical sense.

I remember being instructed about an essay's structure too. We joked that it was this: say what you're going to say, then say it, then say that you've said it. Again, an essay seemed to me like a geometric form: A sentence is formed by its subject/verb/object. A paragraph is composed of sentences: a thematic statement, followed by sentences that explain or elaborate upon that point, and a concluding one that sums up or accentuates what's been said. An essay is made out of successive paragraphs. Pile them up, and there you have your essay—ta-da!

In Kurt's teaching at the Iowa Writers' Workshop, he never talked about separating the writing process from the editing process. That's because that was not how he went about writing. It's probably not how he learned to write for his school newspaper or his teachers at Shortridge High.

Asked in 1974, "Could you talk a little bit about your method of composition, how you write and rewrite successive pages one at a time?," Vonnegut answered:

There are the swoopers and there are the bashers, and I happen to be one of the bashers. That is, you beat your head against a wall until you break through to page two and you break through to page three and so forth. A lot of people write just any which way. I have absolutely no use for an electric typewriter, for instance; I still can't imagine why the damned thing was invented. But the swooper's way, you know—and I envy them too, because it must be exhilarating—is to write a book any which way in a month maybe, whack it out, and then go through it again and again and again and again. I've never been able to do that. I came close to doing it on *The Sirens*. *The Sirens* was a case of automatic writing, almost. That wasn't a bashing book because I just started and I wrote it.[18]

He swooped out *The Sirens of Titan* on long lengths of paper, Kerouac style. He taped and stapled them together end to end. At

Drafts of *Sirens of Titan*. Photo: Suzanne McConnell. Courtesy of the Lilly Library, Indiana University, Bloomington, Indiana.

Indiana University's archive of Vonnegut's work, the drafts are
kept rolled up like scrolls.

———

"How to Write with Style" was itself edited of course. Here are
some examples from it. Please note: the bracketed words *in italics*
are those the editor eliminated.

The first example is from the five-paragraph introduction:

> [*When you start to put words on paper, remember that*] The
> most damning revelation you can make about yourself is
> that you do not know what is interesting and what is not.
> Don't you yourself like or dislike writers mainly for what
> they choose to show you or make you think about? Did you
> ever admire an empty-headed writer for his or her mastery
> of the language? No.

The editor was right to cut Kurt's opening phrase. Don't you
think? The declarative sentence is stronger. Declarative sentences
usually are.[19] Knowing what's interesting has nothing to do with
"When you start," and "remember that" implies "should" and no
one wants to be scolded. Mainly, the phrase *"When you start to put
words on paper, remember that"* doesn't "illuminate your subject."

———

Kurt Vonnegut introduces his piece by saying that reporters and
technical writers are trained not to reveal themselves, but all other
writers "reveal a lot . . . to readers."

> These revelations [*are fascinating to us as readers. They*] tell
> us as readers what sort of person it is with whom we are
> spending time. Does the writer sound ignorant or informed,

[*crazy or sane,*] stupid or bright, crooked or honest, humorless or playful—? And on and on.

The editor eliminated the part about "fascinating" (including a third repetition of "readers"), and cut right to the chase: "These revelations tell us as readers what sort of person . . ." "Crazy or sane" is crossed out. There were too many of those, right? We get the idea.

And here are two sentences the editor cut from "Have the guts to cut."

[*If it were only teachers who insisted that modern writers stay close to literary styles of the past, we might reasonably ignore them. But readers insist on the very same thing. They*] want our pages to look very much like pages they have seen before.

Here's the final version:

Readers want our pages to look very much like pages they have seen before.

Why have the guts to cut? For strength. Uncluttered by distracting riffraff, fewer words, when accurate, pack more punch.

Vonnegut's fifth item of advice is **"Sound like yourself."**

The writing style which is most natural for you is bound to echo the speech you heard when a child. And lucky indeed is the writer who has grown up in Ireland, for the English spoken there is so amusing and musical. I myself grew up in Indianapolis, where common speech sounds like a band saw cutting galvanized tin, and employs a vocabulary as unornamental as a monkey wrench.

All . . . varieties of speech are beautiful, just as the varieties of butterflies are beautiful. No matter what your first language, you should treasure it all your life. If it happens to not be standard English, and if it shows itself when you write standard English, the result is usually delightful, like a very pretty girl with one eye that is green and one that is blue.[20]

Check out this array of voices to see Kurt's point. Each opens a story. None is like Vonnegut's. None is like another, any more than a thumbprint or snowflake is like another. Don't glance at the endnotes to see their sources. Just read them aloud and listen:

You would certainly be glad to meet me. I was the lady who appreciated youth. Yes, all that happy time, I was not like some. It did not go by me like a flitting dream. Tuesdays and Wednesdays was as gay as Saturday nights.[21]

The door of Henry's lunchroom opened and two men came in. They sat down at the counter.[22]

Blind people got a hummin jones if you notice. Which is understandable completely once you been around one and notice what no eyes will force you into to see people, and you get past the first time, which seems to come out of nowhere, and it's like you in church again with fat-chest ladies and old gents gruntin a hum low in the throat to whatever the preacher be saying.[23]

He had dreamed that a hundred orchards on the road to the sea village had broken into flame; and all the windless afternoon tongues of fire shot through the blossom.[24]

Aren't these lovely? Aren't they a variety, though?

In contrast to Vonnegut's criticism of his Midwestern speech, what about these colorfully accurate musical phrases of his, in which the sound echoes the sense and follows the function:

. . . where common speech sounds like a band saw cutting galvanized tin.

She radiated about as much sexuality as her grandmother's card table.[25]

The surface of Earth heaved and seethed in fecund restlessness.[26]

[The word "schizophrenia"] sounded and looked to me like a human being sneezing in a blizzard of soapflakes.[27]

Vonnegut continues:

I myself find that I trust my own writing most, and others

seem to trust it most, too, when I sound most like a person from Indianapolis, which is what I am. What alternatives do I have? The one most vehemently recommended by teachers has no doubt been pressed on you, as well: to write like cultivated Englishmen of a century or more ago.

I don't think teachers today still demand that, but they did when he was in school. And they demand other things that can be just as soul crushing.

Look at how much fun Vonnegut has spoofing these matters in *Breakfast of Champions*:

"I guess that isn't the right word," she said. She was used to apologizing for her use of language. She had been encouraged to do a lot of that in school. Most white people in Midland City were insecure when they spoke, so they kept their sentences short and their words simple, in order to keep embarrassing mistakes to a minimum. Dwayne certainly did that. Patty certainly did that.

This was because their English teachers would wince and cover their ears and give them flunking grades and so on whenever they failed to speak like English aristocrats before the First World War. Also: they were told that they were unworthy to speak or write their language if they couldn't love or understand incomprehensible novels and poems and plays about people long ago and far away, such as *Ivanhoe*.

. . .

The black people would not put up with this. They went on talking English every *which* way. They refused to read books they couldn't understand—on the grounds they couldn't understand them. They would ask such impudent questions as, "Whuffo I want to read no *Tale of Two Cities?* Whuffo?"

• • •

Patty Keene flunked English during the semester when she had to read and appreciate *Ivanhoe*, which was about men in iron suits and the women who loved them. And she was put in a remedial reading class, where they made her read *The Good Earth*, which was about Chinamen.[28]

———

Vonnegut didn't always trust his own Hoosier voice.

I remember I was with the theatrical producer Hilly Elkins one time. He had just bought the film rights to *Cat's Cradle*, and I was attempting to become urbane. I made some urbane remarks, and Hilly shook his head, and he said, "No, no, no. No, No. Go for Will Rogers, not for Cary Grant.

That exchange happened in the mid-'60s while he was teaching at Iowa. Kurt confessed it to us in class right after it happened. I remember his rueful laugh.

I remember this vividly because that same week my sister had visited me and I took her to class so she could have a sense of the workshop and especially of Vonnegut. But Kurt wasn't there. Kurt was in New York. Richard Yates taught that day instead. (Some sub!)

Vonnegut was having success, at last. Things were suddenly opening up for him all over the place, like selling the film rights to *Cat's Cradle*. He was finding his balance.

"I keep losing and regaining my equilibrium, which is the basic plot of all popular fiction. And I myself am a work of fiction," he prefaces the telling of this anecdote in print.[29]

"I understand now that all those antique essays and stories with which I was to compare my own work were not magnificent for their datedness or foreignness, but for saying precisely what their authors meant them to say," Kurt explains under his sixth piece of advice: **"Say what you mean to say."**

> My teachers wished me to write accurately, always selecting the most effective words, and relating the words to one another unambiguously, rigidly, like parts of a machine. The teachers did not want to turn me into an Englishman after all. They hoped that I would become understandable—and therefore understood . . . If I broke all the rules of punctuation, had words mean whatever I wanted them to mean, and strung them together higgledy-piggledy, I would simply not be understood.

And so, Vonnegut says, you had better avoid those too, "if you have something worth saying and wish to be understood."[30]

In *Breakfast of Champions*, the character Rabo Karabekian, an Abstract Expressionist painter, has sold one of his paintings to Midland City's Center for the Arts. The picture, "twenty feet wide and sixteen feet high," was painted with "a green wall paint" from a hardware store.

> The vertical stripe was dayglo orange reflecting tape . . .
> It was a scandal what the painting cost. [Fifty thousand dollars!] . . .
> Midland City was outraged.

In a bar at the inn where many of the "distinguished guests of the arts festival" are staying, Rabo Karabekian asks Bonnie MacMahon, a waitress in Midland, to tell him something about the teenaged Queen of the Festival of the Arts, whose picture—in a white bathing suit with an Olympic gold medal around her neck—adorns the cover of the arts program.

> This was the only internationally famous human being in Midland City. She was Mary Alice Miller, the Women's Two Hundred Meter Breast Stroke Champion of the World. She was only fifteen, said Bonnie. . . .
>
> . . . Mary Alice's father, who was a member of the Parole Board out at Shepherdstown, had taught Mary Alice to swim when she was eight months old, and . . . had made her swim at least four hours a day, every day, since she was three.
>
> Rabo Karabekian thought this over, and then he said loudly, so a lot of people could hear him, "What kind of a man would turn his daughter into an outboard motor?" . . .
>
> Bonnie MacMahon blew up. . . . "Oh yeah?" she said. "Oh yeah?" . . .
>
> "You don't think much of Mary Alice Miller?" she said. "Well, we don't think much of your painting. I've seen better pictures done by a five-year-old."[31]

For those of you who have not had the pleasure of reading *Breakfast of Champions*, I won't give away what the narrator calls "the spiritual climax of this book," the speech that Vonnegut discovered his character Karabekian making to the people in that bar, explaining his painting. But he does explain, eloquently.

The next chapter starts:

> Karabekian's speech had been splendidly received.

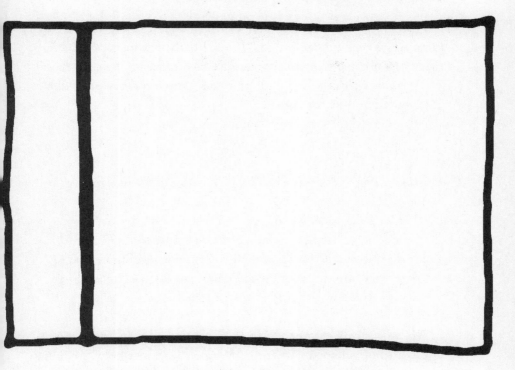

Rabo Karabekian's day–glo stripe painting in _Breakfast of Champions_.

Everybody agreed now that Midland City had one of the greatest paintings in the world.

"All you had to do was explain," said Bonnie MacMahon. "I understand now."

"I didn't think there was anything _to_ explain," said Carlo Maritino, the builder, wonderingly. "But there was, by God."

Abe Cohen, the jeweler, said to Karabekian, "If artists would explain more, people would like art more. You realize that?"[32]

An interviewer asked Hemingway how much rewriting he did. Hemingway said it depended. "I rewrote the ending to *Farewell to Arms*, the last page of it, thirty-nine times before I was satisfied."

"What was it that had stumped you?" the interviewer asked.

"Getting the words right."[33]

———

Vonnegut discovers what it is he means to say by writing:

> The messages that come out on the typewriter are very crude or foolish—misleading—but I know that if I spend enough time at the typewriter the most intelligent part of me will finally make itself known and I will be able to decode what it is trying to talk about.[34]

An early draft, maybe the first—for it is scribbled and doodled upon, and unfinished—of one of Vonnegut's most beloved short stories, "Harrison Bergeron," began, crudely, like this:

> The year was 2081, A.D.
>
> April, of course, was still the cruelest month of all. Dampness, darkness, and fear of spring's never coming were kept at bay in the little house only by the glow of the television screen. These three horsemen of despair seemed ready to smother George and Hazel Bergeron the instant the picture died.
>
> "That was a real purty dance," said Hazel.

Never mind the clumsy "horsemen" metaphor, what dance is Hazel talking about? Vonnegut scribbled in penciled additions that furnish the answers (in italics below), so the revised sentences would read:

> These three horsemen of despair seemed ready to smother

George and Hazel Bergeron the instant the picture died.
On the screen were ballerinas.
"That was a real purty dance *they just did,*" said Hazel.[35]

Now we know for certain that George and Hazel watched the dance on television, precisely when, and just what kind of dance they saw.

In the published story, the inexplicable "horsemen" reference has disappeared. Although tinkered with a bit, the explanations remain. The opening paragraph has been revised extensively. Now it's superb.

> The year was 2081, and everybody was finally equal. They weren't only equal before God and the law. They were equal every which way. Nobody was smarter than anybody else. Nobody was better looking than anybody else. Nobody was stronger or quicker than anybody else. All this equality was due to the 211th, 212th, and 213th Amendments to the Constitution, and to the unceasing vigilance of agents of the United States Handicapper General.[36]

Vonnegut revised and revised because he was fiercely aware of the skill required of his audience, and considerate.

> [Readers] have to identify thousands of little marks on paper, and make sense of them immediately. They have to read, an art so difficult that most people don't really master it even after having studied it all through grade school and high school—twelve long years.

Hence Vonnegut's seventh rule: **"Pity the readers":**

> Our audience requires us to be sympathetic and patient teachers, ever willing to simplify and clarify.[37]

Those "marks on paper" are symbols. They are not the experience itself. They represent sound, and sounds in combination. They require deciphering. They are a system of notation for the silent music of reading.

———

Human beings have not, actually, been reading very long. The first alphabet emerged about 2000 BC.[38] More than 3,000 years later, around 1100 AD, in China, Pi Sheng concocted the first moveable type, but widespread distribution or use still had to wait for centuries. About 350 years after that, in 1450 AD, Gutenberg invented the printing press. So, in sum, it took over 3,000 years from the creation of the alphabet until the mechanism to employ an alphabet was devised, and another 400 years or so before Gutenberg's press became widely utilized, enabling ordinary people to read, and printed matter to be disseminated as a matter of course.

Some people's brains don't function well at deciphering letters arranged on paper. Dyslexia is "a specific learning disability in reading." It's neurological, often genetic, and has nothing to do with intelligence or instruction. It can cause people trouble with reading fluently, out loud, and/or with comprehension. It can stunt vocabulary growth and make for some creative spellers. It can create self-doubt and insecurity. An estimated 15 percent of Americans are dyslexics.[39]

Even if a person has a brain that does translate letters accurately, it takes all of one's school life to learn how to read, as Vonnegut points out. Even then, many people find it difficult. Thirty-two million adults in the US can't read. That's 14 percent of Americans, about one in seven. And 21 percent read below a fifth grade level. These statistics may include those who are dyslexic.[40]

Kurt calls reading an "art." You are not born with it. You must learn how to do it, and as with any art, you can keep gaining skill and pleasure in it for the rest of your life.

Take a look at the pains that Vonnegut took to enable his readers to understand and visualize a key concept, that of ice-nine, in *Cat's Cradle*. He accomplishes this by having a character, Dr. Breed, supposedly an expert on it, teach the narrator. We, the readers, learn with him.

"There are several ways," Dr. Breed said to me, "in which certain liquids can crystallize—can freeze—several ways in which their atoms can stack and lock in an orderly, rigid way."

That old man with spotted hands invited me to think of the several ways in which cannonballs might be stacked on a courthouse lawn, of the several ways in which oranges might be packed into a crate.

"So it is with atoms in crystals, too; and two different crystals of the same substance can have quite different physical properties." . . .

"Now think about cannonballs on a courthouse lawn or about oranges in a crate again," he suggested. And he helped me to see that the pattern of the bottom layer of cannonballs or of oranges determined how each subsequent layer would stack and lock. "The bottom layer is the seed of how every cannonball or every orange that comes after is going to behave, even to an infinite number of cannonballs or oranges."

"Now suppose," chortled Dr. Breed, enjoying himself, "that there were many possible ways in which water could crystallize, could freeze. Suppose that the sort of ice we skate upon and put into highballs—what we might call *ice-one*—is only one of several types of ice. Suppose water always froze as *ice-one* on Earth because it had never had a seed to teach it how to form *ice-two*, *ice-three*, *ice-four* . . . ? And suppose," he rapped on his desk with his old hand again, "that there were one form, which we will call *ice-nine*—a crystal as hard as this desk—with a melting point of, let us say, one-hundred degrees Fahrenheit, or, better still, a melting point of one-hundred-and-thirty degrees."

"All right, I'm still with you," I said.[41]

That's exactly where you want your reader to be: with you.

And thus, with this exhortation of compassion, "Pity the readers," Vonnegut concludes his advice in "How to Write with Style."

When I read Vonnegut's novels, I sometimes lose track of the plot. Following plots is not my strong point as a reader. I'm generally less interested in what happened than in the emotional resonance, so I sometimes don't pay a lot of attention to clues or the sequence of events.

But it's not all my fault. It's partly Kurt's. He doesn't always make what's happening clear enough. Sometimes there's too much happening.

I once read a review, although I can't remember who wrote it or about which novel, in which the reviewer expressed the same sense of getting lost in events, but what she said she did with Vonnegut novels as a result was to speed up, to read faster. My advice is the opposite. Slow down. Way down.

In rereading Vonnegut's oeuvre as preparation for this book, I took notes, which slowed the process considerably. That's when I discovered that, although written to compel the reader to keep reading, a leisurely pace yielded more of everything—delight, comprehension, appreciation.

CHAPTER 2

ABOUT WRITING FICTION

Much wisdom about the craft of writing can apply to every sort of form. But the more specialized the writing, the more it demands specialized advice.

Robert Frost's adage that writing poetry without rhyme is like playing tennis without a net proves inapplicable, for example, unless you're a poet. It wouldn't resonate with most contemporary poets either. Rhyming isn't fashionable now.

Among nonfiction writers, there are journalists, columnists, memoirists, biographers, essayists, critics, and more. Among fiction writers, there are writers of flash fiction, the short story, and the novel, those who write literary fiction, science fiction, romance, mysteries, etc. . . . There are poets, playwrights, scriptwriters. Not to mention bloggers. Most writers explore more than one genre. But the majority favor a certain form, and excel at that one.

Kurt Vonnegut wrote for a lifetime. In that lifetime, his goals, forms of expression, and circumstances in relation to writing changed. The world's tastes and economics in terms of writing kept changing, as well. But his reputation as an iconic American voice emerged and remains with his fiction, particularly his novels, and he regarded himself primarily as a novelist.

When Vonnegut taught, he taught the art of fiction. He was so accustomed to thinking as a fiction writer and teacher that when he wrote "How to Write with Style" for a general audience, he added a sentence under "Have the guts to cut" directed only to fiction writers, which his editor then cut.

The best pearls of wisdom he has to offer on writing, therefore, are about the art of fiction and being a novelist.

⟶

Here's what he said about the difference between fiction and nonfiction in the '70s, when Truman Capote's *In Cold Blood* and Tom Wolfe's *The Pump House Gang* gave rise to the "New Journalism," so labeled by critics because the journalist didn't pretend to be anonymous or objective, as had always been the case, and instead participated in the narrative.

> I am now persuaded again that acknowledged fiction is a much more truthful way of telling the truth than the New Journalism is. Or, to put it another way, the very finest New Journalism is fiction. In either art form, we have an idiosyncratic reporter. The New Journalist isn't free to tell nearly as much as a fiction writer, to *show* as much. There are many places he can't take his reader, whereas the fiction writer can take the reader anywhere; including the planet Jupiter, in case there's something worth seeing there. . . .
>
> I am reminded now, as I think about news and fiction, of a demonstration of the difference between noise and melody which I saw and heard in a freshman physics lecture at Cornell University so long ago. . . . The professor threw a narrow board, which was about the length of a bayonet, at the wall of the room, which was cinder block. "That's noise," he said.
>
> Then he picked up seven more boards, and he threw them against the wall in rapid succession, as though he were a knife-thrower. The boards in sequence sang the opening notes of "Mary Had a Little Lamb." I was enchanted.
>
> "That's melody," he said.
>
> And fiction is melody, and journalism, new or old, is noise.[42]

———

Here's what he said years later:

> As I get older, I get more didactic. I say what I really think.
> I don't hide ideas like Easter eggs for people to find. Now,
> if I have an idea, when something becomes clear to me, I
> don't embed it in a novel; I simply write it in an essay as
> clearly as I can.[43]

My assessment: noise is noise and music is music, in whatever form. Many of Vonnegut's essays are pure melody ("Palm Sunday," for example). Most of his fiction is. It zings with imagination, sings with wit and truth.

———

That is, the work he polished and published. There are also discarded duds.

CHAPTER 3

THE PRIME MOVER

I f you're a writer, then caring about a subject "others should care about" is a necessity. It's the primary tool, before pencil, pen, paper, or computer. You must be compelled "in your heart"; otherwise, why would you do such a difficult thing?

Writing is hard work. Writing well is very hard work. It takes courage and perseverance.

"You have to sit there," as Kurt said. "It's physically uncomfortable, it's physically bad for someone to sit still that long, and it's socially bad for a person to be alone that much. The working conditions are really bad. Nobody has ever found the solution to that."[44]

———

And here let's take a minute to define the word "writer." In *Player Piano*, Vonnegut's first novel, "The Shah of Bratpuhr, spiritual leader of 6,000,000 members of the Kolhouri sect," is driving along with Dr. Halyard of the United States Department of State. The Shah sees a beautiful woman on the street and invites her into his limousine, assuming she's a sex slave, as such a woman would be in his own culture, which consists only of slaves and the elite. She gets in but looks unhappy, Halyard thinks, and finally explains she knows what the Shah wants and that she's willing, because the problem is, her husband is a writer, and has no "classification number," the number required for employment. Halyard asks,

"Then how can you call him a writer?" . . .

"Because he writes," she said.

"My dear girl," said Halyard paternally, "on that basis, we're all writers."

———

Halyard's retort may have popped up in your own mind, dear reader. Vonnegut wrote this scene in the late 1940s. If the fictional Halyard could make such a pronouncement then, think of it now, when we're all writing like never before! We're blogging, e-mailing, logging in to comment. We're "chatting" with our fingers in online "chat" rooms and with experts in "live chats." We're tweeting and texting. And we are all "sitting there" at computers.

Does that make us all writers?

———

The passage continues:

"Two days ago he had a number—W–441 [for a "fiction novice"]," she explains.

> "He was to have it until he'd completed his novel. After that, he was supposed to get either a W–440 [for "fiction journeyman"]. . . . Or a W–255 [for "public relations"]. . . . Two months ago he submitted his finished manuscript to the National Council of Arts and Letters for criticism and assignment to one of the book clubs." . . .
>
> "Anyway," said the girl, "my husband's book was rejected by the Council."
>
> "Badly written," said Halyard primly. "The standards are high."
>
> "Beautifully written," she said patiently. "But it was twenty-seven pages longer than the maximum length." . . .

"And," the girl continued, "it had an antimachine theme."

Halyard's eyebrows arched high. "Well! I should hope they wouldn't print it! What on earth does he think he's doing? Good lord, you're lucky if he isn't behind bars, inciting to advocate the commission of sabotage like that. He didn't really think somebody'd print it, did he?"

"He didn't care. He had to write it, so he wrote it."

"Why doesn't he write about clipper ships, or something like that? This book about the old days on the Erie Canal— the man who wrote that is cleaning up. Big demand for that bare-chested stuff."

She shrugged helplessly. "Because he never got mad at clipper ships or the Erie Canal, I guess."

"He sounds very maladjusted," said Halyard distastefully. . . .

. . . *"And my husband says somebody's just* got *to be maladjusted; that somebody's got to be uncomfortable enough to wonder where people are, where they're going, and why they're going there* [italics mine]. That was the trouble with his book. It raised those questions, and was rejected. So he was ordered into public-relations duty."[45]

———

So a writer is someone who is willing to be uncomfortable enough— or is uncomfortable enough by nature—to wonder where people are, where they're going, and why they're going there. A writer is willing to take risks for that wondering. A writer cares that much about his or her subject.

———

Thirty-five years and ten novels later, Vonnegut has his characters, the veteran novelist Slazinger and the beginning biographer Mrs. Berman, discuss these same matters:

"Everybody thinks he or she can be a writer," he said with airy irony.

"Don't tell me it's a crime to try," she said.

"It's a crime to think it's easy," he said. "But if you're really serious, you'll find out quick enough that it's the hardest thing there is."

"Particularly so, if you have absolutely nothing to say," she said. "Don't you think that's the main reason people find it so difficult? If they can write complete sentences and can use a dictionary, isn't that the *only* reason they find writing hard: they don't know or care about anything?"

Here Slazinger stole a line from the writer Truman Capote . . . "I think you're talking about *typing* instead of *writing*," he said.[46]

Vonnegut uses irony to make the point in other novels:

"You'd be good at public relations," said Kraft.

"I certainly don't have any powerful convictions to get in the way of a client's message," I said.[47]

When he was alive he was like a dead man in 1 respect: everything was pretty much all right with him.[48]

Vonnegut himself was as concerned about how human hearts and their ideas collectively affected societies as he was about the individual.

Oh, God—the lives people try to lead.

Oh, God—what a world they try to lead them in![49]

Those short lines could sum up Vonnegut's entire oeuvre, with an emphasis on the second.

As a young writer, science fiction was the form that beckoned him. He explains why, in the voice of his character Eliot Rosewater addressing sci-fi writers at a science fiction conference:

> "I love you sons of bitches," Eliot said in Milford. "You're all I read any more. You're the only ones who'll talk about the *really* terrific changes going on, the only ones crazy enough to know that life is a space voyage, and not a short one, either, but one that'll last for billions of years. You're the only ones with guts enough to *really* care about the future, who *really* notice what machines do to us, what wars do to us, what cities do to us, what big, simple ideas do to us, what tremendous misunderstandings, mistakes, accidents and catastrophes do to us. You're the only ones zany enough to agonize over time and distances without limit, over mysteries that will never die, over the fact that we are right now determining whether the space voyage for the next billion years or so is going to be Heaven or Hell."

Vonnegut felt so strongly that passion about people and issues ought to be the prime mover for a writer that he would rather you err on the side of caring passionately vs. writing eloquently:

> Eliot admitted later on that science-fiction writers couldn't write for sour apples, but he declared that it didn't matter. He said they were poets just the same, since they were more sensitive to important changes than anybody who was writing well.[50]

What made Vonnegut unique, why people love and need him, along with the fact that he was incredibly funny, was his perspective. It was huge.

> Ever since studying anthropology, I have regarded history and cultures and societies as characters vivid as any in fiction.[51]

Vonnegut earned no degree in anthropology. But he gained something invaluable from the attempt. Years later, he described

> the extraordinarily important idea (I only now understand) which I picked up from Anthropology: culture is a gadget which can be tinkered with like a Model-T Ford.[52]

> A culture can contain fatal poisons . . . a respect for firearms, for example, or the belief that no male is really a man until he has had a physical showdown of some kind, or that women can't possibly understand the really important things which are going on, and so on. . . . [That] enchantingly suggestive thing I learned . . . [became an] attitude I assumed.[53]

> I learned to stand outside of my own society and people have said that I am like a Martian visiting the Earth. . . . It was easy for me to stand outside my own culture. I have discovered that many people are totally incapable of doing this. . . . They assume that their culture is so immutable that it's like their skin and they assume that my asking them to stand outside their culture is like asking them to stand outside their skin.[54]

Here's some concrete evidence of that training:

Master's Thesis Project: <u>Mythologies of North American</u>
<u>Indian Nativistic Cults</u>
Kurt Vonnegut
Summer, 1947

It is in the new myths that come into being during times of
rapid culture change that I am interested, and so propose
to examine the myths associated with the Prophet Dance,
The Smohalla Cult, The Shaker Religion of Puget Sound,
The Ghost Dances of 1870 and 1890, and The Peyote Cult,
as variously manifested by North American Indian tribes.

He cites a letter from an infantry captain on "Indian duty"
in Nevada, describing prophecies that arose among the Indians
regarding the white man. Tavibo, the most influential medicine
man, "went up alone into the mountain and there met the Great
Spirit" several times, and upon his return, after going in a trance,
offered the Spirit's tidings. Each predicted a great disaster "within
a few moons."

In one, "All the improvements of the whites . . . would remain,
but the whites would be swallowed up, while the Indians would
be saved."

In a second, "all, both Indians and whites, would be swallowed
up . . . but at the end of three days the Indians would be resurrected
in the flesh . . . while their enemies, the whites, would be destroyed
forever."

In a third, "Indians who believed in the prophecy would be
resurrected . . . but those who did not believe in it would . . . be
damned forever with the whites."[55]

Entirely different myths were also spawned. One forecast that
life on earth would become a "paradise." "Life was to be eternal,
and no distinction was to exist between races."[56] The Cheyenne
were informed about Christ, and one reported, "I and my people
have been living in ignorance until I went and found out the truth.

All the whites and Indians are brothers, I was told there. I never knew this before."[57] They interpreted the Christ story in their own way and incorporated it into their culture.

What's the common thread? How does each artifact serve and shape the culture? These are the kinds of questions an anthropologist is trained to ask. These are the kinds Vonnegut cared about.

In *Player Piano*, Vonnegut's interest in cultures in flux lands on our own society. What did he care about that he thought others should care about? He was outraged at the tough trade-off when machines increasingly do our work: the incalculable cost/loss in terms of people's sense of "being needed and useful, the foundation of self-respect."[58]

It's based on his experiences and observations growing up in the Depression, and his three years working in public relations at General Electric.

He was born in 1922, and when he was ten years old, in 1932, his architect father lost his job. Adults all around him suffered the indignity of having no work and little income.

> During the Depression when people were looking for radical solutions to economic problems . . . they believed that scientists and engineers and mathematicians should run the world, that they were the only people with common sense. . . .
>
> I had a father and a brother who believed strongly in technology that the world was going to be remade and I was an enthusiast for this too. . . . I was a great believer in truth, in scientific truth, and then as I wrote once "truth was dropped on Hiroshima" . . . and so I was hideously disillusioned.[59]
>
> My first novel, *Player Piano* . . . is a lampoon on GE. I bit the hand that used to feed me.[60]

Some bites:

Rudy Hertz, a superb machinist whose movements were recorded so that machines could duplicate them, therefore eliminating his and other machinists' jobs, holds up his hands when he meets the protagonist, Paul, an executive:

Good as ever, and there's not two like them anywhere.

Each time the protagonist Paul's wife calls, the conversation concludes exactly the same way:

"I love you, Paul."
"I love *you*, Anita." . . .
Anita had the mechanics of marriage down pat, even to the subtlest conventions.

One character, a "dull boy" with privileged connections, gets a top job.

The hell of it was that his attitude won grudging admiration from his fellow engineers, who had got their jobs the hard way.

There's a mechanical checkers player, among other mechanisms, and of course a player piano. A revolutionary secret society springs up: the Ghost Shirt Society.
The factory itself, though, is like a

great gymnasium, where countless squads practiced precision calisthenics—bobbing, spinning, leaping, thrusting, waving. . . . This much of the new era Paul loved: the machines themselves were entertaining and delightful.[61]

Vonnegut cared about these issues, and translated the things he cared about into the form of fiction.

But even though he himself was concerned about technology, science and automation, it wasn't what he himself cared about that mattered to him when teaching or advising budding writers.

Listen to what he said to his former Iowa workshop student, John Casey, in an interview:

> Machinery is important. We must write about it.
> But I don't care if you don't; I'm not urging you, am I?
> To hell with machinery.[62]

CHAPTER 4

DETOURING FORWARD

It's a risky business, writing about subjects you care about terribly. There are grave dangers. Kurt discovered some of them. I certainly have. I'll bet my bottom dollar that all fiction writers suffer some of these:

You may be too close to the raw experience to write about it with any perspective or distance.

You may want so badly to tell about it that you find yourself tongue-tied, because words are just words, and they are insufficient. They are not experience itself.

You may not yet be skilled enough as a writer.

You may feel loyalty to an actual experience that interferes with your ability to refashion it into telling the truth of it fictionally.

You may want to convey your concern or opinion so much that your writing becomes didactic and preachy.

You may suffer from reliving trauma, and delving into what it holds for you may cause you more emotional stress than you can handle or than is worth it for your well-being.

You may be blown out of the water by readers' responses, suggestions for revising, or rejection from editors, because you're unable to allow in or digest criticism. In other words, you may not be able to distinguish feedback that has to do with the craft of your writing from the personal experience your writing is based upon.

Vonnegut said:

> Paul Engle—the founder of the Writers' Workshop at
> Iowa . . . told me that, if the Workshop ever got a building of
> its own, these words should be inscribed over the entrance:
> "Don't take it all so seriously."[63]

But we did, we did.
    And so did Kurt.

———

He was writing the book that would become *Slaughterhouse-Five*.
He had been trying to write it for twenty-three years.

———

What should you do, if any of the risks listed previously apply to
you?
    The answers may be found by looking at Kurt Vonnegut's jour-
ney. Here are some guideposts.

———

It may have taken Kurt Vonnegut twenty-three years to find the
way to write directly about the firebombing of Dresden and his
experience of war in *Slaughterhouse-Five*. But if you read his fiction
in sequence up to that point, you'll see him flirting with it, using it,
skewing it, working his way up to it.
    In "Basic Training," a realistic early novella (circa 1950) that
Vonnegut failed to publish, the "General," as his teenaged daughters call him, runs his Indiana farm like the army, dividing his few
workers into "squads" and keeping a bulletin board where all can
see his "orders," sometimes quite ludicrous. The farm is named,

one daughter says, "in honor of battle, just like everything else around here." The General is a blowhard, a figure of fun, but also a responsible man and a vet, who has adopted Haley, his orphaned nephew, the main character. When the General tells his war stories, the teenagers hear them as noise.

> "Now take the case of the 240 howitzer," said the General. "Far more effective against concrete bunkers than aerial bombardment. I remember just before the Bulge . . ."
> Haley nodded and turned his face toward the sunroom windows to hide his yawn from the General.[64]

The 240-millimeter howitzer is the weapon Vonnegut himself was trained to use. And like the General, he would have remembered the time just before the Battle of the Bulge. Because during it, Vonnegut was captured.

In this way, nestled among other plots, settings, and topics, Vonnegut's story sneaks out.

None of the published novels he wrote before *Slaughterhouse-Five* were precisely about Vonnegut's experiences in the war.

But consider the following snippets from the novels (in sequence as published) and notice how Vonnegut employs his own experiences, how they spill out imaginatively.

From *Player Piano* (a science fiction novel about industrialization):

> The limousine stayed where it had been trapped . . . while the dull thunder of explosions walked about the city like the steps of drunken giants, and afternoon turned to twilight under a curtain of smoke. Each time escape seemed possible, and Halyard raised his head to investigate a lull, fresh contingents of vandals and looters sent him to the floor again.

"All right," he said at last, "I think maybe we're all right now. Let's try to make it to the police station. We can get protection there until this thing plays itself out."

The driver leaned on the steering wheel and stretched insolently. "You think you've been watching a football game or something? You think maybe everything's going to be just the way it was before?"[65]

From *The Sirens of Titan* (a science fiction novel about the meaning and nature of mankind and the universe):

Unk was bound to admit that a soldier would be crazy not to do his duty at all times.

At the hospital they had said the most important rule of all was this one: Always obey a direct order without a moment's hesitation. . . .

Brackman came up to Unk and ordered him to march up to the man at the stake in a military manner and strangle him until he was dead.

Brackman told Unk it was a direct order.

So Unk did it.[66]

From *Mother Night* (about a double agent):

Mengel was speaking of Rudolf Franz Hoess, the commandant of the extermination camp at Auschwitz. In his tender care, literally millions of Jews were gassed. Mengel knew a little about Hoess. Before emigrating to Israel in 1947, Mengel helped to hang Hoess.

And he didn't do it with testimony, either. He did it with

his two big hands. "When Hoess was hanged," he told me, "the strap around his ankles—I put that on and made it tight."

"Did that give you a lot of satisfaction?" I said.

"No," he said. "I was like almost everybody who came through that war."

"What do you mean?" I said.

"I got so I couldn't feel anything," said Mengel. "Every job was a job to do, and no job was any better or any worse than any other.

"After we finished hanging Hoess," Mengel said to me, "I packed up my clothes to go home. The catch on my suitcase was broken, so I buckled it shut with a big leather strap. Twice within an hour I did the very same job—once to Hoess and once to my suitcase. Both jobs felt about the same."[67]

From *Cat's Cradle* (a sci-fi novel about religion and scientists' responsibilities):

I joined her at the top of the ridge. She was looking down raptly into a broad, natural bowl. She was not crying.

She might well have cried.

In that bowl were thousands upon thousands of dead.[68]

In *God Bless You, Mr. Rosewater* (about a man who helps the poor):

Eliot [Rosewater] didn't look up again until the bus reached the outskirts of Indianapolis. He was astonished to see that the entire city was being consumed by a fire-storm.

He had never seen a fire-storm, but he had certainly read and dreamed about many of them.

He had a book hidden in his office, and it was a mystery even to Eliot as to why he should hide it, why he should feel guilty every time he got it out, why he should be afraid of being caught reading it. His feelings about the book were those of a weak-willed puritan with respect to pornography, yet no book could be more innocent of eroticism than the book he hid. It was called *The Bombing of Germany.* It was written by Hans Rumpf.

And the passage Eliot would read over and over again, his features blank, his palms sweating, was this description of the fire-storms in Dresden. . . .

Eliot, rising from his seat in the bus, beheld the firestorm of Indianapolis. He was awed by the majesty of the column of fire. . . .

. . . Everything went black for Eliot. . . . And then he awoke to find himself sitting on the flat rim of a dry fountain. . . .

Eliot looked up at the bird and all the green leaves, understood that this garden in downtown Indianapolis could not have survived the fire he saw. So there had been no fire. He accepted this peacefully.[69]

So before Billy Pilgrim of *Slaughterhouse-Five*, Eliot Rosewater became "unstuck in time." But Vonnegut didn't call it that. And it happened just once. But it's the predecessor to what will become a theme in his next book, the breakthrough book, *Slaughterhouse-Five*.

What did Vonnegut gain by detouring? Time to mature. Skill at his craft. Confidence. A growing reputation. Five published novels, one published collection of short stories, innumerable stories published in magazines, plays, and essays.

Distance from his crucibles. Making a kind of bushwhacking preparatory headway into wrangling with them.

Here's what Vonnegut had to say to students about such indirection:

> You will be writing about your own life anyway, but you won't know it, if you write a hack western—or not a hack western, if you write an excellent western like *High Noon*. Because somewhere in there is the coded psychiatric problem of the author. And if you write an episode for some space program on television, this will somehow parallel things that are on your mind, as unresolved conflicts. But that's the place to write and that's the way to deal with your conflicts too, if you want to write fast, if you don't want to get blocked.[70]

Please take note: This wisdom derived from hindsight. Vonnegut said if you write a hack western or whatever else "you won't know" you're writing about your own life. Neither did he, at the time he was writing. Neither will you. And you don't have to concern yourself about whether you are or not.

———

In a beginning fiction workshop at Hunter College, one of my students wrote her first two stories on abortion and addiction. I received at least one story each class about abortion and one every other class on drug addiction. But it was unusual for someone to hand in stories on both topics in their first workshop. This lovely earnest young woman cared and thought others should care about these issues and she wanted urgently to tell her stories about them. But her reach exceeded her grasp. Like many beginners' stories, these could have been novels in their scope. The characters were wooden, the prose didactic. I suggested she scale down her ambition. Finally she turned in a fresh, compelling story, with realized characters and wit, about a fat girl—ordinarily overweight, not obese—who goes to Weight Watchers.

I got into the Iowa workshop based on one story. I wrote four more, then started a novel. I spent six months on the first chapter, revising and revising. It meant so much to me. But when it was workshopped, it did not have the impact on my classmate readers that I wanted, at all.

What was it about?

A boy has been sentenced to a year in prison. It's his initial day behind bars.

What was it based on?

My first love's incarceration. I'd visited him every two weeks, which entailed a long drive with his father, being searched before entering, guarded during the visit, and enduring his shame, humiliation, need, and our separation. For starters.

I knew these experiences would make a good story. Great conflict within the characters, and societally. A world foreign to most, and even to me. Tragedy.

But I was ill-equipped to write about it. We had split up, for the last time, that very year. The imprisonment and relationship rendered me traumatized, guilty, outraged. I did not yet even comprehend those effects.

Too much attachment to my personal experience. Not enough distance.

Not nearly enough craft to know how to approach the material.

Ambition far ahead of my expertise. I had just begun to write "your first twenty bad stories" as my first creative writing teacher, William Harrison, at the University of Arkansas, had suggested necessary before mastering the craft of the short story. And a novel is a different beast.

Right after the workshop session, I saw my fellow student Gail

Godwin in the student cafeteria buying dinner. Gail was older and a more experienced, confident writer than I was, and I'd told her how important the story was to me. She asked me how the session had gone. She could see I was shaken and told me to get my tray and come back to her table. She heard me out about the students' feedback, essentially that the story was too dense, though the dramatic part worked. She listened intently.

Then she asked, "Why do you write?" Startled, I gave her an answer. She asked again, leaning slightly more forward, "Suzanne, why do you write?" I gave another answer. Bending even closer, she asked again, and again, her blue eyes penetrating, until finally I burst into tears.

"It's the only thing I can *do*!"

She leaned back, as if satisfied. She suggested I go write something crazy, something entirely different, just start writing, write anything, she said. I walked down to the crowded buzzing café of the student union in a daze, feeling oddly separate from myself and everyone and everything. While students were haranguing about Vietnam and clattering their coffee cups, I sat down and wrote a line, then another. I wrote, for the first time, out of my imagination, an entirely other place. It had nothing to do with reality, or so it seemed, or my desperate need to tell of traumas, or so it seemed.

Two weeks later I presented the resulting fantastical story in workshop and everyone loved it.

―――――

Years later, in a novel focused on another plot, the main character looks back on the teenaged years when she fell in love and visited a boy (who would become her fictional ex-husband), in prison. Now written from the girl's and woman's point of view, and infused by imagination, the chapters convey all that I once so badly wanted to communicate.[71]

Be kind to yourself. Give yourself room. There are years to go. Don't pummel yourself with expectation. Go easy. Your material will eventually find its way to voice.

CHAPTER 5

DEAD AHEAD

L isten: Throughout these years, Vonnegut was also trying to write straightforwardly about Dresden.

———

The Atlantic Monthly
August 29, 1949

Dear Mr. Vonnegut:

    . . . *Both the account of the bombing of Dresden* [italics mine] and your article, "What's a Fair Price for Golden Eggs?" have drawn commendation although neither one is quite compelling enough for final acceptance. . . .

Faithfully yours, (Signed, "Edward Weeks")[72]

———

Novelists are not only unusually depressed, by and large, but have, on the average, about the same IQs as the cosmetics consultants at Bloomingdale's department store. Our power is patience. We have discovered that writing allows even a stupid person to seem halfway intelligent, if only that person will write the same thought over and over again, improving it just a little bit each time. It is a lot like inflating a blimp with a bicycle pump. Anybody can do it. All it takes is time.[73]

—~—

And my husband says somebody's just got to be maladjusted; that somebody's got to be uncomfortable enough to wonder where people are, where they're going, and why they're going there.[74]

What did it cost Kurt Vonnegut to create fiction out of the events in his letter home? To consider this, please reread his letter (chapter 1). Slowly. It's compressed. Perhaps imagine that you are one of Kurt's family members. It's 1945. The last news received about K, as he is called in the family, was a returned letter that his father, Kurt Sr., wrote to K months before.

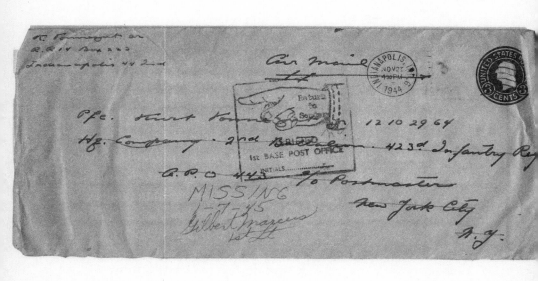

Letter from Kurt Vonnegut Sr. to Kurt Vonnegut Jr., November 1944. Photo: Chris LeFave, Vonnegut Memorial Library. Courtesy of the Vonnegut family.

Now at the mailbox you see there's a letter from K. You're over-joyed! He's *alive*! You tear it open. You race inside, yelling, "There's a letter from K!" to whoever else is there. You read it aloud. Then you read it again to yourself, carefully, digesting all that he says has happened to him.

———

Asked in 1969, "After the lean years, how does it feel to have a success like *Slaughterhouse-Five*?," Vonnegut starts by replying this way:

> Well, as a business story it interests me, but my books have stayed in print all along. This is the first to make it in hard cover.

Then he gets closer to the truth.

> I must have used up tons of paper. I can't tell you how many versions I wrote. . . . I even wrote two heroic versions.

He pauses, then asks if anyone recalls the bombing raid of *Catch-22* in which Yossarian, having elaborately bandaged the arm of a wounded pilot, unzips the man's jacket, whereupon all the pilot's guts fall out.[75]
There's his answer. It required all his guts to fall out.

> I would hate to tell you what this lousy little book cost me in money and anxiety and time. When I got home from the Second World War twenty-three years ago, I thought it would be easy for me to write about the destruction of Dresden, since all I would have to do would be to report what I had seen. And I thought, too, that it would be a masterpiece

or at least make me a lot of money, since the subject was so big.[76]

In an early interview, he says:

> Well, it seemed a categorical imperative that I write about Dresden, the firebombing of Dresden . . . since it was the largest massacre in the history of Europe and I am a person of European extraction and I, a writer, had been present. I *had* to say something about it. And it took me a long time and it was painful.[77]

Later he says,

> I tried to write, but I just couldn't get it right. I kept writing crap.[78]

A novel, he discovered, is "a quest."[79] He did not think that he'd have to write his guts out. Or so he says.

———

By the time he created Bokonon in *Cat's Cradle*, he must have suspected the jig was up. Because he has Bokonon espouse this gem:

> Peculiar travel suggestions are dancing lessons from God.[80]

And it opens by evoking Jonah.

> Call me Jonah. My parents did, or nearly did. They called me John.
>   Jonah—John—if I had been a Sam, I would have been a Jonah still—not because I have been unlucky for others,

but because somebody or something has compelled me to be certain places at certain times, without fail. . . .

When I was a much younger man, I began to collect material for a book to be called *The Day the World Ended*.

The book was to be factual.

The book was to be an account of what important Americans had done on the day when the first atomic bomb was dropped on Hiroshima, Japan.

It was to be a Christian book. I was a Christian then.[81]

Well, the narrator John never writes that book. Lots of other things happen to him instead. Bokonism, for one thing. And lots of things happened to Kurt Vonnegut on his journey to writing *Slaughterhouse-Five*, and happen to every writer as they dance to the music of their own particular material.

———

At Indiana University's Lilly Library, which holds Vonnegut's papers, I located some of what he called "crap." It was moving, even heartbreaking, to hold in my hands so many pages that testify to how much Vonnegut was trying, one way and then another, to fashion a coherent tale.

He tried out titles: *Captured, We Are Captured, Rolling Pisspots and Flaming Prams, Calvados, Slaughterhouse-Five* subtitled *A Comedy of Manners*.

He tried out protagonists: Milos Vernon, an architect on Cape Cod; Billy Pilgrim, a Pontiac dealer in the Midwest; David McSwan, a Unitarian minister's son, narrated by an unidentified first-person character.

He tried to deal in differing ways with the same events, situations, and people. These show up in the final book. But they are treated differently in various drafts.

He made notes. He told us in class that he once drew elaborate plot outlines on huge pieces of paper with multicolored pencils, and tacked them all over his walls. He describes that in chapter 1 of *Slaughterhouse-Five*.

Books ends with image of Mike Palaia shitting and eating at the same time, the thing O'Hare remembers.

The kid who won't share tobacco, who will trade.

Stopping off at Stalag Luft, sponging tobacco — the thief who gets thrown into shithouse for stealing. Russians selling urine-soaked cigarettes.

Tom Jones and his revolver.

The homo-sexual marriages.

Lehr and his one strange eye.

Joe Crone spilling the soup. Joe goes to a hospital, stares and stares. They bury him in a white paper suit with full military honors.

Sometimes, when I am very pessimistic, I think about modern man's cruelty to himself, and think of all of us as hungry people in ruins, eating cold, stolen beans from a can while we squat and shit. I think of our being arrested for stealing those beans, of being given a fair trial in a foreign language, of being shot by four enemies, of being buried by four shocked but philosophical friends.

Most days I don't feel like that. Praise be to God, the bad days are few.

Tell me again about Jesus Christ. I
Want to be a Christian
Tell me again

Draft of *Slaughterhouse-Five*. Courtesy of the Lilly Library, Indiana University, Bloomington, Indiana.

```
Do a 6000-Word piece on Dresden.


    If you take a twenty-year-old kid, who has seen Indinnapolis
and Louisville and Cinncinnati and Chicago, and that's about all,
and you send him over to Europe real fast, have him camp in French
woods one night, and then go into the line a couple of days after
that, missing Paris, and you have him go into a losing battle,
be captured, and then have him sent in by his captors to Dresden,
Germany, to work for his keep, you have the child I once was --
and you have him in the first old and beautiful city he was ever
in.
    Since my father was an architect
```

Draft of *Slaughterhouse-Five.* Courtesy of the Lilly Library, Indiana University, Bloomington, Indiana.

He tried visuals. In one draft, plotted chronologically, he typed the lines and letters closer and closer together as the story neared the date of the Dresden firebombing. When it got to that date, February 13, 1945, they became solid black.[82]

CHAPTER 6

BREAKTHROUGH

How did Kurt Vonnegut finally make his breakthrough to *Slaughterhouse-Five*? As is self-evident, he got old enough, distant enough from the actual events, and experienced enough as a writer. Then there occurred a fortuitous confluence of Fate and Commitment.

He got a job teaching at the University of Iowa's Writers' Workshop (1965–67). He gained a community of writers, an atmosphere, shoptalk. He earned a steady paycheck. He committed himself to writing his war book.

Besides the cauldron of the civil rights movement, the Vietnam War, and the counterculture, lots of things were bubbling up about the shape and content of writing in those days. At the workshop, people were keenly aware of them. Truman Capote and Tom Wolfe capsized the notion of objectivity in journalism. John Barth (who gave a delightful performance of his work once at Iowa), Jorge Luis Borges (who visited as a guest speaker), Robert Coover (who was hired to teach the year Kurt left), and Julio Cortázar, to mention a few, were having a great time messing around with form, breaking conventions right and left. Critics grouped and labeled them. The New Journalism, magical realism, metafiction. Robert Scholes, a critic teaching at Iowa, wrote *The Fabulist*s, and included Kurt Vonnegut.

The *New York Times* asked Vonnegut to write a review of the new *Random House Unabridged Dictionary*. He wrote it in his honest, idiosyncratic style. He quoted Random House's publisher, Bennett Cerf. When asked whether Lyndon Johnson should be colloquial when speaking of the Vietnam War, Cerf said, "Now's not the time for the

President of the United States to worry about the King's English."
The review caught the eye of Seymour Lawrence, formerly a vice
president at Random House under Cerf. Lawrence now worked for
Delacorte, scouting for new authors. Lawrence and Vonnegut met.
Vonnegut told him he was working on *Slaughterhouse-Five* but that
his books didn't sell. Lawrence offered him a three-book contract.[83]

So now, besides his own dedication to the story, he had an obligation to Lawrence and Lawrence's faith that he would make good
on that obligation.

Making a commitment like that is powerful. Commitment invites
Fate to be your Fairy Godmother Collaborator, to close and open
just the doors you need.[84]

And so Fate did.

She brought him fresh, key perceptions about form and content
on the one hand, and a top book publisher on the other.

These appear sequentially because the conventions of narrative
nonfiction dictate that they do so. I don't know the order. They
ought to look like scrambled eggs.

1. Mary O'Hare, the wife of his war buddy Bernard O'Hare,
    confronts him and says, "in effect, 'Why don't you tell the truth
    for a change?'"—that is, that he and the other soldiers were
    children, not heroes like those portrayed by movie stars.[85]
2. He discovers that, in fact, he can't remember much about it.
    Necessity is the mother of invention. And he has to invent,
    to fill out the story. He conjures up Tralfamadore out of his
    old sci-fi hat along with his sci-fi writer-character Kilgore
    Trout. (Together they add 7,251 words, about 25 pages. The
    Tralfamadore sections add 4,851 words, the Trout about 2,400.)
3. He came up with the notion of writing the first chapter
    straightforwardly, violating a cardinal rule of fiction,

which is to maintain the *dream* of the fictional story. He confides right off the bat, "All this happened, more or less." He describes the basis for it, his POW Dresden firebombing story, and his struggle and process writing it. He invites the reader in, like a friend.

How did he arrive at this? Random House reissued his out-of-print third novel, *Mother Night*, in 1966, and Vonnegut wrote a preface, reproduced ever since, in which he says outright what he thinks its lesson is, so this precedent may have contributed to the idea. The Writers' Workshop and atmosphere of experimentation must have as well. He'd already tried writing about Dresden both as nonfiction and as fiction. Now he simply combined those impulses. But I suspect the most significant factor was his underlying urgency to ensure that he conveyed how much he cared about this subject and how much he wanted the reader to understand it.

4. His wife Jane told me, when I visited them in Barnstable a year or so after *Slaughterhouse-Five* was published, that she'd disliked the first autobiographical chapter intensely until she realized it was about time. Vonnegut quotes Céline and Roethke in that chapter, both in regard to time. He says, "And I asked myself about the present: how wide it was, how deep it was, how much was mine to keep."[86] This soulful line sings of middle age. That's where Vonnegut was then, in the continuum of life. His sense of time passing must have spurred him to get on with it and go for broke.

5. He gave up. He yielded to his sense that it would not be the book he'd always imagined, that he would fail to realize it in the way he'd wanted. Surrendering perfection happens, more or less, to all writers.[87] Some passages from Vonnegut's drafts are as vivid as any in the finished manuscript. He had to sacrifice his dream of what the book might be for the sake of what he could in fact now deliver.

But deliver he did.

He concludes his first chapter alluding to Lot's wife, who failed to heed God's warning about looking back and was turned into a pillar of salt.

> I've finished my war book now. The next one I write is going to be fun. This one is a failure, and had to be, since it was written by a pillar of salt.

> It's . . . it's very thin . . . about as long as *The Bobbsey Twins*.

It was such a short book that *Ramparts Magazine*, who serialized it, inquired of him if they'd got it all.[88]

> Writers can't write great things all the time. You do the best you can, then you have to move on. Otherwise you'll end up writing the same book your whole life.[89]

VONNEGUT'S BREAKTHROUGH-CLUSTER CONVERTED INTO ADVICE:

1. Make a commitment.
2. Trust fate, your Fairy Godmother Collaborator.
3. Tell the truth.
4. Keep on truckin'.
5. Surrender perfection.

Heed what you need. Alter to fit your own left foot.

I think a lot of people, including me, clammed up when a
civilian asked about battle, about war. It was fashionable.
One of the most impressive ways to tell your war story is
to refuse to tell it, you know. . . .

But I think the Vietnam War freed me and other writers,
because it made our leadership and our motives seem so
scruffy. . . . We could finally talk about something bad that
we did. . . . And what I saw, what I had to report, made war
look so ugly. You know, the truth can be really powerful
stuff. You're not expecting it.

Then he added,

Of course, another reason not to talk about war is that it's
unspeakable.[90]

[The prisoners] were brought at last to a stone cottage at
a fork in the road. It was a collecting point for prisoners
of war. Billy and Weary were taken inside, where it was
warm and smoky. There was a fire sizzling and popping
in the fireplace. The fuel was furniture. There were about
twenty other Americans in there, sitting on the floor with
their backs to the wall, staring into the flames—thinking
whatever there was to think, which was zero.

Nobody talked. Nobody had any good war stories to tell.[91]

In *Mother Night*, the central character, Howard Campbell, originally a playwright before he altered his occupation to double agent
with the advent of World War II, has this dialogue as an old man:

"You don't write anymore?" she said.
"There hasn't been anything I've wanted to say," I said.
"After all you've seen, all you've been through, darling?"
she said.

"It's all I've seen, all I've been through," I said, "that makes it damn nearly impossible for me to say anything. I've lost the knack of making sense. I speak gibberish to the civilized world, and it replies in kind."[92]

CHAPTER 7

FEAR OF FINDING A WORTHY SUBJECT OR A DEARTH OF DEATH

What if you love to write, you want to be a writer, but you don't feel that something sufficiently monumental has happened to you? That is, sufficiently monumental about which it is worthwhile to write? Vonnegut has some things to say about that.

PATIENCE

A young woman to whom I was
teaching Creative Writing at CCNY
years ago, confessed to me,
half-ashamed, as though
this was keeping her
from being a truly creative writer,
that she had never seen
a dead person.
I put my hand on her shoulder,
and I said,
"One must be patient."[93]

That's one piece of Kurt's advice. Here's another:

> When the city [of Dresden] was demolished, I had no idea of
> the scale of the thing. . . . I had no scale except for what I'd
> seen in the movies. When I got home (I was a writer since
> I had been on the *Cornell Sun*, except that was the extent
> of my writing) I thought of writing my war story, too. All
> my friends were home; they'd had wonderful adventures,
> too. I went down to the newspaper office, the Indianapolis
> *News*, and looked to find out what they had about Dresden.
> There was an item about half an inch long, which said our
> planes had been over Dresden and two had been lost. And
> so I figured, well, this really was the most minor sort of
> detail in World War II. Others had so much more to write
> about. I remember envying Andy Rooney, who jumped into
> print at that time; I didn't know him, but I think he was
> the first guy to publish his war story after the war; it was
> called *Air Gunner*. Hell, I never had any classy adventure
> like that. But every so often I would meet a European and
> we would be talking about the war and I would say I was
> in Dresden; he'd be astonished that I'd been there, and
> he'd always want to know more. Then a book by David
> Irving was published about Dresden, saying it was the
> largest massacre in European history. I said, By God, I
> saw something after all![94]

Maybe you, too, have seen something after all. Maybe what
you've witnessed merely in your own back*yard* is something. Henry
David Thoreau lived in Concord, Massachusetts. And he had this
to say: "I have traveled extensively in Concord." Vonnegut used
that as the epigraph for his first nonfiction collection, *Wampeters,
Foma & Granfalloons*. He explains:

> That quotation was probably first brought to my attention

by one of my magnificent teachers in high school. Thoreau, I now feel, wrote in the voice of a child, as do I. And what he said about Concord is what every child feels, what every child seemingly *must* feel, about the place where he or she was born. There is surely more than enough to marvel at for a lifetime, no matter where the child is born.

Castles? Indianapolis was full of them.[95]

———

You do not have to experience death or destruction or agony to write. You simply have to care about something. Perhaps what you care about is joyful.

At the Iowa Writers' Workshop, in a Form of Fiction class (a required literature class geared toward examining fiction from a writer's perspective, comprised of about eighty students), Kurt taught a Chekhov story. I can't remember the name of it. I didn't quite understand the point, since nothing much happened. An adolescent girl is in love with this boy and that boy and another. She points at a little dog, as I recall, or maybe something else, and laughs. That's all. There's no conflict, no dramatic turning point or change. Kurt pointed out that she has no words for the sheer joy of being ripe with life, her own juiciness, the promise of romance. Her inarticulate feelings spill into laughter at something innocuous. That's what happened in the story. His absolute delight in that girl's joy of feeling so alive was so encouraging of delight. Kurt's enchantment taught me that such moments are nothing to sneeze at. They're worth a story.

———

Maybe it's impossible, if you're young, as that student at City College was, to have experienced or accomplished what older people have accomplished. At the Iowa Workshop, having been admitted with only one story under my belt and having majored in sociology, so that I knew little about the profession of writing and, like Kurt, felt outclassed by my peers and ignorant of English literature, I used to compare myself with my writing teachers. They'd had at least twenty more years of life to roam around in, to read and write in!

Vonnegut opines about the generations:

> What is it the slightly older people want from the slightly younger people? They want credit for having survived so long, and often imaginatively, under difficult conditions. Slightly younger people are intolerably stingy about giving them credit for that.
>
> What is it the slightly younger people want from the slightly older people? More than anything, I think, they want acknowledgement and without further ado that they are without question women and men now. Slightly older people are intolerably stingy about making any such acknowledgement.[96]

I once read an interview with John Barth and Kurt Vonnegut and others in which Vonnegut stated that the reason all writers write, of course, is that they want to change the world. Whereupon Barth objected. No, he said. That wasn't why he wrote. As I recall, Barth said, in effect, that he just liked to horse around with words.

Asked what affinity he felt toward his "brother and sister writers," Vonnegut answered, "Friendly, certainly. It's hard for me to talk to some of them, since we seem to be in very different sorts of businesses ["like podiatry and deep-sea diving," he suggested elsewhere]. This was a mystery to me for a while."[97] Then Saul Steinberg, his graphic artist friend, cleared it up: "There are two types of artists, neither superior to the other. One responds to life itself. The other responds to the history of his or her art so far."[98]

> I fell into the [first] . . . group, and had to. I couldn't play games with my literary ancestors, since I had never studied them systematically.[99]

Maybe you adore your literary ancestors. Maybe responding to them is the kind of artist you are. Maybe that's what *you* care about.

———

Less reasonably, Vonnegut opined:

> I think it can be tremendously refreshing if a creator of literature has something on his mind other than the history of literature so far. Literature should not disappear up its own asshole, so to speak.[100]

———

Vonnegut is notoriously playful in how he *handles* his serious responses to life in writing. He goofs around. In *Breakfast of Champions* especially he keeps coming onstage and messing around with his characters and therefore us, his readers, showing how much fun and even silly a thing it is to be the creator of his book's universe.

> "Give me a Black and White and water," he heard the waitress say, and Wayne should have pricked up his ears at that. That particular drink wasn't for any ordinary person. That drink was for the person who had created all Wayne's

misery to date, who could kill him or make him a millionaire or send him back to prison or do whatever he damn pleased with Wayne. That drink was for me.[101]

———

There's a tall children's book with a gorgeous bright blue cover adorned by one sun, moon, and star called *Sun Moon Star*. Originally published in 1980, it's by Kurt Vonnegut and Ivan Chermayeff, a graphic designer and creator of the PBS, Mobil, and NBC logos, among many others, who happened to be my summer neighbor. I'd wondered how they knew each other and went about collaborating. I imagined them bouncing story and picture ideas off one another over a period of time.

Ivan Chermayeff told me a different story:

They met in the '70s through a mutual friend, and at that time Ivan had been making collages, and the friend said he ought to show them to Kurt. Ivan said, "I was just interested in the different shapes of the sun, moon, and stars, and their relationships, so I made hundreds of collages without any idea whatsoever of what I was going to do with them." He followed his friend's advice and "handed Kurt the stack of about a hundred collages, and then I didn't hear from him for three months. And I thought, oh well, Kurt isn't interested or got occupied. Then Kurt called. He came over and put his feet up on my big desk and watched me go through what he'd done." Ivan laughed. "What he'd done had nothing whatsoever to do with sun, moon, and stars. Kurt had put them in his own order and used his own idea, which was about as far from my idea as he could get. The only thing he didn't do was change my title." Ivan chuckled. "He really enjoyed watching my reaction. And I loved that he surprised me."

The story Kurt construed from Ivan's images? A tale of the birth of the Creator of the Universe, from the point of view of the newborn.

The book flap copy, as it turns out, reveals their process:

> This book is an experiment in making music for the eye rather than the ear.
>
> Ivan Chermayeff made the illustrations first, without saying what they meant. Then Kurt Vonnegut wrote words to fit the images he saw.
>
> This is a song then, whose music came first.
>
> A simple hymn for printing press. Others may find it entertaining to put their own words to Chermayeff's tune.

Just a couple of grown men at play: one with shapes and their relationships, the other with words and their relationships to shapes.

Play around! *or* On with the Music!

CHAPTER 8

THE LAST WORD ON THE PRIME MOVER OR FEAR NOT

If you *do* feel an urgency "in your heart" that others should hear what you have to say about a subject, that deep-felt urgency will sustain you to follow the quest over years, stops and starts, the wrong approach, the roller coaster of drudgery, elation, despair.

There's scientific evidence that being motivated by intrinsic interest results in the greatest success, even more than when combined with practical incentives.[102]

Here's what Vonnegut wrote to his disheartened friend, the Chilean writer José Donoso. It's "the closest he came to a personal manifesto about the writer's challenge to keep working," according to his biographer.[103] José also taught at the Iowa workshop, and he and Kurt and their wives became close friends. Kurt Vonnegut had been working on *Slaughterhouse-Five* for twenty-two years. José Donoso had been working on his book, *The Obscene Bird of Night*, for ten years. José wrote Kurt, telling him that he despaired of it. He was having suicidal thoughts. The writing of it had been wrenching, and now he was feeling incapable, inferior, and impotent. He had just boxed it up, all one thousand pages.

Kurt was on his way to revisit Dresden to do research for *Slaughterhouse-Five* with his war buddy Bernard O'Hare. They'd been "royally hosed by a communist travel agent" whose bungled papers didn't permit the trip they'd paid for to Leningrad. Now

they'd rerouted and were in Helsinki, as he scribbles in pencil to
José along with other news. Then he says:

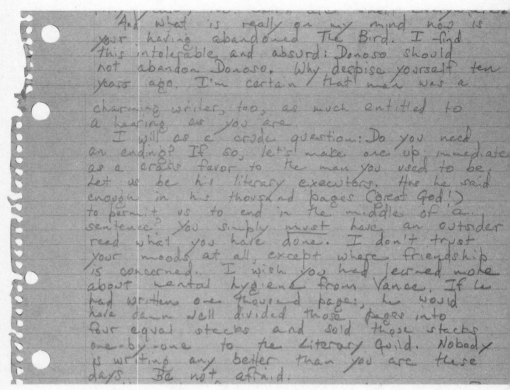

"And what is really on my mind now is
your having abandoned The Bird. I find
this intolerable and absurd: Donoso should
not abandon Donoso. Why despise yourself ten
years ago. I'm certain that man was a
charming writer, too, as much entitled to
a hearing as you are.
    I will as a crude question: Do you need
an ending? If so, let's make one up immediate
as a crazy favor to the man you used to be.
Let us be his literary executors. Has he said
enough in his thousand pages (Great God!)
to permit us to end in the middle of a
sentence? You simply must have an outsider
read what you have done. I don't trust
your moods at all, except where friendship
is concerned. I wish you had learned more
about mental hygiene from Vance. If he
had written one thousand pages, he would
have damn well divided those pages into
four equal stacks and sold those stacks
one-by-one to the Literary Guild. Nobody
is writing any better than you are these
days. Be not afraid.

Letter from Kurt Vonnegut to José Donoso, October 1967. **Courtesy of José
Donoso papers, Department of Rare Books and Special Collections, Princeton University, Princeton, New Jersey.**

If you *do* possess such urgency about your subject, dear writer,
then, lifted from this letter, here's breakthrough Rule #6: "Be
not afraid."

CHAPTER 9
SOUL GROWTH

The primary benefit of practicing any art, whether well or badly, is that it enables one's soul to grow.[104]

Vonnegut espoused this belief many times in many ways, especially as he grew older. "Writing was a spiritual exercise for my father," his son Mark says, "the only thing he really believed in."[105]

———

Wine writer Allan Yarrow shares this Vonnegut anecdote annually on his blog for those aspiring to write—for little monetary recompense—about wine:

> I was taking a fiction writing class one spring, and our teacher managed to convince a good friend of hers to substitute teach a bunch of us eager, bright-eyed college students for one class session. The first thing Kurt Vonnegut said to the twelve of us in his mellow raspy voice, as he slouched in the uncomfortable, dim room was "The novel is dead. No one reads fiction anymore. America has divested itself of its imagination. It's over."
>
> In my memory, he said this and rambled on some more while chain-smoking cigarettes. While I've probably invented the cigarettes, I definitely remember his words

though, and his answer to the timid question one of us managed to squeak out at the end of his rant.

"So, uh, are you saying that, um, we should just forget about this fiction writing thing?"

At this, Mr. Vonnegut (stubbing out his cigarette, of course) sat up a little straighter and got a bit of a glint in his eye, and said,

"Oh no. Don't get the wrong idea here. You'll never make a living at being a writer. Hell you may even die trying. But that doesn't mean you shouldn't write. You should write for the same reasons you should take dancing lessons. For the same reason you should learn what fork to use at a fancy dinner. For the same reason you need to see the world. It's about grace."[106]

Vonnegut was addressing a beginners' college class. To committed writers, he said the same kind of thing, with added weight:

Bill Gates says, "Wait till you can see what your computer can become." But it's you who should be doing the becoming, not the damn fool computer. What you can become is the miracle you were born to be through the work that you do.[107]

The arts are not a way to make a living. They are a very human way of making life more bearable. Practicing an art, no matter how well or badly, is a way to make your soul grow, for heaven's sake.[108]

Practicing an art as a "way to make the soul grow" may sound like a vague platitude. What does Vonnegut mean, "make the soul grow"? What is the "soul"?

It's this, according to *Webster's*:

* the spiritual or immaterial part of a human being or animal, regarded as immortal
* a person's moral or emotional nature or sense of identity

It's *this*, according to Vonnegut's character in *Breakfast of Champions*, the painter Rabo Karabekian, in explaining his abstract expressionist painting, a huge green painting intersected by a single strip of day-glo orange tape:

> It is a picture of *the awareness of every animal*. It is *the immaterial core of every animal*—the 'I am' to which all messages are sent. It is all that is alive in any of us—in a mouse, in a deer, in a cocktail waitress. It is unwavering and pure, no matter what preposterous adventure may befall us. . . . *Our awareness is all that is alive and maybe sacred in any of us*. Everything else about us is dead machinery [all italics mine].[109]

How does the soul—our awareness—grow? Here are some ways and means.

Vonnegut says in the preface to his first nonfiction collection:

> I find scant evidence in my nonfiction that I have matured at all. I cannot find a single idea I hadn't swiped from somebody else and enunciated plonkingly by the time I reached the seventh grade.
>
> My adventures in the writing of fiction, however, have been far more surprising and amusing, to *me*, at least. I may actually have done some sort of growing up in that field. That would be nice, if that were so. It might prove that works of the imagination themselves have the power to create.

If a person with a demonstrably ordinary mind, like mine, will devote himself to giving birth to a work of the imagination, that work will in turn tempt and tease that ordinary mind into cleverness. A painter friend, James Brooks, told me last summer, "I put the first brush stroke on the canvas. After that, it is up to the canvas to do at least half the work." The same might be said for writing paper and clay and film and vibrating air, and for all the other lifeless substances human beings have managed to turn into teachers and playmates. . . .

So I now believe that the only way in which Americans can rise above their ordinariness, can mature sufficiently to rescue themselves and to help rescue their planet, is through enthusiastic intimacy with works of their own imaginations. I am not especially satisfied with my own imaginative works, my fiction. *I am simply impressed by the unexpected insights which shower down on me when my job is to imagine, as contrasted with the woodenly familiar ideas which clutter my desk when my job is to tell the truth* [all italics mine].[110]

Why should this be so? For simply setting down the truth on paper can be quite validating. Writing is a generosity, even to yourself. This happened, and you bear witness by writing it down. You think and observe this particular way, and by that specific presentation you assert your individuality and confirm the value of your experience.

But with fiction, a portal opens onto the mystery of the imagination and the unconscious—in other words, onto all that which may be hidden from awareness.

A professor at Hunter College, Louise DeSalvo, wrote a marvelous book called *Writing as a Way of Healing*. She asserts that not all writing leads to healing—freewriting doesn't, or objective description of trauma, or venting—and lists specific methods that do. "Writing that describes traumatic or distressing events in detail *and* how we felt about these events then and feel about them now is the only kind of writing about trauma that clinically has been associated with improved health."

DeSalvo's prescription is precisely what often happens in the process of writing fiction.

Fiction requires the mask of character: that is, taking on an imagined character's view. That lends to empathizing. "Give a man a mask," Oscar Wilde said, "and he will tell the truth."

Fiction begs for change. There's no story if there's no change. Without confrontation of someone else, of some issue, or of something within the character, and a shift in that confrontation, the story is static, stillborn.

Fiction is narrative. That is, it occurs over a period of time, even if only a short period of time. It lends itself to a "then" and "now."

Of course, not all fiction adheres to the principles DeSalvo presents. And nonfiction certainly can, especially memoir: her book, after all, is addressed to people writing nonfiction. In whichever form, however, according to controlled clinical experiments, she says, "We must write in a way that links detailed descriptions of what happened with feelings—then and now—about what happened."[111]

That's what Kurt Vonnegut did in many of his novels.

We'll look at two of them as examples of means to Vonnegut's own soul growth, and perhaps inspiration for your own.

———

"One way to approach a story," the writer Josephine Humphreys suggests, "is to think of it as the writer's response to the most important question he can ask. The response is often complex, ambiguous and changeable, but the question is simple and almost always the same. The bigger the question, the riskier the fiction."[112]

Listen to the question Vonnegut asks about the firebombing of Dresden during an interview soon after the publication of *Slaughterhouse-Five*:

The American and British air forces together killed 135,000 people in two hours. This is a world's record.

We got through it, the Americans there, because we were quartered in the stockyards where it was wide and open and there was a meat locker three stories beneath the surface, the only decent shelter in the city. So we went down into the meat locker, and when we came up again the city was gone and everybody was dead. We walked for miles before we saw anybody else: all organic things were consumed.

How the hell do I feel about burning down that city? I don't know. The burning of the cities was in response to the savagery of the Nazis, and fair really was fair, except that it gets confusing when you see the victims. That sort of arithmetic is disturbing. When I finally came home from the war, I was upset about it because what we had seen cleaning out the shelters was as fancy as what we would have seen cleaning out the crematoria. *How do you balance off Dresden against Auschwitz? Do you balance it off; or is it all so absurd it's silly to talk about?* [italics mine]

As the Fairy Godmother would have it, while composing this section, I happened to meet (at the opening of my husband's retrospective at the Liechtenstein Museum) another victim of the Dresden firebombing: a German, Mr. Frank Preuss. He was five years old when it happened.

I told Herr Preuss about Kurt Vonnegut's experience. He told me he had a few vivid memories. He shared them afterward in a phone call:

My first memory is the night the British started bombing. We are in the *luftschutz*—the cellar—of our apartment building. My brother and I are kneeling before our mother, who is six months pregnant, hiding our faces in our mother's lap.

There was a lot of noise and bustle, neighbors coming in and my father trying to rescue them and their belongings the entire night.

The next morning we spent trying to get to my father's parents, a suburb ten kilometers distant. I remember debris and smoke everywhere. I saw an old lady in a black dress, her face covered in blood. I asked my mother, "Do you see this old lady with her bloody face?" I saw a soldier in a gray uniform, lying on the street without his head. "Mommy, Mommy," I said, "look at this soldier without his head." Thirty years later my father started to write his memories and he wrote that down, my saying "Daddy, Daddy, look at this soldier without a head!"

We had to cross an open meadow and a bridge over the Elbe. Bombers were flying over. The bombs were huge, like *Litfasssaeule*, the columns that display advertisements all over Europe, about 1.2 meters in diameter, 3.5 meters high.

It was terrifying. My little brother, who was three, quit speaking for days.

About two weeks later, at the end of February, my family headed north with others on a ship towards Hamburg. Bombers shot and killed one of our crew. I opened the cabin door in a moment when my parents weren't looking, and I saw the face of the pilot. It was that close.

He was told later it was very difficult to navigate the river because of the debris.

I asked what the adults said about the firebombing in retrospect. "We didn't talk about it later. My father and mother never talked about it." He paused. "Many people of my generation didn't talk to their parents about it.

"It was unexpected, I learned later," he said, "because Dresden was not a military spot, and it was full of refugees. The population was usually five hundred thousand but had swelled to over a million."

I told him that's what Vonnegut reported. I quoted Vonnegut about Churchill ordering it:

> The trouble with Dresden was restraint surely, or lack of restraint. . . . The politicians went mad, as they often do. The man responsible for the bombing of Dresden against a lot of advice was Winston Churchill. It's the brain of one man, the rage of one man, the pride of one man.[113]

"Yes," Mr. Preuss said to me. "Churchill, for revenge and to demoralize."

We concluded our conversation. There was no blame in his voice. There was, it seemed to me, the same large question Vonnegut posed. Understanding the savagery of the Nazis, and therefore the British and Americans' desire for revenge: but Frank Preuss was five years old. Disturbing arithmetic.

A major insight Vonnegut accrued in wrangling with transforming his Dresden experience into fiction was about the nature of memory and trauma:

> The most difficult thing about it was that I had forgotten about it. And I learned about catastrophes from that, and from talking to other people who had been involved in avalanches and floods and great fires, that there is some device in our brain which switches off and prevents our remembering catastrophes above a certain scale. I don't know whether it is just a limitation of our nervous system, or whether it's actually a gadget which protects us in some way. But I, in fact, remembered nothing about the bombing of Dresden although I had been there, and did everything short of hiring a hypnotist to recover the information. I wrote to many of the guys who

went through it with me saying "Help me remember" and the answer every time was a refusal, a simple flat refusal. They did not want to think about it. There was a writer in *Life* magazine—I don't know how much he knows about rabbits and the nervous system—who claimed that rabbits have no memory, which is one of their defensive mechanisms. If they recalled every close shave they had in the course of just an hour, life would become insupportable. As soon as they'd escaped from a Doberman Pinscher, why, they forgot all about it. And they could scarcely afford to remember it.[114]

This thin book is about what it's like to write a book about a thing like that. I couldn't get much closer. I would head myself into my memory of it, the circuit breakers would kick out; I'd head in again, I'd back off. The book is a process of twenty years of this sort of living with Dresden and the aftermath. It's like Heinrich Böll's book, *Absent Without Leave*—stories about German soldiers with the war part missing. You see them leave and return, but there's this terrible hole in the middle.[115]

Vonnegut observed this phenomenon in his orphaned nephews, three of whom he and his wife Jane raised after his sister and her husband died within two days of each other.

As adults, his nephews revealed to Vonnegut

a creepy business which used to worry them a lot: They cannot find their mother or their father in their memories anywhere—not anywhere.

The museums in children's minds, I think, automatically empty themselves in times of utmost horror—to protect the children from eternal grief.[116]

Vonnegut's playwright character in *Deadeye Dick* says:

> I have this trick for dealing with all my worst memories. I insist that they are plays. The characters are actors. Their speeches and movements are stylized, arch. I am in the presence of art.[117]

When Frank Preuss and I first spoke, he said, "I remember these few incidents vividly. They never affected me, no trauma. They are simply vivid memories." After I e-mailed him these pages, he wrote back: "Strange: I have told my story a few times and it was just like telling some story. When I read your lines, however, I was shivering."

They were not my lines. They were his. I simply wrote them down.

You already have evidence of Vonnegut's soul growth in writing *Slaughterhouse-Five* from what I've presented here and from what he himself tells in his first chapter.

Even the title he landed on conveys his discoveries. Not the one it's been reduced to on the front of the book for years now: *Slaughterhouse-Five.* I mean the original, with "or" and *"The Children's Crusade"* placed front and center. Here's the way it appears in my treasured, autographed, hardback copy from 1969:

First–edition hardcover of *Slaughterhouse-Five* (New York: Delacorte Press, 1969). Photo by the author.

Vonnegut himself said, about his growth, a few years after *Slaughterhouse-Five*'s publication:

> I felt after I finished [it] that I didn't have to write at all any-more if I didn't want to. It was the end of some sort of career. I don't know why, exactly. I suppose that flowers, when they're through blooming, have some sort of awareness of some pur-pose having been served. Flowers didn't ask to be flowers and I didn't ask to be me. At the end of *Slaughterhouse-Five*, I had the feeling that I had produced this blossom. So I had a shutting-off feeling, you know, that I had done what I was supposed to do and everything was OK. And that was the end of it. I could figure out my missions for myself after that.[118]

That "shutting-off feeling" didn't end his writing. Or his struggles. It opened a Pandora's box of others.

He suffered a kind of postpartum depression.

Vonnegut began going through the "big ka-BOOM," as his eldest daughter, Edie, called it: he was thrust into overnight success and fame. His family, sense of self, and his world were coming apart and reconfiguring themselves.

He swore that he was through writing novels. His interest turned to commedia dell'arte and plays for a while.

However, he discovered, as he said much later,

> in a piece in *Harper's*, or a letter I wrote to *Harper's*, about "the death of the novel": *People will continue to write novels, or maybe short stories, because they discover that they are treating their own neuroses.*[119]

This time what showed up on Vonnegut's plate for him to deal with were his parents.

Treat one trauma and another surfaces.

A writer's voice is "grounded in a single scene," Reynolds Price posits, "most often a lingering sight from childhood or early youth. And that scene is almost always one that a seasoned reader may well suspect lies near the start of a given writer's reason for writing, the physical moment in which a single enormous question rose before a watchful child and fueled the lifelong search for an answer."[120]

Perhaps the scene or scenes Vonnegut wanted to know about were the ferocious arguments his parents had in the middle of the night.[121] Why, the child Kurt must have asked, are they so unhappy? Is it my fault?

Asked about his aura of sadness, Vonnegut replied in a 1973 interview,

> Well, there are sad things from my childhood, which I assume have something to do with my sadness. . . . There are two [gravestones] out there in Indianapolis, and I looked at those two stones side by side and I just wished—I could hear it in my head, I knew so much what I wished—that they had been happier than they were. It would have been so goddamned easy for them to be happier than they were. So that makes me sad. . . .
>
> . . . They wrecked their lives thinking the wrong things. And, damn it, it wouldn't have taken much effort to get them to think about the right things.[122]

At the interview's conclusion, he circles back to this topic.

> One thing writing *Breakfast* did for me was to bring right to the surface my anger with my parents for not being happier than they were. . . . I'm damned if I'll pass their useless sadness on to my children if I can possibly help it.[123]

Reading *Breakfast of Champions* feels to me like going on a reckless spree, a wild, hilarious ride. People's delusions drive them, and childlike drawings abound. Vonnegut skewers guises and bullshit and misguided beliefs by exposing those in his characters, in all their damaging, heartbreaking absurdity.

Could his parents have helped themselves or were they programmed by their chemistry and their own upbringings to behave as they did? Is it possible for anyone to transcend his or her own chemistry and programming?

Vonnegut was going to a therapist, trying to understand depression and his own regularly periodic bursts of temper. In this novel, he said,

> The motives of all the characters are explained in terms of body chemistry. . . .
> Suicide is at the heart of the book.[124]

In it, the narrator says to himself,

> You're afraid you'll kill yourself the way your mother did.[125]

Vonnegut comments:

> As for real death—it has always been a temptation to me, since my mother solved so many problems with it. The child of a suicide will naturally think of death, the big one, as a logical solution to any problem, even one in simple algebra.[126]

It's unclear whether his mother committed suicide or overdosed on barbiturates. Whichever it was, the timing of her death was terrible. Kurt was in basic training. He had come home on a surprise leave with a three-day pass over Mother's Day. His sister Alice had come home as well. The third morning—on Mother's Day—they found their mother dead.

His son Mark says that earlier in his life, Kurt didn't refer to his mother's death as suicide. Kurt's brother and father weren't certain. She was a writer and left no note. But she was a very absent, depressed mother, locking herself in her room for long periods. Mark thinks Kurt may have lumped all that absence together as "suicide."

Whether intentional or not, death is the ultimate leave-taking. It can feel like abandonment. If someone—especially your own mother—isn't willing to live for your sake, it can make you feel worthless. It can feel like your fault. Talk about survivor's guilt.

Having been around suicide and its survivors—my sister is the survivor of her first husband's suicide—I can hardly bear, dear Kurt, thinking of the impact of this.

> *Breakfast of Champions* isn't a threat to commit suicide, incidentally. It's my promise that I'm beyond that now. Which is something for me. I used to think of it as a perfectly reasonable way to avoid delivering a lecture, to avoid a deadline, to not pay a bill, to not go to a cocktail party.[127]

As usual, this "quest" in novel form did not occur in a straight line. Once upon a time, *Breakfast of Champions* and *Slaughterhouse-Five* were going to be one book.[128] Later, *Breakfast of Champions* was going to be about a world in which everyone, except the narrator, is a robot. Even Jesus Christ: "He was a robot who died for my sins."[129]

When it was finally finished, he said,

> I have a feeling that *Breakfast* will be the last of the therapeutic books, which is probably too bad. Craziness makes for some beautiful accidents in art. At the end of *Breakfast*, I give characters I've used over and over again their freedom. I tell them I won't be needing them anymore. They

can pursue their own destinies. I guess that means I'm free to pursue my destiny, too. I don't have to take care of them anymore.[130]

Everyone wants absolutes. Even Kurt Vonnegut, who abhorred absolutes. He wants his characters' freedom and his freedom from them, and for this to be the last "therapeutic book." But none of these prove true. His characters return, including suicidal characters and veterans, and their subjects. But never again are the issues of suicide and war the main focus in Vonnegut's work. This seems psychologically on target. When addressed, the most vital concerns one has—the impact of events and people that have most deeply touched your life—don't disappear. But they certainly may lighten up.

There's evidence that diving into trauma can backfire.[131]

In *God Bless You, Mr. Rosewater*, Eliot Rosewater suffers a breakdown and is in a mental hospital. A musician who entertains mental patients meets him there. The musician's son says,

> "Father thought Eliot was the sanest American he had ever met. . . . I remember Father's introduction: 'I want you all to meet the only American who has so far noticed the Second World War.'" . . .
>
> ". . . He said, 'This young Captain I'm bringing home—he despises art. Can you imagine? *Despises* it—and yet he does it in such a way that I can't help loving him for it. What he's saying, I think, is that art has failed him, which, I must admit, is a very fair thing for a man who has bayoneted a fourteen-year-old boy in the line of duty to say.'"[132]

CHAPTER 10
SANCTUARY

Besides nurturing the soul, Vonnegut notes, the act of writing can be a solace and refuge.

I found me a place where I can do good without doing any harm. —Boaz in Sarah Horne Canby's *Unk and Boaz in the Caves of Mercury*[133]

In *Bluebeard*,

I asked her if she would write. I meant letters to me, but she thought I meant books. "That's all I do—that and dancing," she said. "As long as I keep that up, I keep grief away." All summer long, she had made it easy to forget that she had recently lost a husband who was evidently brilliant and funny and adorable.[134]

Using the Socratic method, [James Slotkin, Vonnegut's professor at the University of Chicago] asked his little class this: "What is it an artist does—a painter, a writer, a sculptor—?"

He already had an answer, which he had put down in the book he was writing, a book which would never be published. But he would not tell us what it was until the end of the hour, and he might discard it entirely if our answers to his question made more sense than his. This was a class

107

composed entirely of veterans of the Second World War in the summertime. The class had been put together in order that we might continue to receive our living expenses from our government when most of the rest of the university was on vacation.

If any of us came up with good answers, I now have no idea what they might have been. His answer was this: "The artist says, 'I can do very little about the chaos around me, but at least I can reduce to perfect order this square of canvas, this piece of paper, this chunk of stone.'"

Everybody knows that.

• • •

Most of my adult life has been spent in bringing to some kind of order sheets of paper eight and a half inches wide and eleven inches long. This severely limited activity has allowed me to ignore many a storm. . . .

• • •

About nine years ago I was asked to deliver an address to the American Institute and Academy of Arts and Letters here. I was not then a member, and was terrified. I had left home, and was spending most of my time counting flowers on the wall and watching Captain Kangaroo in a tiny apartment on East Fifty-fourth Street. My friend with the gambling sickness had just cleaned out my bank account and my son had gone insane in British Columbia.

I asked my wife please not to come, since I was rattled enough as it was. I asked a woman with whom I had been keeping company some not to come, either—for the same reason. So they both came, all dressed up for a fancy execution.

What saved my life? Pieces of paper eight and a half inches wide and eleven inches long.

• • •

I am sorry for people who have no knack for reducing to seeming order some little thing.[135]

But everybody can. And people do. Vonnegut knew that. The most unread among us, the most unlikely to write, will take pen to paper in times of duress or to record important occurrences or to make sense of a perplexing time in their lives.

In *The Sirens of Titan*, the character Unk writes a letter to himself before his memory is wiped out:

> It was literature in its finest sense, since it made Unk courageous, watchful, and secretly free. It made him his own hero in very trying times.[136]

If you're professional, like Vonnegut, you will be exacting about word choice, sequence, punctuation, and rhythms. You will strive for "Those masterful images because complete," as Yeats says, and that will take "all [your] thought and love."[137] Or at least, your absorption. That's sanctuary.

One can also whittle, bake.

> What is that perfect picture which any five-year-old can paint? Two unwavering bands of light.[138]

CHAPTER 11
WHAT MAKES GREAT ART or ART AND SOUL

Although any child, every child, can draw that picture, all results are not equal.

Here's a third definition for "soul," according to *Webster's*: "emotional or intellectual energy or intensity, especially as revealed in a work of art or an artistic performance."

What makes a work of art great? Soul.

What constitutes soul in a work of art? Here's the deal according to Vonnegut, speaking here through his character Rabo Karabekian, who is assessing another fictional painter, Dan Gregory:

> But he lacked the guts or the wisdom, or maybe just the talent, to indicate somehow that time was liquid, that one moment was no more important than any other, and that all moments quickly run away.
>
> Let me put it another way: Dan Gregory was a taxidermist. He stuffed and mounted and varnished and mothproofed supposedly great moments. . . .
>
> Let me put it yet another way: life, by definition, is never still. Where is it going? From birth to death, with no stops on the way. Even a picture of a bowl of pears on a checkered tablecloth is liquid, if laid on canvas by the brush of a master. Yes, and by some miracle I was surely never able to achieve as a painter, nor was Dan Gregory, but which

was achieved by the best of the Abstract Expressionists, in the paintings which have greatness birth and death are always there.[139]

Gary Kuehn. *Practitioner's Delight*, 1966, steel, fiberglass, and enamel. Collection MMK Museum für Moderne Kunst Frankfurt am Main, Former Rolf Ricke collection at Kunstmuseum St. Gallen, Kunstmuseum Liechtenstein, Vaduz, MMK Museum für Moderne Kunst Frankfurt am Main. Courtesy of the artist.

I mourned the destruction of Dresden because it was only temporarily a Nazi city, and had for centuries been an art treasure belonging to earthlings everywhere. It could have been that again. The same was true of Angkor Wat, which military scientists have demolished more recently for some imagined gain.[140]

Now, at this writing, it's Syria's time to be ravaged of art treasures "belonging to earthlings everywhere." So it goes.

⸻

In *Deadeye Dick*, while dedicating an arts center, a Reverend Harrell

declared that the most important arts centers a city could have were human beings, not buildings. [He points out a playwright.] "There in the back sits an arts center named 'Rudy Waltz,'" he said.[141]

CHAPTER 12
AGENTS OF CHANGE

Writers get a nice break in one way, at least: They can treat their mental illnesses every day. If I'm lucky, the books have amounted to more than that. I'd like to be a useful citizen, a specialized cell in the body politic.[142]

For Kurt Vonnegut, the personal and political were inextricably bound. Soon after *Slaughterhouse-Five* became a best seller, an interviewer asked him, "Beyond the fact that it's become a profitable way to make a living, why do you write?"

My motives are political. I agree with Stalin and Hitler and Mussolini that the writer should serve his society. I differ with dictators as to *how* writers should serve.

He went on.

Writers are specialized cells in the social organism. They are evolutionary cells. Mankind is trying to become something else; it's experimenting with new ideas all the time. And writers are a means of introducing new ideas into the society, and also a means of responding symbolically to life. . . .
. . . We're expressions of the entire society. . . . And when a society is in great danger, we're likely to sound the alarms.

I have the canary-bird-in-the-coal-mine theory of the arts.[143]

In another interview, he said,

> I would not be interested in writing if I didn't feel that what
> I wrote was an act of good citizenship or an attempt, at any
> rate, to be a good citizen. What brought my ancestors over
> here from Germany was not oppression over there, but
> simply the attractiveness of the United States Constitution,
> and the dream of brotherhood here. And also plenty of
> land. They were attracted materially too. I was raised to
> be bughouse about the Constitution, and to be very excited
> about the United States of America as a Utopia. It still
> seems utterly workable to me and I keep thinking of ways
> to fix it, to see what the hell went wrong, to see if we can
> get the thing to really run right.[144]

Kurt Vonnegut Jr. grew up with evidence that contributing to
your community was worthwhile, was something a man should do.
His architect grandfather designed what is still one of the largest
public spaces in Indianapolis. It's beautiful. His father and grandfather together designed a department store—now gone—along with
the clock outside it, the Ayres Clock, which still stands at a major
intersection. His father was a founder of the Children's Museum,
still one of the largest in the country. He was raised around useful
monuments to citizenship that patriarchs of his family bestowed.
Now a gigantic mural of him adorns a wall a few blocks from his
grandfather's building.

I was invited to speak in Indianapolis in spring 2014 for the Kurt
Vonnegut Museum and Library's fund-raising event. And where
was the fund-raiser held, where did I give the speech in which I told
my audience about Kurt Vonnegut as a teacher at the Iowa Writers'
Workshop, and what I learned from him, and how important his
singular voice is to us all? In the building his grandfather Bernard

designed, the Atheneum—originally named, before World War II, Das Deutsche Haus.[145]

Incidentally, he also grew up surrounded by monuments to war. There are an astonishing number in Indianapolis. Listen to this: "The Indiana War Memorial Plaza Historic District contains two museums, three parks, and 24 acres of monuments, statues, sculptures, and fountains in the heart of downtown Indianapolis, making the state's capital second only to Washington D.C. in acreage and number of monuments dedicated to veterans."[146]

I think writers are the most important members of society, not just potentially but actually. Good writers must have and stand by their own ideas.[147]

Mainly, I think they should be—and biologically have to be—agents of change.[148]

Think of *Uncle Tom's Cabin*, *The Jungle*, *Black Like Me*, *Catch*-22, *Invisible Man*, *The Fire Next Time*, *The Feminine Mystique*, *Silent Spring*. Now, *you* name some off the top of your head.

Vonnegut's own work serves as evidence of his canary-in-the-coalmine theory. Looking back on his first novel, *Player Piano*, years later, he said:

The book predicted what has indeed come to pass, a day when machines, because they are so dependable and efficient and tireless, and getting cheaper all the time, are taking the halfway decent jobs from human beings.[149]

That doesn't seem particularly prescient. Machinery had been used increasingly since the Industrial Revolution, certainly during and just after World War II, when he wrote *Player Piano*.

But get this:

The protagonist Paul drives an old Plymouth. Bud, an inventor, drives by and shows off his futuristic car to Paul. It's astonishingly automatic—as cars are today—but very far from automobiles of the late '40s and early '50s when Kurt was composing the novel, in which you were obliged to operate everything, and with force: shift gears, roll a window up or down, lock and unlock the door, steer, and brake.[150]

And listen to *this* passage, in which Paul's secretary, Katherine, hands him his speech that she's typed, commenting that she thinks it's good:

> What you said about the Second Industrial Revolution . . . that part where you say how the First Industrial Revolution devalued muscle work, then the second one devalued routine mental work . . . Do you suppose there'll be a Third Industrial Revolution?

Paul says,

> I guess the third one's been going on for some time, if you mean thinking machines. *That would be the third revolution I guess—machines that devaluate human thinking* [italics mine]. Some of the big computers like EPICAC do that all right, in specialized fields.

Katherine replies after a bit, "First the muscle work, then the routine work, then, maybe, the real brainwork."

Paul says, "I hope I'm not around long enough to see that final step."[151]

Thus Vonnegut imagined and wrote, years before the advent of the personal computer and the Internet—years before "an autonomous automobile" drove itself, as occurred last week while I was composing this.[152]

———

Let's hope that Vonnegut's novel *Galápagos* is prescient.

In it, mankind does not survive our environmental desecration. At least not in the physical form that we call human.

But it does survive.

Vonnegut considered *Galápagos* his best book, by the way. Because his canary-in-the-coal-mine is on urgent tweet.[153]

———

Writers can broker change in other ways. By writing about something or someone, even if dead or disappeared, you make it or that person alive. Writers can be redeemers.

"Surely the most exciting and instructive teacher I have ever had," Vonnegut said about James Slotkin, the untenured, unpopular anthropologist on the faculty at the University of Chicago after the war.

> He gave courses whose lectures were chapters in books he was writing about the mechanics of social change, and which no one, as it turned out, would ever publish. . . .
>
> One night on Cape Cod, when I was drunk and reeking of mustard gas and roses, and calling up old friends and enemies, as used to be my custom, I called up my beloved old thesis advisor. I was told he was dead—at the age of about fifty, I think. He had swallowed cyanide. He had not published. He had perished instead.
>
> And I wish I had an unpublished essay of his on the mechanics of social change to paste into this collage of mine now.[154]

Vonnegut granted himself his own wish a few years after he wrote the words above: he resurrected his mentor's work through a fictional character, Slazinger, in his novel *Bluebeard*. This may not be his mentor Slotkin's essay verbatim. But it puts across his mentor's ideas:

> Slazinger claims to have learned from history that most people cannot open their minds to new ideas unless a mind-opening team with a peculiar membership goes to work on them. Otherwise, life will go on exactly as before, no matter how painful, unrealistic, unjust, ludicrous, or downright dumb that life may be.
>
> The team must consist of three sorts of specialists, he says. Otherwise, the revolution, whether in politics or the arts or the sciences or whatever, is sure to fail.
>
> The rarest of these specialists, he says, is an authentic genius—a person capable of having seemingly good ideas not in general circulation. "A genius working alone," he says, "is invariably ignored as a lunatic."
>
> The second sort of specialist is a lot easier to find: a highly intelligent citizen in good standing in his or her community, who understands and admires the fresh ideas of the genius, and who testifies that the genius is far from mad. "A person like that working alone," says Slazinger, "can only yearn out loud for changes, but fail to say what their shapes should be."
>
> *The third sort of specialist is a person who can explain anything, no matter how complicated, to the satisfaction of most people, no matter how stupid or pigheaded they may be* [italics mine].[155]

Who has the third talent? A good writer.

A good writer certainly can explain anything to anybody. The passage above is evidence.

This passage, I discovered, is reproduced on a business website.[156] It's quite possible that Vonnegut's reclamation and promulgation of these ideas fictionally has spread farther via the Internet than his mentor's book, if published, might ever have been able to do!

~

Kilgore Trout took a leak in the men's room of the New York City movie house. . . .

There was a message written in pencil on the tiles by the roller towel. This was it:

Trout plundered his pockets for a pen or pencil. He had an answer to the question. But he had nothing to write with, not even a burnt match. So he left the question unanswered, but here is what he would have written, if he had found anything to write with:

> *To be*
> *the eyes*
> *and ears*
> *and conscience*
> *of the Creator of the Universe,*
> *you fool.*[157]

That was the fictional writer Kilgore Trout's answer, and Kilgore Trout was admittedly Kurt Vonnegut's alter ego.

The creator, it seems, doesn't have eyes, ears, or a conscience. The creator, another one of Kurt's characters says, is "the laziest man in town."[158]

So it's up to us, in Vonnegut's view, to be that conscience.

Especially us writers.

———

Here are a few more quotes from various Vonnegut novels affirming that idea:

> "Howard—" he said to me, "future civilizations—better civilizations than this one—are going to judge all men by the extent to which they've been artists. You and I, if some future archaeologist finds our works miraculously preserved in some city dump, will be judged by the quality of our creations. Nothing else about us will matter."[159]

> "Ten thousand years from now," Eliot predicted boozily, "the names of our generals and presidents will be forgotten, and the only hero of our time still remembered will be the author of *2BRO2B*." This was the title of a book by Trout, a title which, upon examination, turned out to be the famous question posed by Hamlet.[160]

> "I'm thinking of calling a general strike of all writers until mankind finally comes to its senses. Would you support it?"
>
> "Do writers have a right to strike? That would be like the police or the firemen walking out."
>
> "Or the college professors."
>
> "Or the college professors," I agreed. I shook my head. "No, I don't think my conscience would let me support a

strike like that. When a man becomes a writer, I think he takes on a sacred obligation to produce beauty and enlightenment and comfort at top speed."[161]

The most dangerous thing they found on his person was a two-inch pencil stub.[162]

———

On the other hand, Vonnegut had his doubts about the impact of writing:

> I want to go into the slums and help the people who are really being screwed by society. You can't comfort the poor with a play or novel.[163]

Marilee, a character in *Bluebeard*, wants to leave "some sort of mark" on the rotunda she owns.

> "I considered hiring women and children to paint murals of the death camps and the bombing of Hiroshima and the planting of land mines, and maybe the burning of witches and the feeding of Christians to wild animals in olden times," she said. "But I think that sort of thing, on some level, just eggs men on to be even more destructive and cruel."[164]

In *Mother Night*, perhaps the darkest of all Vonnegut's novels (and one of his best, to my mind), the protagonist is an American double agent, formerly a playwright. His boss, the Nazi Goebbels, orders him to write a pageant honoring German soldiers who died putting down the uprising of Jews in the Warsaw Ghetto. He does. He calls it "Last Full Measure." It is never performed.

About this pageant: it had one peculiar result. It brought the Gettysburg Address of Abraham Lincoln to the attention of Goebbels, and then to the attention of Hitler himself.

Goebbels asked me where I'd gotten the working title, so I made a translation for him of the entire Gettysburg Address.

He read it, his lips moving all the time. "You know," he said to me, "this is a very fine piece of propaganda. We are never as modern, as far ahead of the past as we like to think we are."

"It's a very famous speech in my native land," I said. "Every schoolchild has to learn it by heart." . . .

"There are phrases in here that might be used most impressively in dedications of German military cemeteries," he said. "I haven't been happy at all, frankly, with most of our funeral oratory. This seems to have the extra dimension I've been looking for. I'd like very much to send this to Hitler."

"Whatever you say, sir," I said. . . .

Two weeks later, the Gettysburg Address came back from Hitler. There was a note from *der Fuehrer* himself stapled to the top of it. "Some parts of this," he wrote, "almost made me weep. All northern peoples are one in their deep feelings for soldiers. It is perhaps our greatest bond."[165]

And then there's the anecdote Vonnegut himself tells in the opening pages of *Slaughterhouse-Five*, familiar to all fans:

Over the years, people I've met have often asked me what I'm working on, and I've usually replied that the main thing was a book about Dresden.

I said that to Harrison Starr, the movie-maker, one time, and he raised his eyebrows and inquired, "Is it an anti-war book?"

"Yes," I said. "I guess."

"You know what I say to people when I hear they're writing anti-war books?"

"No. What *do* you say, Harrison Starr?"

"I say, 'Why don't you write an anti-*glacier* book instead?'"

What he meant, of course, was that there would always be wars, that they were as easy to stop as glaciers. I believe that, too.

And even if wars didn't keep coming like glaciers, there would still be plain old death.

***

Vonnegut got his wish to be "a useful citizen." We all know that. But here's a lovely anecdote that attests to it, written by Marshall Smith, owner of the Wellfleet Marketplace and the Boston-area bookstore Booksmith:

> I first heard about Vonnegut's novels in 1967 from Larry S., a clerk in our Harvard Square Store. Vonnegut had built a loyal following among science fiction enthusiasts, a genre of little interest to me or our very literary book buyer. "This one is going to be big," Larry said. "It's called *Cat's Cradle*." . . . Cleo, the buyer, and I read it reluctantly.
>
> It was, is, fabulous. A few years later came *Slaughterhouse-Five*, the book that brought Vonnegut national recognition. . . .
>
> Vonnegut had a firm policy of not signing books in bookstores. Undaunted, I wrote him a letter suggesting that he not sign books, but meet and talk with some of his longest-term, most loyal supporters; and that he do it at midnight in Harvard Square. To everyone's surprise, he thought that was a pretty neat idea. . . . His appearance in person was in line with his public persona—large mustache;

long, somewhat messy hair; slightly disheveled over-all. A nice man.

... We ensconced him outside the bookstore in the Square, and thousands of his fans came from all over the Greater Boston area. We tied up traffic for hours. He bantered with the students for almost two hours. They loved him, and I think he had a great time.

Why did a crowd—mostly students—show up? Why did they banter for two hours? Because *Slaughterhouse-Five* arrived like the zeitgeist for those of us embroiled in the anti-war movement, and, along with his earlier books, for all the movements (civil rights, counterculture) against the prevailing society at that time. Through his novels, he was the very embodiment of citizenship in its righteous, critical protest mode.

"Many years later," Marshall Smith writes, "I was privileged to present to Kurt Vonnegut the Massachusetts Civil Liberties Union Annual Bill of Rights Award for his outspoken defense of free speech. He hadn't changed over the years."

CHAPTER 13

WRITERS AS TEACHERS OR THE NOBLEST PROFESSION

"**A** writer is first and foremost a teacher," Vonnegut said.[166]

These days many writers, besides instructing through writing, teach in the classroom. When Vonnegut taught at the Iowa Writers' Workshop in the late '60s, only three universities granted master's degrees in creative writing. Graduates began reproducing them. In 1975, there were fifteen MFA programs in writing. Today there are over two hundred.[167] The Associated Writing Programs, an association of universities and colleges with writing programs, lists over five hundred members. Besides graduate programs, offering creative writing courses and majors is de rigueur for any undergrad English department worth its contemporary salt.

Add to that the proliferation of nonacademic writing schools, plus countless course offerings at YMCAs, community centers, creative arts centers, spas, and private classes writers hold in their own homes. In all of these, writers are teaching writing.

So the topic of teaching is relevant to writers in their role as writers, as well as their role as teachers in a class.

Teaching, may I say, is the noblest profession of all in a democracy.[168]

But what kind of teacher? Are all teachers equal?

Vonnegut specifies the kind he admires.

In *Cat's Cradle*, the narrator inquires of the character Julian Castle about Bokonon, the elusive dictator-guru of the tiny island of San Lorenzo:

"You know him, too?"

"That happiness is mine. He was my tutor when I was a little boy." He gestured sentimentally at the mosaic. "He was Mona's tutor, too."

"Was he a good teacher?"

"Mona and I can both read and write and do simple sums," said Castle, "if that's what you mean."[169]

In this backhanded way, Vonnegut provokes the question of what it means to be a good teacher.

What does a good teacher mean to you? Is teaching conveying a skill? Information and wisdom on a particular subject? Is a great teacher someone who can help you pass the SAT? The GED?

———

One reason Vonnegut admired teachers is because he himself had some terrific ones, teachers who made an impact on his life.

Everything I believe I was taught in junior civics during the Great Depression.[170]

At that time, with people out of work, some of the best and brightest were teaching. Shortridge High School, the public high school Vonnegut attended (since his parents had lost all their money and couldn't afford the private school they would have sent him to), was remarkable, and from all reports, continues to be so. I saw it in Indianapolis. Displayed across its grand façade, separated by columns, are the subjects it aspires to teach: Music Poetry Drama/ Education Culture/Commerce Industry/Philosophy Ethics.

> It had a faculty worthy of a university.... Our chemistry teachers were first and foremost chemists. Our physics teachers were first and foremost physicists.... Our English teachers were very commonly serious writers.[171]

Vonnegut cut his teeth by writing for his high school newspaper. Shortridge High School had been given a printing press, and the students put out a daily paper, one of the few in the country, the *Shortridge Echo*. Kurt said, "It was so old my parents had worked on it."[172]

The writer Dan Wakefield, who compiled the volumes of Kurt's *Letters* and his speeches in *If This Isn't Nice, What Is?*, graduated from Shortridge too, though some years later. Wakefield had also worked on the *Shortridge Echo*. "Kurt was very proud of it, and so was I," Wakefield told me. He and Kurt met at a dinner party. Having Shortridge High and the *Echo* in common cemented their friendship.

One of Vonnegut's influential English teachers, Marguerite Young, went on to

> write the definitive biography of Indiana's own Eugene Victor Debs, the middle-class labor leader and socialist candidate for President of the United States, who died in 1926, when I was 4. Millions voted for Debs when he ran for President.

Vonnegut would use the labor movement and "another middle-class Indiana labor leader," Powers Hapgood, as the basis for his novel *Jailbird*.[173]

———

A naturalist, Hillis L. Howie, turned out to be one of Vonnegut's most extraordinary teachers. From 1926 to 1970, Howie led teenagers on two-month camping and wilderness explorations of the Wild West. In 1938, at the age of sixteen, Vonnegut took such a trip. His father paid for it by designing cabins, built by two Navajos, reportedly still standing to this day. Vonnegut dedicated his novel *Galápagos* to Howie.[174]

———

Anthropology professors at the University of Chicago blew the young, postwar Vonnegut's mind with the idea of cultural relativity. That notion became fundamental to Vonnegut's worldview. He said once that he'd often thought of writing a manual for little kids, telling them what kind of a planet they were on.

> And one thing I would really like to tell them about is cultural relativity. . . . A first-grader should understand that his culture isn't a rational invention; that there are thousands of other cultures and they all work pretty well; that all cultures function on faith rather than truth; that there are lots of alternatives to our own society. I didn't find that out for sure until I was in the graduate school of the University of Chicago. It was terribly exciting.[175]

His outstanding professor, James Slotkin, lectured brilliantly on a culture's requirements for change and the necessary leadership. He compared totally dissimilar movements, the Ghost Dance religion among Native Americans and the Cubists among European artists, to make his point.

Addressing a graduating class at his and Slotkin's former school, the University of Chicago, in 1994—years after fictionalizing Slotkin in *Bluebeard* and his ideas in other novels—Vonnegut seized the opportunity to redeem and honor his mentor on his own turf. He cited Slotkin's notions about what was required for a society's transformation, whether for good or ill:

1. A charismatic, gifted leader who described cultural changes which should be made;
2. Two or more respected citizens who testified that this leader was not a lunatic, but was well worth listening to;
3. A glib, personable explainer, who told the general public what the leader was up to, why he was so wonderful, and so on, day after day.[176]

This teacher, whom Vonnegut called a mentor, barely gave him the time of day, and didn't remember him when Kurt phoned him years later.[177]

Vonnegut's fiction offers gorgeous examples of teachers teaching.

Mary Hepburn, the most honorable character in *Galápagos*, "had been a biology teacher in the public high school in Ilium, New York, now defunct, for a quarter of a century."[178] Vonnegut based her character on Hillis L. Howie. Through her, Vonnegut demonstrates how winning and thought-provoking a good teacher ought to be.

> The high point of . . . Mary Hepburn's lectures on the [Galápagos] islands at Ilium High School, was film footage of the courtship dance of the blue-footed boobies.[179]

As the male made his advances in the film, Mary Hepburn ad-libbed comically for the female boobie.

> Mary Hepburn used to give her students extra credit if they would write a little poem or essay about the courtship dance. Something like half of them . . . thought the dance was proof that animals worshipped God. The rest of the responses were all over the place. One student turned in a poem which Mary would remember to her dying day. . . .
>
> *Of course I love you,*
> *So let's have a kid*
> *Who will say exactly*
> *What its parents did;*
> *"Of course I love you,*
> *So let's have a kid*
> *Who will say exactly*
> *What its parents did;*
> *'Of course I love you,*
> *So let's have a kid*
> *Who will say exactly*
> *What its parents did—'"*
> *Et cetera.*
>
> Noble Claggett
> (1947–1966)
>
> Some students would ask permission to write about some other Galápagos Islands creature, and Mary, being such a good teacher, would of course answer, "Yes."

Mary winds up her presentation by returning to her creator Vonnegut's primary query, a Darwinian puzzle:

> And that brings us back to the really deep mystery of the blue-footed boobies' courtship dance, which seems to have absolutely no connection with the elements of booby

survival, with nesting or fish. What does it have to do with, then? Dare we call it "religion"? Or, if we lack that sort of courage, might we at least call it "art"?

Your comments, please.[180]

An exemplary instructor holds center stage in *Hocus Pocus*, the next-to-last novel in Vonnegut's oeuvre. The protagonist-narrator, Gene Hartke, teaches at a prison. He explains his approach:

> I did not loaf. I like to teach.
>
> I dared some of the more intelligent prisoners to prove to me that the World was round, to tell me the difference between noise and music, to tell me how physical traits were inherited, to tell me how to determine the height of a guard tower without climbing it . . . and so on.
>
> I showed them a chart a fundamentalist preacher from downtown Scipio had passed out to Tarkington students at the Pavilion one afternoon. I asked them to examine it for examples of facts tailored to fit a thesis. . . .
>
> The dumber ones . . . used me as an ambulatory *Guinness Book of World Records*, asking me who the oldest person in the world was, the richest one, the woman who had had the most babies, and so on.[181]

> In Music Appreciation I played a recording of Tchaikovsky's 1812 *Overture*. I explained to the class that the composition was about an actual event in history, the defeat of Napoleon in Russia. I asked the students to think of some major event in their own lives, and to imagine what kind of music might best describe it. They were to think about it for a week before telling anybody about the event or the music. I wanted their brains to cook and cook with music, with the lid on tight.[182]

He gets in trouble with the trustees over some sexual escapades and has to defend himself to the Board of Trustees.

> I argued that it was a teacher's duty to speak frankly to students of college age about all sorts of concerns of humankind, not just the subject of a course as stated in the catalogue. "That's how we gain their trust, and encourage them to speak up as well," I said, "and realize that all subjects do not reside in neat little compartments, but are continuous and inseparable from the one big subject we have been put on Earth to study, which is life itself."[183]

Vonnegut reiterates this view through another character, Dr. Helen Dole, who applies for a job and is interviewed by the Trustees:

> But Dr. Dole had blown up at the Board of Trustees instead. They asked her to promise that she would never, whether in class or on social occasions, discuss politics or history or economics or sociology with students. She was to leave those subjects to the college's experts in those fields.
>
> "I plain blew up," she said to me.
>
> "All they asked of me," she said, "was that I not be a human being."[184]

⁓

By its nature, literary fiction "teaches": it shows how people feel, think, respond, and vary; how circumstances affect them; how their brains, personalities, surroundings and culture make them tick. How an experience strikes a particular person a certain way, and another differently. How a person feels inside as opposed to how they act or are perceived. And so on.

All writing teaches—communicates something about something.

Even bad writing "teaches." So if you're writing, you're teaching. You can't help it.

But then there's intentional teaching through writing.

A show of hands, please: How many of you have learned a fact from reading the work of Kurt Vonnegut? Or something about history? How many of you have learned a concept? An attitude? Something else?

Make a list, fast. Then turn to someone else and tell that person what you learned. Do that face-to-face. (If you can't right this minute, do it as soon as you can). Kurt would like that very much.

Post it on Facebook. (Forgive me, Kurt.)

Vonnegut purposely teaches.

He may not have written that particular children's book (*Welcome to Earth*, he wanted to call it) but he impresses the concept of cultural relativity, the "thing I would really like to tell them," on his adolescent and grown-up readers again and again. It's a subtext in everything he wrote.

Besides teaching on the sly through plot and character, Vonnegut is often overt.

He informs readers about historical matters and figures he cares about and feels in his heart others ought to know and care about, habitually.

You've heard of Sacco and Vanzetti, right? No? Well, in *Jailbird* he uses his considerable carrot-on-a-stick fictional skill to make you want to know who they were. Or to remind you.

Vonnegut blatantly educates and simultaneously entices the reader (enticement being the storyteller's most important skill, according to Vonnegut—see "Plot"), spacing the carrot at intervals and weaving it skillfully into the main plot in order to keep your curiosity chomping away at the pages.

In the prologue, he mentions Sacco and Vanzetti on pages 5, 9, 11, and 21, each time speaking generally of their heroism in the labor movement and of the tragic injustice done to them. Just before the fictional tale begins, he presents an excerpt of Sacco's letter to his son, written three days before Sacco's execution.

In the first chapter, the narrator, Walter F. Starbuck, muses on time and their case:

> I thought now about Sacco and Vanzetti. When I was young, I believed that the story of their martyrdom would cause an irresistible mania for justice to the common people to spread throughout the world.

Seventeen chapters later, Starbuck reflects again:

> I recently asked . . . the former night clerk . . . what he knew about Sacco and Vanzetti, and he told me confidently that they were rich, brilliant thrill-killers from Chicago. He had them confused with Leopold and Loeb.
>
> Why should I find this unsettling? When I was a young man, I expected the story of Sacco and Vanzetti to be retold as often and as movingly, to be as irresistible, as the story of Jesus Christ some day.[185]

Finally, in chapters 18 and 19, after tantalizing you throughout with the importance of their tragedy, he first presents a horrifying postscript—the actual killer's confession to the murders they were accused of and would die for—and then tells the entire story of what happened to Sacco and Vanzetti, imagining it as a passion play, comparable to Christ's story.

It's worth reading. It feels familiar. It feels like the present.

I admit I'd always been uncertain about what happened to them, as though—as a friend of mine says when ignorant about something he feels he ought to know—I missed that day in school. But it was simply not my generation.

Thus Vonnegut reclaims the labor movement and resurrects its heroes who were so important to him and to the country when he was young.

> I define a saint as a person who behaves decently in an indecent society.[186]

I saw the movie *Selma* last night. I was in Selma in 1965. I marched, coming from the University of Arkansas. It was terrifying, exhilarating. I learned powerful lessons. It made an indelible impact on me.

I feared seeing the movie. But except for erroneously depicting Lyndon Johnson as a roadblock rather than as a gate opener for Dr. King in the civil rights cause (a Hollywood simplifier if there ever was one), I thought it captured the nonviolent movement, the time, and the issues as well as a movie could.

Hurrah for redemption of our evils and struggles. We need to know what they were and are.

Hurrah for redemption of our saints. We need to know what it takes to overcome.

Teaching is a two-way street.

When you teach, you learn. Magically, it seemed, I became a

better writer after dissecting novels, stories, poems, and essays in order to point my students to their treasures of content and craft.

The same happens when you "teach" in your writing. It occurred for me just now. In order to explain Kurt's use of Sacco and Vanzetti, I reread his version of the story in *Jailbird* several times, summarized it, revised that, then cut most of it. Consequently, Sacco and Vanzetti's story is now etched on my brain and heart. So is Vonnegut's skill.

Vance Bourjaily, a twenty-two-year veteran teacher at the Iowa workshop, as well as Vonnegut's close friend and fellow traveler, said, "It was striking, through the years, how much I learned from my workshop students, and I used to recall that in Appalachian English the verb is used both in the customary way and as a synonym for *teach* (e.g., 'she learned me my ABC's.')."[187]

I believe it was in that same spirit that Kurt autographed the copy of *Slaughterhouse-Five* he gave to me: "For Suzanne, Good Pupil, Good Teacher."

CHAPTER 14
VONNEGUT IN CLASS

What was Vonnegut like in the classroom?

He was marvelous. Serious, funny, entertaining. Sharp, kind. Rumply. Down-to-earth. He smoked. He doodled. He was as a teacher the way he was as a writer.

He was like his characters Mary in *Galápagos* and Gene in *Hocus Pocus*. At least that's how he was at the Writers' Workshop at the University of Iowa, in 1965 to 1967.

He had taught once before, for a year.

> It was a school for disturbed kids—disturbed rich kids since it cost a lot of money to go there—in Sandwich, on Cape Cod. I was the whole English department for kids who were of high school age, many of whom could not read or write very much. These kids, for one reason or another, became highly inconvenient to their parents. Occasionally the police department said, "Either this kid goes to a structured school, a structured environment, or we're going to put him in jail." There were brain-damaged kids and all sorts of kids who had something wrong with them.[188]

I've a vivid memory of Kurt in class telling us a story that one of the kids wrote, a mentally ill kid. A boy has a closet full of glass objects he loves. He takes them out, one by one, to admire them, setting them carefully on the floor. One accidentally breaks, then another. Or maybe the boy himself accidentally breaks them. At any rate, they all crash against one another, splintering. He's in their midst on his hands and knees, frantically trying to rescue them. He cuts himself to ribbons.

I remember Kurt's face, telling this: half-smiling, helpless, ironic, pained, compassionate.

———

"You'll be an excellent teacher. Your ego will demand it, and so will your students," he wrote fellow writer Richard Gehman about joining the Iowa faculty. "You'll have an appalling number of real writers entrusted to your care."

Vonnegut would teach later at Harvard and at City College, but he said he did his best teaching at Iowa. His circumstances changed. While at Harvard, his marriage was coming apart. At City College, he was swamped by other projects.[189]

Several of Vonnegut's former students have written about him: Gail Godwin, John Irving, Barry Jay Kaplan, Jim Siegelman, Dick Cummins, John Casey, and more, I'm sure. I have too.[190]

"The classes don't matter much. The real business, head-to-head, is done during office hours in the afternoons," Vonnegut advised Richard Gehman.[191]

"In those one-to-one sessions," Gail Godwin says, "he was as loose and playful as a Zen master." He read her novella, which would later become her first novel, *The Perfectionists*, and commented in the margins (with *pencil*, he was so respectful): "Lovely." "First-rate." Or "No: sandbagging flashback." She told him she was thinking of expanding it into a novel, and asked his opinion. "'Oh, I think, it's just great as it is,' Vonnegut said." In the next conference, she told him she'd decided "to go ahead and turn it into a novel anyway. 'Great idea,' he exclaimed enthusiastically."

"Naturally it helped to have an older, more confident writer reading over my shoulder," John Irving told an interviewer. "But I found that I needed that very little by the time I got to Iowa and

that led me to . . . Kurt Vonnegut." He'd say, "'This part bored me.'
And then one hundred pages later he'd say 'This was really funny.'
Sometimes he said, 'You certainly like *this* word a lot, don't you?'
Mostly, he just let me be."[192]

In Barry Jay Kaplan's first conference with Vonnegut, he told me,
both of them smoked and looked at their shoes, their knees splayed
and almost touching, while an uncomfortable silence went on and on.
Finally Kurt said, "Your stories make me very nervous." Barry waited
anxiously. Kurt worked tobacco off his tongue. More silence ensued. At
last Kurt said, "I don't know what to say about them." Barry replied,
"Oh," and sat there, frozen. Then Kurt looked directly at him. "What
I mean is . . . I just think you ought to keep writing them, don't you?"

After that Barry gave him story after story. Kurt encouraged
him without imposing himself in any way. Barry became Kurt's
research assistant. Kurt asked him to do two things, the entire
semester: find a map of Dresden pre–World War II, and locate the
rules of Little League.

Vonnegut wrote later to Gail Godwin:

> All I did in those private conferences with you guys was
> to say *Trust me*. What I'm going to do now is open your
> mouth, very gently, with these two fingers, and then I'm
> going to reach in—being very careful not to bruise your
> epiglottis—and catch hold of this little tape inside you and
> slowly, very carefully and gently, pull it out of you. It's your
> tape, and it's the only tape like that in the world.[193]

If I'd ever had a conference with him, perhaps I would have
experienced that gentle pulling out of what I had to say. But I was
too shy. I never asked him for a conference.

Here's my advice to students: don't be shy.

But. If you are, you can learn an entire world anyway—the same
way he learned from his mentor, and I learned from him—in the
safety of the relatively anonymous classroom.

———

Kurt advised John Irving, who was working on his first novel, "that I was interested in a certain young woman's underwear to an excess of what my readers would be." Irving revised it accordingly, but "Not to the degree that I probably should have . . . But he also said I wrote with so much enthusiasm. He told me,

> Never lose that enthusiasm. So many writers are *unenthusiastic* about their work.[194]

———

At the Iowa workshop during that time, men students far outnumbered women. Not one teacher was female. Similarly, there were few people of color, and the gay and lesbian community was underground.

My fellow-female classmate Ronni Sandroff recalls this anecdote:

> "Do you believe that a woman wrote such a powerful story?" Vonnegut asked, pointing me out at the end of the semester when he revealed the anonymous authors of the stories we had read in class. I glowed from the praise—"powerful!"— but my stomach was twisted in a knot. It was just a couple of years pre-feminism. Once that movement dawned, I at least understood why my stomach twisted at the idea that it was amazing that a woman could write well. The world was a less comfortable place for women and men back then.

Similar affronts happened to me and other women in the workshop in those years. Some were blatant. A male student told me when I first arrived at the workshop that he didn't think women should write. It was sufficiently acceptable to say such a thing in those days that he said it to my face. He seemed to think we might usurp men's places.

Society didn't yet have a vocabulary for this. "Sexist" wasn't yet a word. Especially without language, those experiences were bewildering.

Once at a party at the Vonneguts' house, after I had turned in a story that Kurt didn't like much, I was telling him that he'd like the next one. He twinkled at me, drink in hand, and said, "You're a pretty girl, Suzanne, you can get married anyway." I was dumbfounded. What did that have to do with my burning desire to write? I was openmouthed. He would never have said that to a man. I understood he was flirting, that he thought he was giving me a compliment. That made it worse.

Fourteen years later, after the feminist movement, at another party in New York in honor of José Donoso, who was visiting the US, I reminded Kurt what he'd said. He blinked. "Did I say that?" In an attempt to defend himself, he responded, "Well, that *is* an avenue open to women." He got up and got another drink. Then he apologized. With time and distance, I saw that his response was a practical one, in his view. Writing for him was tied up with making a living.

Most of the sexism, like Vonnegut's in these anecdotes, came from a cultural blind spot. Vonnegut was a product of his generation and culture, even as he strived against being so in many ways. He was not intentionally sexist or hurtful.

Such blind spots, to phrase it most benignly, occur in every culture. You may harbor some yourself. Sexism, racism, ageism, nationalism. Homophobia. Political and regional prejudices. Your teachers, being human, will have such blind spots. They may not, as Vonnegut's own mentor did not, recognize your value, remember you, or care about you. That doesn't mean you can't learn from them. It doesn't mean they themselves are evil.

The blind spot itself, though, is.

An insidious, damaging wrongdoing, undermining confidence and selfhood.

One upside: consciousness soars with obvious abuse.

Four pieces of advice: Recognize the blind spot. Call it out. Keep your eyes on your own prize. Expect change.

People and times do change. Raggedly, incrementally. Vonnegut changed too.

"The women's liberation movement of today in America," Vonnegut wrote in 1981, "in its most oceanic sense, is a wish by women to be liked for something other than their reproductive abilities. . . . And the rejection of the Equal Rights Amendment by male state legislators is this clear statement by men, in my opinion: 'We're sorry, girls, but your reproductive abilities are about all we can really like you for.'"[195]

Late in his life Kurt sent me postcards and clippings about women's issues.

Jim Siegelman, a "nugget," as Vonnegut's Harvard students called themselves, reports that Vonnegut told them creative writing classes often did more harm than good because "people tore into each other's best efforts in the meanest ways." Which was true sometimes, at Iowa.

Vonnegut warned Barry Jay Kaplan not to present his idiosyncratic stories in the Iowa workshop. When Barry did anyway, a couple of times, students responded that they were "nihilistic" and "anti-writing."

Surviving some of those chicken-pecking workshop sessions turned out to be awfully good for thickening the skin. But pretty bad for the blooming of your spirit, self-esteem, the sense of your fellows—let alone your writing.

At Harvard, Vonnegut set up the class to avoid that. He eliminated the workshop altogether. Students investigated what made great classic stories stupendous, instead. Vonnegut spoke about writing, but relied on individual conferences to discuss the students' own.

Siegelman mainly wrote short humor pieces for the *Harvard Lampoon*. Vonnegut urged him "to give people an opportunity to do more than laugh at what I wrote . . . to write feelings, not just pictures, to create full-bodied characters . . . to tell tales of love and mystery and human experience, not just 'vaudeville.'"

He cautioned that writing was tortuous and opportunities to publish were sorely lacking (and that was in 1970!). He urged them to follow their instincts, free of literary history and Harvard's weight.

"Your minds are marvelous machines," he said, "and you can just turn them on and let them run, and they will produce something wonderful."[196]

"When we were your students, you let us work it out for ourselves," Gail Godwin once told him. "Yet your being there for us did the trick."[197]

Trusting is a two-way street. All he did in those classes and conferences was to trust us. He trusted that we were working out our tapes at our own pace in our own ways. And what would come, would come. Or it wouldn't.

I've been having trouble concluding this topic. Kurt Vonnegut taught me about so much more than writing. At a time when I sorely needed models to know that one could keep on trucking, one could even thrive, in spite of personal and societal traumas, he was there, a template, teaching and writing.

What he taught was more important than writing.

He led us to abhor war, to be compassionate toward our characters, to respect people, to question rigid constructs, to care deeply, to try to be decent, to laugh. To tell useful lies.

He taught these things by his responses to people's stories, by his anecdotes, by his quiet remarks, by his treatment of us, by being himself.

I sang gospel every few weeks at a friend's loft in SoHo in the '80s, with a loose group of superb singers. We sang a cappella. We riffed and harmonized. One night someone suggested that one person hold a single note while the others kept harmonizing. It seemed like a boring static part to take, so I didn't volunteer, but when my turn came, I discovered that holding one note—while all other voices were moving up and down and around—not only took a fierce focus but felt physical, as though I were a ridgepole holding up the rest of a swaying tent threatening to pull to one side and then the other. That's what Kurt Vonnegut was like to me: a singular, sustaining note.

Kurt Vonnegut teaching a class in the Quonset huts at the Iowa Writers' Workshop, 1966. Courtesy of Robert Lehrman. Photo: John Zielinski

Here are two of Vonnegut's assignments at the Writers' Workshop in a Form of Fiction class—literature classes geared toward examining fiction from a writer's perspective, comprised of about eighty students. I kept them, along with the papers I wrote, all these years. I gave a copy of the second one to Dan Wakefield, who published it, since it's formed like a letter, in *Letters*. The first one is a virgin, as far as publication goes.[198]

FORM OF FICTION TERM PAPER ASSIGNMENT   November 30, 1965

Beloved:

    This course began as Form and Theory of Fiction, became Form of Fiction, then Form adn Texture of Fiction, then Surface Criticism, or How to Talk out of the Corner of Your Mouth Like a Real Tough Pro. It will probably be Animal Husbandry 108 by the time Black February rolls around. As was said to me years ago by a dear, dear friend, "Keep your hat on. We may end up miles from here."

    As for your term papers, I should like them to be both cynical and religious. I want you to adore the Universe, to be easily delighted, but to be prompt as well with impatience with those artists who offend your own deep notions of what the Universe is or should be. "This above all..."

    I invite you to read the fifteen tales in Masters of the Modern Short Story (W. Havighurst, editor, 1955, Harcourt, Brace, $14.95 in paperback). Read them for pleasure and satisfaction, beginning each as though, only seven minutes before, you had swallowed two ounces of very good booze. "Except ye be as little children..."

    Then reproduce on a single sheet of clean, white paper the table of contents of the book, omitting the page numbers, and substituting for each number a grade from A to F. The grades should be childishly selfish and impudent measures of your own joy or lack of it. I don't care what grades you give. I do insist that you like some stories better than others.

    Proceed next to the hallucination that you are a minor but useful editor on a good literary magazine not connected with a university. Take three stories that please you most and three that please you least, six in all, and pretend that they have been offered for publication. Write a report on each to be submitted to a wise, respected, witty and world-weary superior.

    Do not do so as an academic critic, nor as a person drunk on art, nor as a barbarian in the literary market place. Do so as a sensitive person who has a few practical hunches about how stories can succeed or fail. Praise or damn as you please, but do so rather flatly, pragmatically, with cunning attention to annoying or gratifying details. Be yourself. Be unique. Be a good editor. The Universe needs more good editors, God knows.

    Since there are eighty of you, and since I do not wish to go blind or kill somebody, about twenty pages from each of you should do neatly. Do not bubble. Do not spin your wheels. Use words I know.

POLONIUS

ABOVE AND TOP OF NEXT PAGE: **University of Iowa Writers' Workshop assignments, November 30, 1965, and March 15, 1966. Courtesy of the author.**

FORM OF FICTION TERM PAPER ASSIGNMENT
VONNEGUT'S SECTION
MARCH 15, 1966

Dear Sam:

Referring to the works we have read in this course, since
they are the only books with which teacher is familiar, do the
following chores:

1. Write a four-page essay on the mechanical and spiritual
limitations, if any, imposed by the short story as compared with
the novel.

2. Even though it is a grotesque and stupid thing to do, describe in twenty-five words or less the plot of each of four books
we have read. Then write a four-page essay on the usefulness or
uselessness of plots to the writer and to the reader.

3. Without peeking at the books, name four minor characters
you remember vividly. Then investigate and report upon techniques
the authors used to make the characters stick in your mind. Four
pages again.

4. One student announced in class that he found some of the
books we were reading so bloody depressing that he didn't want to
read any more. Comment on this.

Hokay? Fair enough?

Write like a human being. Write like a writer.

In Christ,
(Which is the way you
end a letter to the
Pope)

Gus

CHAPTER 15
HEFT AND COMFORT

As a writer, you bestow the pleasure and balm of reading. You provide the incalculable value of communication by the cheap and accessible means of the written word.

> In the Vonnegut house, with its charge-account deadbeats, and in the Goldstein house next door, with its bankruptcy, there were many books. As luck would have it, the Goldstein children and I, and the Marks children three doors down, whose father would soon die quite suddenly, could all read about as easily as we could eat chocolate ice cream. Thus, at a very tender age and in utter silence, disturbing no one, being children as good as gold, we were comforted and nourished by human minds which were calmer and more patient and amusing and unafraid than our parents could afford to be.[199]

> If you ever wonder what in hell you think you're doing with your life, let me remind you that you are telling people as reasonable and humane as yourself what they desperately need to hear, that others feel as they do.[200]

> My favorite *New Yorker* cartoon depicts, in the first panel, a woman sitting alone in a room reading a book. In the second, she puts down her book, rises from her chair, and crosses the room. In the third, she returns to her chair with a pencil in hand. And in the last, she writes in the margin of the book she's been reading, "How true."

Late in his life, Vonnegut wrote:

> Do you realize that all great literature . . . [is] all about what
> a bummer it is to be a human being? (Isn't it such a relief to
> have somebody say that?)[201]

Dear cranky funny-valentine Kurt, I disagree that all great lit boils
down to that. I disagree that it's such a bummer to be human. But it's
a huge relief for somebody that you said it, and it would've been for
me when I was much younger. Maybe it will be again, who knows?

If you're a writer or an artist of any kind, your self-expression
will ring a bell with some other self. You can count on that.

───

> If you can [read], you can go whaling in the South Pacific
> with Herman Melville or you can watch Madame Bovary
> make a mess of her life in Paris.[202]

> Whatever the future may hold for literature in classrooms,
> uncounted millions of Americans will continue to meditate
> with books in perfect privacy, escaping from their own
> weary minds for at least a little while.[203]

> "I'm not a drug salesman. I'm a writer."
>   "What makes you think a writer isn't a drug salesman?"
>   "I'll accept that. Guilty as charged."[204]

> A plausible mission of artists is to make people appreciate
> being alive at least a little bit.[205]

───

Vonnegut wove his staunch belief in the freedom to read, and consequently his fear and loathing of censorship, into his first novel, *Player Piano*. Readers as well as writers in that novel's society are constricted.

When the writer's wife in the novel explains that her husband has been "classified" and has submitted a manuscript to one of the book clubs, Halyard from the State Department clarifies the state's book clubs for a foreign guest:

> "There are twelve of them," Halyard interrupted. "Each one selects books for a specific type of reader."
>
> "There are twelve types of readers?" said Khashdrahr.
>
> "There is now talk of a thirteenth and fourteenth," said Halyard.[206]

Vonnegut tried Transcendental Meditation in the late '60s. Everyone was trying it then, including his wife and daughter. He wrote about it in *Fates Worse than Death*:

> My own impression was that TM was a nice little nap, but that not much happened, whether for good or ill. It was like scuba diving in lukewarm bouillon. A pink silk scarf might drift slowly by. . . .
>
> . . . I realized that I had done the same sort of thing thousands of times before.
>
> I had done it while reading books!
>
> Since I was eight or so, I had been internalizing the written words of persons who had seen and felt things new to me. . . . The world dropped away when I did it. When I read an absorbing book, my pulse and respiration rate slowed down perceptibly, just as though I were doing TM.
>
> I was *already* a veteran meditator. When I awoke from my Western-style meditation I was often a wiser human being.

He endorses printed books as the preferred delivery system for the elixir of reading.

> So many people nowadays regard printed pages as nothing more than obsolescent technology, first developed by the Chinese two thousand years ago. Books came into being, surely, as practical schemes for transmitting or storing information, no more romantic in Gutenberg's time than a computer in ours. It so happens, though—a wholly unforeseen accident—that the feel and appearance of a book when combined with a literate person in a straight chair can create a spiritual condition of priceless depth and meaning.
>
> This form of meditation, an accident, as I say, may be the greatest treasure at the core of our civilization.

He concludes that we should surrender "only crass and earthly matters to the printout and the cathode tube."[207]

> Don't give up on books. They feel so good—their friendly heft. The sweet reluctance of their pages when you turn them with your sensitive fingertips. A large part of our brains is devoted to deciding what our hands are touching is good or bad for us. Any brain worth a nickel knows books are good for us.[208]

In the introduction to the short fiction collection *Bagombo Snuff Box*, Vonnegut describes perfectly marvelously the way families read short stories in the heyday of magazines, the '40s and '50s. I was a kid during that time, and his description makes me nostalgic for that era of the short story—that quieter, gentler, more private form of communal entertainment.

A short story, because of its physiological and psychological effects on a human being, is more closely related to Buddhist styles of meditation than it is to any other form of narrative entertainment. What you have in this volume, then, and in every other collection of short stories, is a bunch of Buddhist catnaps.

———

Meditators may disagree with Vonnegut's equation: the reading state equals the meditative. Similar, no doubt. But does reading affect the brain the same way meditating does? That would have to be put to a scientific test.

Controlled experiments prove Vonnegut right on this most important count: Our brains do know reading is good for us. Especially literary fiction. That's what the scientific journals *NeuroImage*, *Brain and Language*, and the *Annual Review of Psychology* report.

One study found that "after reading literary fiction, as opposed to popular fiction or serious nonfiction, people performed better on tests measuring empathy, social perception and emotional intelligence." Literary fiction improves social skills. Why? Because it leaves more to the imagination, activating inferences about characters and sensitivity "to emotional nuance and complexity."[209]

Researchers discovered other particulars.

The brain, it seems, does not make much of a distinction between reading about an experience and encountering it in real life; in each case, the same neurological regions are stimulated.

Fiction—with its redolent details, imaginative metaphors and attentive descriptions of people and their actions— offers an especially rich replica. Indeed, in one respect novels go beyond simulating reality . . . : the opportunity to enter fully into other people's thoughts and feelings.[210]

For five years I led seminars for health care professionals at two hospitals under the auspices of a program called "Literature and Medicine, Humanities at the Heart of Healthcare," founded on such premises about the impact of literature. Begun in Maine in 1996, the mission is to encourage "health care professionals to . . . reflect on their professional roles and relationships through reading plays, short stories, poetry, fiction and personal narratives, and [to] share those reflections with colleagues."[211]

Though not scientific, there was plenty of anecdotal evidence of the positive effects of participants' literary reading: a social worker at a VA hospital said, after I'd assigned a novel about a female soldier in Iraq and her civilian Iraqi counterpart, that she would never again be impatient with the healing process of the women vets she dealt with in the hospital's rape victim unit. A nurse announced that she'd cared for comatose patients and patients unable to communicate, but reading one written by such a patient and seeing the film based on it jarred her into deeper consideration of those patients' consciousness and humanity. A short-short story about female nurses assisting an inebriated surgeon called up an amazing chorus of responses. The issue of a literary journal dedicated to the theme of war elicited a flood of their own and their patients' experiences. And on and on.[212]

Narrative Medicine is fast becoming a component in medical school curriculums, and literature and writing are increasingly recognized as avenues to sensitize future doctors and enhance their interpersonal skills. Writing and literature serve across the spectrum of populations, from prisoners to veterans to at-risk youth, for the same purposes. They are good for us all.

Reading at Risk: A Survey of Literary Reading in America, a report made over a decade ago by the National Endowment for the Arts, found literary reading in America is declining rapidly, especially among the young. The census bureau conducted this survey of 17,000 across a broad swath of the population, at the NEA's request. "For the first time in modern history, less than half the adult population now reads literature."[213]

As a result of their findings, the NEA created "The Big Read," providing "citizens with the opportunity to read and discuss a single book within their community."[214]

———

Here's some of Vonnegut's "circuitous tribute to the art of reading," as he called his speech for Connecticut College, dedicating a library.

Our ability to read, when combined with libraries like this one, makes us the freest of women and men—and children. . . .

. . . Because we are readers, we don't have to wait for some communications executive to decide what we should think about next—and how we should think about it. We can fill our heads with anything from aardvarks to zucchinis—at any time of night or day.

Even more magically, perhaps, we readers can communicate with each other across space and time so cheaply. Ink and paper are as cheap as sand or water, almost. No board of directors has to convene in order to decide whether we can afford to write down this or that. I myself once staged the end of the world on two pieces of paper—at a cost of less than a penny, including wear and tear on my typewriter ribbon and the seat of my pants.

Think of that.

Compare that with the budgets of Cecil B. DeMille. . . .

Reading exercises the imagination—tempts it to go from strength to strength. . . .

The language is holy to me. . . .

Literature is holy to me. . . .

Our freedom to say or write whatever we please in this country is holy to me. It is a rare privilege not only on this planet, but throughout the universe, I suspect. And it is not something somebody gave us. It is a thing we give to ourselves.[215]

Winding up a commencement speech, Kurt Vonnegut asked graduates a question and gave them a task. He transposed it into a poem too. In homage to his tribute to reading, consider naming a book as well as naming a teacher.

BACCALAUREATE

A show of hands, please:
How many of you have had a teacher
at any stage of your education,
from the first grade until this day in May,
who made you happier to be alive,
prouder to be alive,
than you had previously believed
possible?
Good!
Now say the name of that teacher
to someone
sitting or standing near you.
All done?
Thank you, and drive home safely,
and God bless you all.[216]

CHAPTER 16
TALENT

The *Paris Review* asked Vonnegut two fundamental questions for aspiring fiction writers:

> Interviewer: Surely talent is required?
>   Vonnegut: . . . I was a Saab dealer on Cape Cod for a while, and I enrolled in their mechanic's school, and they threw me out of their mechanic's school. No talent.[217]

Vonnegut had failed enough in his life at all the things for which he hadn't much talent to know in his bones that being blessed with a God-given knack for something is a prerequisite for success at it.

> It just turned out that I could write better than a lot of other people. Each person has something he can do easily and can't imagine why everybody else is having so much trouble doing it. In my case, it was writing. In my brother's case, it was mathematics and physics. In my sister's case, it was drawing and sculpting.[218]

"He had an extra gear, language-wise," Vonnegut's son Mark says of his father. "At eighty-plus he was still doing the *New York Times* crossword puzzles quickly. . . . As soon as I told him the verb came last, he could translate my Latin homework at sight, without having ever taken Latin."[219]

Further in the *Paris Review* interview, Vonnegut calls writing a "trade."

> Interviewer: Trade?
>
> Vonnegut: Trade. Carpenters build houses. Storytellers use a reader's leisure time in such a way that the reader will not feel that his time has been wasted. Mechanics fix automobiles.
>
> Interviewer: Do you really think creative writing can be taught?
>
> Vonnegut: About the same way golf can be taught. A pro can point out obvious flaws in your swing.[220]

If you don't have an athlete's knack for that swing, you're not going to be a pro. Kurt "didn't really believe you could teach a person how to write if the ability wasn't there to begin with."[221]

———

Talent is required. But it's only one of the components for creating good fiction. And being possessed of less than superlative gifts doesn't mean you shouldn't pursue writing.

> I was a mediocrity in the anthropology department of the University of Chicago after the Second World War. Triage was practiced there as it is practiced everywhere. There were those students who would surely be anthropologists, and the most winsome faculty members gave them intensive care. A second group of students . . . might become so-so anthropologists, but more probably, would use what they had learned about *Homo sapiens* to good advantage in some other field. . . .

> The third group, of which I was a member, might as well
> have been dead—or studying chemistry.[222]

The anthropology student Vonnegut doesn't belong in the third group. Placing himself in the third group makes for drama and an in-joke about his failure at chemistry. In truth, he turned out to be a solid member of the second group, those using "what they had learned . . . to good advantage in some other field." Chemistry provoked his interest in science. Anthropology shaped his worldview, his writing—so where's the failure?

What is "failure" anyhow? A different outcome than expected, in this case.

⁓

Again and again, these questions arise. "Can you *really* teach anyone how to write?" a *New York Times* editor asked Vonnegut, just as he was composing a piece for that very newspaper about that very subject. This suspicion is left over from a legend, Vonnegut says in the finished article,

> from the old days, when male American writers acted like tough guys, like Humphrey Bogart, to prove that they, although they were sensitive and liked beauty, were far from being homosexual. The Legend: A tough guy, I forget which one, is asked to speak to a creative writing class. He says: "What in hell are you doing here? Go home and glue your butts to a chair, and write and write until your *heads* fall off!" Or words to that effect. . . .
>
> The *Times* guy who wondered if anybody could be taught how to write was taught how to write by editors. The tough guy who made students and their instructor feel like something the cat dragged in, possibly spitting on the floor after having done so, almost certainly, like me, handed

in manuscripts to his publisher that were as much in need of repairs as what I got from students at the workshop.

My reply: "Listen, there were creative writing teachers long before there were creative writing courses, and they were called and continue to be called *editors*."[223]

The tough guy he's referring to may well have been Nelson Algren, a fellow writer/teacher at the workshop. From up at the podium along with Bourjaily and Vonnegut in a Form of Fiction class, Algren scoffed bold-facedly at us students for coming to school to learn to write. I recognized that Algren was the real deal. But man, I wanted to ask him why he was up there, being paid by our tuitions and wasting his own time teaching us if it were so pointless, rather than skulking around the mean streets of Chicago, where he presumably had picked up the knack.

Vonnegut was not without poses, but pretending his writing emerged full-bodied from Zeus's forehead was not one of them.

Neither did he confuse life experience with craft.

Asked in 1970 if he was "influenced by a particular writer or style," Vonnegut answered:

No, although I do see myself as an "instructed" writer, and there aren't many producing authors who would confess to such a thing. What I mean is: I went to a high school that put out a daily newspaper and, because I was writing for my peers and not for teachers, it was very important to me that they understand what I was saying. So the simplicity, and that's not a bad word for it, of my writing was caused by the fact that my audience was composed of sophomores, juniors and seniors. In addition, the idea of an uncomplicated style was very much in the air back then—clarity, shorter sentences, strong verbs, a de-emphasis of adverbs and adjectives, that sort of thing. Because I believed in the merits of this type of prose, I was quite "teachable" and so I worked hard to achieve as pure a style as I could. When I got to Cornell my experiences on a daily paper . . . enabled me to become a big shot on Cornell's *Daily Sun.* I suppose it was this consistent involvement with newspaper audiences that fashioned my style. Also, since I was a Chemistry major, I had very little instruction from the profoundly literary people.

. . . The people who were senior to me at the *Sun* were full of advice and, again, it had to do with clarity, economy, and so forth. . . . The magazines were thriving then and the editors knew a good deal about story telling. . . . And keep in mind that you had to do what they told you to do or you couldn't sell them a story. . . . So I was drilled from the start in basic journalistic techniques and, in a very real sense, my instructors were masters at their craft. I hope I'm making this clear: these editors were neither tyrannical nor contemptible. They were dedicated, knowledgeable professionals. *My point, then, is that I was taught to write the way I do* [italics mine].[224]

What about storytelling, as differentiated from writing? Because writing prose is one thing, and writing a yarn is another. Vonnegut and his friend, the writer Sidney Offit, discussed that. Offit taught much longer than Vonnegut—at NYU, Hunter College, and the New School. "And," Offit says, "I have to tell you: the gift for narrative, for storytelling, is rarer than the gift for poetic prose or elegant language—it isn't even close." He adds, "The students I have had over the years who could write stories were eventually published."[225]

Offit's right. Many, many students write well. Not nearly as many have the hang of telling a story.

Students have been writing all their lives. But they have not been writing stories all their lives.

———

Vonnegut suggests:

A creative writing course provides experienced editors for inspired amateurs.[226]

———

Today, with the proliferation of writing programs, I might agree with Nelson Algren. There's some backlash about the MFA-ing of writing.[227] If you've some talent, passion, and a good story to tell, must you spend a fortune on an MFA program to hone your craft? Not necessarily.

CHAPTER 17
DILIGENCE

As a writer, I share a problem, perhaps you could call it a tragedy, with most human beings: a tendency to lose contact with my own intelligence. It's almost as if there were a layer of fat upon the part of us that thinks and it's the writer's job to hack through and discover what is inside. So often it's this belief, or some such belief, that keeps me going after a day when I've been at it for hours and am dissatisfied with what I've produced. But I do keep at it and, if I'm patient, a nice egg-shaped idea emerges and I can tell my intelligence has gotten through. It's a slow process, though, and an annoying one, because you have to sit still so long.[228]

"'Writing takes a kind of demented patience.' That Vonnegut line stayed with me my whole career," Vonnegut's Iowa student Ronni Sandroff says. "I wrote very slowly and longed for the mythical automatic writing of Jack Kerouac, tumbling out gripping prose in a heated rush. But I learned to labor. And it made me an editor as well as a writer."[229]

Just because Vonnegut had talent and expertise didn't mean he wasn't plagued by daily doubt.

I keep suspecting I'm out of business and better become a

rock star or buy a greenhouse or something. Right now I
don't feel particularly in business, but I know how to get
into business—and that is by hacking around to see what
is in me. . . . It's a little like a Ouija board. I will try to get a
clue to what my intelligence wants to talk about, and then
I will try to talk about it more and more.[230]

Ask any artist, anyone accomplishing anything of value: patience,
perseverance, and work, those humble virtues, rate at least as high
as talent on the list of necessary equipment, any day.

1509
Michelangelo:
To Giovanni da Pistoia When the Author Was Painting the
Vault of the Sistine Chapel

I've already grown a goiter from this torture,
hunched up here like a cat in Lombardy
(or anywhere else where the stagnant water's poison).
My stomach's squashed under my chin, my beard's
pointing at heaven, my brain's crushed in a casket,
my breast twists like a harpy's. My brush,
above me all the time, dribbles paint
so my face makes a fine floor for droppings!

My haunches are grinding into my guts,
my poor ass strains to work as a counterweight,
every gesture I make is blind and aimless.
My skin hangs loose below me, my spine's
all knotted from folding over itself.
I'm bent taut as a Syrian bow.

Because I'm stuck like this, my thoughts
are crazy, perfidious tripe:
anyone shoots badly through a crooked blowpipe.

My painting is dead.
Defend it for me, Giovanni, protect my honor.
I am not in the right place—I am not a painter.

(translated by Gail Mazur)[231]

——～——

The small, stunning Abbey Library of St. Gaul in St. Gallen, Switzerland, a World Heritage Site, contains over 2,100 handwritten manuscripts, spanning well over a thousand years, according to the visitors' brochure.[232]

The library itself is rococo and beautiful, and the collection is arranged superbly to display the history of print—papyrus, palimpsest, parchment—and the instruments and painstaking work of calligraphy.

But what charmed me most were scribbled complaints on the margins and back page of an enormous Latin grammar book copied circa 850 by a laboring Irish monk: "Alas! my hand" (*uit mo chrob*); "A blessing on the soul of Fergus. Amen. I am very cold" (*bendacht for anmmain ferguso. amen. mar uar dom*); "The ink is thin" (*is tana andub*); "The parchment is rough and the writing" (*is gann in memr' & ascribend*).

And another manuscript bearing this scribe's complaint: "I, Eadberct, have finished this book . . . with the aid of God, not without physical strain. Who doesn't know how to write doesn't think it's a hardship; for three fingers write and the whole body labours."

——～——

Here's Kurt Vonnegut's lament:

> My own means of making a living is essentially clerical, and hence tedious and constipating. Intruders, no matter how ill-natured or stupid or dishonest, are as refreshing as the sudden breakthrough of sunbeams on a cloudy day.[233]

Never hurts to let off steam. Meanwhile, in spite of tedium, cramped backs, self-doubt, patiently and persistently these laborers produced illuminated manuscripts, the Sistine Chapel ceiling, and a singular body of writing, in Kurt Vonnegut's case, and bestowed them to us.

CHAPTER 18
PITFALLS

"Good Taste will put you out of business," [Vonnegut] declared. . . . "For some reason almost all good writers are drop-outs," he said. "English departments have never produced a (good) writer." He suggested that this is because people learn what is considered "good taste" at a stage "when they themselves aren't capable of doing very good work. So what they learn makes them hate what they write. And they stop before they ever get started."[234]

Any artist of any kind has to be able to stomach falling short of the mark, continually, in all kinds of ways. But perhaps especially when starting out. As the poet William Stafford often said to students: You've got to lower your standards! You can't compare yourself with the most renowned writers in the history of literature, for example.

Another thing that will put you out of business: the "third player." Vonnegut invented this phrase in a preface composed for the Franklin Library edition of *Bluebeard*, reprinted in *Fates Worse than Death*:

Children . . . get smashed for hours on some strictly limited aspect of the Great Big Everything . . . such as water or snow or mud or colors or rocks . . . or banging on a drum and so on. Only two people are involved: the child and the Universe. . . .

... Professional picture painters, who are what a lot of this made-up story is about, are people who continue to play children's games with goo, and dirt, with chalks and powdered minerals mixed with oil and dead embers and so on, dabbing, smearing, scrawling, scraping, and so on, for all their natural lives. When they were children, though, there was just they and the Universe, with only the Universe dealing in rewards and punishments, as a dominant playmate will. When picture painters become adults, and particularly if other people depend on them for food and shelter and clothing and all that, not forgetting heat in the wintertime, they are likely to allow a third player, with dismaying powers to hold up to ridicule or reward grotesquely or generally behave like a lunatic, to join the game. It is that part of society which does not paint well, usually, but which knows what it likes with a vengeance. That third player is sometimes personified by an actual dictator, such as Hitler or Stalin or Mussolini, or simply by a critic or curator or collector or dealer or creditor, or in-laws.

In any case, since the game goes well only when played by two, the painter and the Great Big Everything, *three's a crowd.*[235]

Children, too, can get stunted by the "third player." In second grade, for example, my teacher told me that my blue sky across the top of the page was not how the sky appeared. It was everywhere, not just at the top. She took me outside to prove it. But I didn't see blue all around. It looked bluer up higher. I have a vivid memory of her staring down at me. She was a lot bigger than me, an authority. Her perception trumped mine.

I avoided drawing or painting from then on until I was in my late thirties at an art colony, and suddenly became impatient with words as tools to describe a magnificent purple cabbage in the garden. I snatched it up, began drawing it. An artist walked by. "I'm drawing!!" I exclaimed. "What should I do?"

She drew in breath. "Just follow your own eye. Everything else you can learn later."[236]

Only after that permission did I recall the scene with the teacher.

The most insidious "third player" is the one in your own head. You may not even know where it came from. Become acquainted with it. Beware of it.

CHAPTER 19
METHODOLOGISM

Decades after suggesting writers fall into two groups according to their methods, Vonnegut discussed that dichotomy again in his last novel.

> Swoopers write a story quickly, higgledy-piggledy, crin-kum-crankum, any which way. Then they go over it again painstakingly, fixing everything that is just plain awful or doesn't work. Bashers go one sentence at a time, getting it exactly right before they go on to the next one. When they're done they're done.
>
> I am a basher.

Only this time he elaborates and calcifies his original nonjudgmental observation of the two differing processes into verdicts.

> Writers who are swoopers, it seems to me, find it wonderful that people are funny or tragic or whatever, *worth reporting*, without wondering why or how people are alive in the first place.
>
> Bashers, while ostensibly making sentence after sentence as efficient as possible, may actually be breaking down seeming doors and fences, cutting their ways through seeming barbed-wire entanglements, under fire and in an atmosphere of mustard gas, in search of answers to these eternal questions: "What in heck should we be doing? What in heck is really going on?"[237]

—

I believe here that Vonnegut, being human, has fallen into what I'm going to call "methodologism": when someone (a) confuses a method with results, or (b) prescribes for all a method that worked well for that person.

I may also be committing (b), believing strongly as I do in the swooping method, and being human.

—

To avoid such mental traps, take a look at *W.O.W., Writers on Writing*, a compendium of contradictory quotes from extraordinary writers on every possible writerly topic, from "angst" to "work habits."[238] It will avert your yen to know The Way. Everyone wants to know The Way. But there is no single Way. There is only discovering your own. That entails imitating paths others have tread, taking advice, and exploring what works best for you. The quotes in it on process don't even fall neatly into two camps. Some novelists write the major scenes first, for example, confounding the swoop/bash division all to heck. Some must know how their story will end before they start. Some declare they'd never start if they knew the end.

—

Audience:

> Write to please just one person. If you open a window and make love to the world, so to speak, your story will get pneumonia.

That's Vonnegut's "Creative Writing 101" Rule #7 for the short story.[239] Here's how he arrived at that conclusion.

He used to write for his sister, Alice. He'd chuckle to himself, imagining her over his shoulder, enjoying what he'd written.[240]

Tragically, Alice died of cancer at the age of forty-one. Vonnegut writes about her and her death in the preface to *Slapstick*. He based that novel on their relationship.

"Hers would have been an unremarkable death, statistically," he says. Except that her husband, an editor who worked on Wall Street, died two mornings before she did, in a train wreck on the way to work.

They left four boys. Jane and Kurt took them in. Now they had seven children. Surveying the Vonneguts' straits, a cousin of Alice's husband, a judge in Alabama, persuaded Jane and Kurt to let him and his wife raise the youngest, a baby.

Vonnegut disclosed in the *Paris Review* interiew:

I didn't realize that [Alice] was the person I wrote for *until after she died* [italics mine].

That discovery turned into his edict:

Every successful creative person creates with an audience of one in mind. That's the secret of artistic unity. Anybody can achieve it, if he or she will make something with only one person in mind.[241]

He continued writing for her after her death in 1958, until her presence "began to fade away." He never reports who replaced her as his audience. But the dictate stuck. It crops up in the mouths of his characters:

"Writers will *kill* for an audience."
  "An audience of *one*?" I said.
  "That's all she needed," she said. "That's all anybody needs. Just look at how her handwriting improved and her vocabulary grew. Look at all the things she found to

talk about, as soon as she realized you were hanging on every word. . . ."

"That's the secret of how to enjoy writing and how to make yourself meet high standards," said Mrs. Berman. "You don't write for the whole world, and you don't write for ten people, or two. You write for just one person."[242]

———

This advice as a method to gain artistic unity is uniquely Vonnegut's, insofar as I know. His arriving at it is understandable emotionally, because he cherished his sister so. But it seems like another "methodologism." He didn't consciously write with Alice in mind; he only discovered he did so *after* she died, as he says. This advice always makes me worry that I'm doing something wrong. Because it's not true for me.

To give Kurt the benefit of the doubt, perhaps I've been unaware—as you may be, as *he* was—that I've someone for whom I'm telling any given story. But I don't think so. Like many writers, I'm telling myself the story, the universe, whoever has ears to hear.

Kurt Vonnegut wrote with Alice in mind. Maybe it helps you to write with one person in mind too. Maybe it doesn't. Do what works for you.

CHAPTER 20
MATERIALIZATIONS

Where do stories come from? How can you conjure them up? First, by paying attention.

It was a treat to take a walk with Kurt, his friend Sidney Offit says. Because he noticed things most people didn't, and responded to what he saw more than most people did. He took the same delight in discovering information. He loved disseminating it too.

Kurt Vonnegut had "big ears." That's the term jazz musicians apply to one of their own who's especially tuned in to the music.

> So I wandered up on the balcony, and I sat on a hard-backed chair there. It must have been something I used to do in the carriage house when I was genuinely innocent and twelve years old—to sit very still on the balcony, and *to appreciate every sound that floated up to me. It wasn't eavesdropping. It was music appreciation* [italics mine].[243]

"Eavesdropping," by the way, is a word begotten from King Henry the Eighth, who installed gargoyles in the eaves of his palaces to peer down upon everyone as a warning that spies were overhearing, so people should watch their Ps and Qs. I just learned that on a PBS special. Vonnegut loved facts like this. He had big ears for them too.

A passage in *Jailbird*, written from the point of view of the released prisoner-narrator, reads as if Kurt strolled to the park behind the main New York Public Library in Manhattan and simply recorded his eavesdropped observations and responses.

I looked about myself in Bryant Park. Lilies of the valley had raised their little bells above the winter-killed ivy and glassine envelopes that bordered the walks. . . .

I was aroused at last by a portable radio that was turned up loud. The young man carrying it sat down on a bench facing mine. He appeared to be Hispanic. . . . The radio was tuned to the news. The newscaster said that the air quality that day was unacceptable.

Imagine that: unacceptable air.

The young man did not appear to be listening to his own radio. He may not even have understood English. The newscaster spoke with a barking sort of hilarity, as though life were a comical steeplechase, with unconventional steeds and hazards and vehicles involved. He made me feel that even I was a contestant—in a bathtub drawn by three aardvarks, perhaps. I had as good a chance as anybody to win.

He told about another man in the steeplechase, who had been sentenced to die in an electric chair in Texas. . . .

Two joggers came down the path between me and the radio. They were a man and a woman in identical orange-and-gold sweatsuits and matching shoes. . . .

About the young man and his radio. I decided that he had bought the thing as a prosthetic device, as an artificial enthusiasm for the planet. He paid as little attention to it as I paid to my false front tooth.

Soon the radio reports something so horrifying that he "got off [the] bench, left the park, and joined the throng . . . toward Fifth Avenue."[244]

Imitate Kurt Vonnegut and the Big Bad Wolf. BIG EARS and BIG EYES snag a lot of fodder for fiction.

Kurt was an idea guy, a writer enthralled with possibilities in humankind and with their shortfalls. His work exemplifies fiction that springs from ideas.

You take a common notion from a culture, and you make it literal. "Everybody is created equal." Vonnegut made a humdinger of a story, "Harrison Bergeron," based on that notion, by positing a government attempting to make it literally true.

You take a wish and let your imagination run off with it. Tired of your body getting tired? Don't like your shape? Gender? What if you could park your body somewhere or trade it for someone else's? Read "Unready to Wear."[245]

You take an issue about which you feel urgency, mix it with your experience, add the imaginative "what if," and whammy, you've got ammunition for a book. *Cat's Cradle* might result, for example, if you're Vonnegut.

> The novel was inspired by GE, the science of GE. In those days it was quite conventional for research scientists to be indifferent about what became of their discoveries . . . and I think that the government was very interested in having the scientists feel that they were in no way associated with weapons.[246]

Or *Deadeye Dick*:

> The book . . . is about a kid, he's grown now, grown and in his 40s and his father was a gun nut. It was a house with dozens of guns in it.

Kurt Vonnegut Sr. was such a "gun nut." What if Kurt Vonnegut Jr. had shot off one of his father's guns as a kid and accidentally murdered someone?

> At the age of 11 this kid was playing with one of his father's guns, which he wasn't supposed to do, put a cartridge into

a 30-06 rifle and fired out a goddamn attic window and killed a housewife, you know, eighteen blocks away, just drilled her right between the eyes. And this has colored his whole life, and made his reputation. And of course this weapon should not have existed. He was brought into [a] planet where this terribly unstable device existed, and all he had to do was sneeze near it. I mean, it wanted to be fired; it was built to be fired. It had no other purpose than to be fired and the existence of such an unstable device within the reach of any sort of human being is intolerable.[247]

Your Fairy Godmother can usher you into a story or novel by leading you from one thing to another:

I would eventually write a book about a painter, *Bluebeard*. I got the idea for it after *Esquire* asked me for a piece about the Abstract Expressionist Jackson Pollock. The magazine was putting together a fiftieth-anniversary issue to consist of essays on fifty native-born Americans who had made the biggest difference in the country's destiny since 1932. I wanted Eleanor Roosevelt but Bill Moyers already had her.[248]

Your Fairy Godmama may poke you.

Knox Burger, Kurt's ex–Cornell classmate and cohort at the *Sun*, challenged him at a party: When are you going to write your next novel? It had been ten years since his first. Kurt's response: *The Sirens of Titan*.

Or she may wave her magic wand.

Mother Night was touched off by meeting "a big shot in Naval Intelligence" at a party in Chatham on Cape Cod, who had "beautiful views on espionage," just as Vonnegut was thinking to himself, "Christ, I've got to get going on another book."

Apparently, he was ready to start tackling the nightmare of World War II.

———

A certain person's character, their way of viewing or handling things, can provide the avenue into a story. Vonnegut based *God Bless You, Mr. Rosewater* on an accountant who had office space above him when he first lived on Cape Cod, a sweet man who used to encourage and comfort his customers. He'd hear him murmuring through the floorboards.[249]

———

Sometimes a story delivers itself whole out of your own life. How Kurt courted his first wife, Jane—a sweetly ordinary love story—is the basis of "A Long Walk to Forever." At a party at their house, Jane once acted out for me the manner in which Kurt had proposed, going down on one knee. Of course, he changed such details in the story, along with their names.

———

You can start anywhere and keep on going and see where it leads you, parting the layers of fat on your brain until your consciousness emerges, reeling your own tape out of your own mouth. To mix Vonnegut's metaphors. That's how he poured out *The Sirens of Titan*.

———

You can steal a plot.

[For *Player Piano*] I cheerfully ripped off the plot of *Brave New World*, whose plot had been cheerfully ripped off from Eugene Zamiatin's *We*.[250]

———

Getting the scent of a story becomes a habit. Vonnegut's noggin was so full of that habit that he bestowed the overflow from his prolific imagination to Kilgore Trout, his sci-fi writer character, concocting summaries of dozens of zany sci-fi plots.

CHAPTER 21

PROPAGATION

[The storyteller's] initial lie, his premise, will suggest many new lies of its own. The storyteller must choose among them, seeking those which are most believable, which keep the arithmetic sound. *Thus does a story generate itself* [italics mine].[251]

Memory, fact, observation, an imaginative spree: these are a writer's resources. You seize the one that springs up out of your tool chest.

You know the amazing passage in *Slaughterhouse-Five* about Billy Pilgrim's imagining the war movie backward?

He came slightly unstuck in time, saw the late movie backwards, then forwards again. It was a movie about American bombers in the Second World War and the gallant men who flew them. Seen backwards by Billy, the story went like this:

American planes, full of holes and wounded men and corpses took off backwards from an airfield in England. Over France, a few German fighter planes flew at them backwards, sucked bullets and shell fragments from some of the planes and crewmen. They did the same for wrecked American bombers on the ground, and those planes flew up backwards to join the formation.[252]

And on it goes.

There's no explaining the imaginative leap that spawned that marvelous scene. However, films *were* rewound in the good old celluloid days. You could turn the light off your 8mm home movie projector so you didn't have to see, or you could watch it reel backward. It was amusing to do that. Fellow employees and friends of Vonnegut's at GE, guys in their late twenties, used to have stag nights watching blue movies, and they'd deliberately rewind the films to view them backward. "Such fun watching the bellboy getting dressed and backing out of the room, carrying a tray."[253] The un-fucking, too, must've been entertaining. This experience may have embedded itself more deeply in Kurt's memory than your everyday rewound home movie, and triggered this transformative use of it.

The word "karass" in *Cat's Cradle*? A student in our workshop at Iowa asked Kurt where it came from. In that split second before reply, there was the hushed expectation, the possibility, that it might've descended from something magical, meaningful. Kurt responded candidly. It was a name on a mailbox he often passed in Barnstable, Cape Cod.

The prayer, commonly known now as AA's Serenity Prayer, in *Slaughterhouse-Five* that adorns Billy Pilgrim's office wall and the locket between Montana Wildhack's breasts?[254]

GOD GRANT ME
THE SERENITY TO ACCEPT
THE THINGS I CANNOT CHANGE,
COURAGE
TO CHANGE THE THINGS I CAN,
AND WISDOM ALWAYS
TO TELL THE
DIFFERENCE.

Kurt lifted it from a story, he confessed to me, written by Mary Kathleen O'Donnell, his student and my friend, soon after the novel's publication. He said he'd never done that before, taken something from a student's work. He was mildly ashamed.

Some stolen property. Soon after he told me that, I saw the prayer in embroidery and framed in my mother's farmhouse kitchen. AA had adopted it, it turns out, years before.[255] That's probably how Mary knew it. It's public domain.

Fictional theories about social change, which Vonnegut concocted in *The Sirens of Titan*, for example? They certainly derived from his mentor Slotkin's actual theories.

> As he says in his *Pocket History of Mars*: "Any man who would change the World in a significant way must have showmanship, a genial willingness to shed other people's blood, and a plausible new religion to introduce during the brief period of repentance and horror that usually follows bloodshed."[256]

Two novels later, in *Cat's Cradle*, it seems Vonnegut applied these theories in creating its characters and "plausible new" religion, Bokonism. Chapter 58, "Tyranny with a Difference," lets us know that "the new conquerors" of the fictional island of San Lorenzo

> "dreamed of making San Lorenzo a Utopia.
> "To this end, McCabe overhauled the economy and the laws.
> "Johnson designed a new religion."
>> I wanted all things
>> To seem to make some sense,
>> So we all could be happy, yes,
>> Instead of tense.
>> And I made up lies
>> So that they all fit nice,
>> And I made this sad world
>> A par-a-dise.

It was the belief of Bokonon [McCabe's friend] that good societies could be built only by pitting good against evil, and by keeping the tension high between the two at all times.[257]

To that end, the religion was outlawed. Laws were instituted. This was one:

ANYBODY CAUGHT PRACTICING BOKONON-ISM IN SAN LORENZO . . . WILL DIE ON THE HOOK![258]

Let the good times roll.

———————

I don't know how people explain the imagination, anyway. My books are protests against explanations. It drives me nuts when someone tells me what's going on.[259]

"Kurt's way of looking at people, of creating characters," Sidney Offit says, "was his own. Take Billy Pilgrim in *Slaughterhouse-Five*. He comes off like a character in a fable. If you or I were writing that story about Dresden, we'd be trying to dredge the emotion from the scene. Not Kurt.

"With Kurt's stories there was always something else going on—a spiritual quality. Religion itself has a quality, a spiritual jump. . . . You could call them science fiction leaps."[260]

CHAPTER 22
REGENERATION

If you keep writing, your concerns will sneak up again and again in various forms.

Long after Vonnegut said he'd put his mother's suicide to rest by writing *Breakfast of Champions*, it kept materializing.[261] In fact, in *Deadeye Dick*, three novels later, he took it on more directly.

> I would be glad to attempt a detailed analysis of Celia Hoover's character, if I thought her character had much of anything to do with her suicide by Drāno. As a pharmacist, though, I see no reason not to give full credit to amphetamine.
>
> Here is the warning which the law requires as a companion now for each shipment of amphetamine as it leaves the factory:
>
> "Amphetamine has been extensively abused. Tolerance, extreme psychological dependence, and severe social disability have occurred. There are reports of patients who have increased dosages to many times that recommended. Abrupt cessation following prolonged high dosage results in extreme fatigue and mental depression; changes are also noted in the sleep EEG.
>
> "Manifestations of chronic intoxication with amphetamine include severe dermatoses, marked insomnia, irritability, hyperactivity, and personality changes. The most severe manifestation of chronic intoxication is psychosis, often indistinguishable from schizophrenia."
>
> Want some?[262]

Further on, the pharmacist narrator, who converts all his worst memories into plays, remembers "the snaggletoothed ruins" of Celia knocking on his back door, begging for more:

> Rudy: You came here because you've been shut off every-place else. And I wouldn't give you any more of that poison, if you had a prescription signed by God Almighty. Now you're going to tell me you don't love me after all.

> Celia: I can't believe you're so mean.

> Rudy: And who was it who was so nice to you for so long? Dr. Mitchell, I'll bet—hand in hand with the Fairchild Heights Pharmacy. Too late, they got scared to death of what they'd done to you.[263]

All the above is fiction. Vonnegut's mother did *not* drink Drano. She was *not* addicted to amphetamines. This is what actually happened, in his words:

> So when my mother went crazy, long before my son went crazy, long before I had a son, and finally killed herself, I blamed chemicals, and I still do, although she had a terrible childhood. I can even name two of the chemicals: pheno-barbital and booze. Those came from the outside, of course, the phenobarbs from our family doctor, who was trying to do something about her sleeplessness.[264]

Vonnegut ups the ante from the truth, in his fictional story, as any good fiction writer does.

About truth and fiction: at a *Slate* magazine panel discussion I attended about *Slaughterhouse-Five* and fan fiction, the editorial participants declared that Kurt's mother had been addicted to amphetamines and downed Drano.

They conflated fiction with fact. They had not done their homework.

Besides "sneaking up," you can intentionally recycle and elaborate upon your concerns. Whichever way it developed, intuitively or purposefully, here's a Vonnegut example: his use of taking literally the adage "everybody is created equal."

It appears in his first novel, *Player Piano*, as an idea two characters discuss.

> "Well—I think it's a grave mistake to put on public record everyone's I.Q. I think the first thing the revolutionaries would want to do is knock off everybody with an I.Q. over 110, say . . ."
>
> ". . . Things are certainly set up for a class war based on conveniently established lines of demarcation. . . . The criterion of brains is better than the one of money . . ."
>
> *"It's about as rigid a hierarchy as you can get," said Finnerty. "How's somebody going to up his I.Q.* [italics mine]?"[265]

In his second book, *The Sirens of Titan*, Vonnegut actualizes the idea within his sci-fi society.

> He . . . rattled the blue canvas bag of lead shot that was strapped around his wrist.
>
> There were similar bags of shot around his ankles and his

other wrist, and two heavy slabs of iron hung on shoulder straps—one slab on his chest and one on his back.

These weights were his handicaps in the race of life.

He carried forty-eight pounds—carried them gladly. A stronger person would have carried more, a weaker person would have carried less. . . .

The weakest and meekest were bound to admit, at last, that the race of life was fair.[266]

Vonnegut describes realistic handicaps, as well:

There were . . . several true believers who had chosen handicaps of a subtler and more telling kind. . . .

A dark young man, whose lithe, predaceous sex appeal could not be spoiled by bad clothes and bad manners, had handicapped himself with a wife who was nauseated by sex.

The dark young man's wife, who had reason to be vain about her Phi Beta Kappa key, had handicapped herself with a husband who read nothing but comic books.[267]

Two years after *The Sirens of Titan* was published in 1959, the short story "Harrison Bergeron," with its opening premise of everybody being equal, appeared in *Fantasy and Science Fiction Magazine*. In the short story Vonnegut forgoes the realism of "subtler and more telling" handicaps. He zeroes in on the physically obvious, keeping the story tight and to the point. It's hilarious. And haunting.

CHAPTER 23
THE MOTHER OF ALL PEARLS

Picture a huge, luminescent pearl, its gleam so great that its glow prevails over all the lesser pearls nestled around it.

Well, here is the Mother of All Pearls of wisdom that Kurt offered us at Iowa on the nuts and bolts of writing fiction:

You're in the entertainment business.

He stood in front of the class, shaking his head over someone's story, as he said that. Many times.

This was startling to hear. "Entertainment business" implied Hollywood, with its crass glitter and flash.

I myself wasn't thinking about entertaining anyone. I just wanted to get sorrow and outrage off my chest. Everyone in the workshop had things to get off their chests. Our instructors did too. It seemed that Kurt had the most. He was writing *Slaughterhouse-Five*. We knew his firebombing, prisoner-of-war backstory.

These were soul-scouring experiences. And we were in the entertainment business?

Eventually I understood he meant this: You have to play by the rules of the game of fiction well enough so that you can get across what is in the rag-and-bone shop of your heart. You have to be like a magician or pickpocket, distracting the audience by entertaining, while you are really saying those things you most want to say.

At a party recently, I told two MFA candidates that this was Kurt's most important advice. They stared at me, aghast.

One of the hardest lessons for novice writers to realize is that caring alone, no matter what you've been through or what story you have to tell, doesn't matter in terms of rendering the successful creation of your work. It's not your story that matters. It's how you tell it.

Vonnegut knew the distinction between spinning a yarn and the voltage that caused the yarn to spin, between the self and the persona. Of all he taught about writing, what he said about the "entertainment business," I would come to discover, was the most complex and important.

In *Player Piano*, a character exclaims,

> I mean, Christ, boy, that was a show. You know, it's enter-tainment, and still you learn something, too. Christ! When you do both, that's art, boy.[268]

> He [a publicity man in *Galápagos*] had transformed what was to have been a routine, two-week trip out to the islands and back into the nature cruise of the century. How had he worked such a miracle? By never calling it anything but "the Nature Cruise of the Century."[269]

Vonnegut had to learn the entertainment lesson too. When Kurt and Jane first married and he was in the service stationed at Fort Riley, Jane spotted an ad for what nowadays would be called a "book doctor." Scammon Lockwood's office was near publishers in Manhattan and he reviewed writing samples for free. Jane sent him some of Kurt's stories.

Lockwood replied, "I warmly applaud Kurt's desire to 'say something' that will have some influence, however small, that will do something to help uplift humanity," he wrote. "Every writer worth a hoot has ambition. But . . . what it adds up to or boils down to is this: you have got to master the current technique if you want acceptance for anything, good or drivel, in the current market. The 'message to humanity' is a by-product: it always has been. . . . *If you want to make a living writing you will first of all write to entertain*, to divert, to amuse. And that in itself is a noble aim.[270]

In the 1950s, Vonnegut published over fifty stories. Magazines *needed* fiction writers then. It behooved an editor to cultivate a writer.

> I developed sociability skills writing for the slicks, because they wouldn't publish it if it wasn't sociable.[271]

Richard Yates heard from students at Iowa that Vonnegut admonished, "Never forget you're writing for strangers." Yates adopted that line, using it in every class he ever taught after that. "It's the best single piece of advice I know for beginning writers, expressed in the fewest possible words."[272]

Vonnegut said,

> We must acknowledge that the reader is doing something quite difficult for him, and the reason you don't change point of view too often is so he won't get lost; and the reason you paragraph often is so that his eyes won't get tired, is so you get him without him knowing it by making his job easy for him. He has to restage your show in his head—costume and light it. His job is not easy.[273]

Vonnegut calls the reader "my indispensable collaborator."[274] His rules for "Creative Writing 101" in *Bagombo Snuff Box*, adapted from his classroom admonishments, begin with courtesy toward them. Rule #1:

> Use the time of a total stranger in such a way that he or she will not feel the time was wasted.[275]

In other words, "You're in the entertainment business."

CHAPTER 24

BEGINNINGS

Being in the entertainment business, your primary tasks are to hook the reader, then keep the reader reading, Kurt exhorted in workshops.

Let's start with hooking the reader.

Novices often think engaging the reader means immediately staging something outlandish or stunningly dramatic.

Beginners also confuse withholding information with suspense. They suppose a murky situation will make the reader want to find out what's going on. But what it really does is make the reader feel stupid and left out.

In 1980, an interviewer said to Vonnegut, "I was interested in hearing you insist that a writer should set the stage early because I can think of very few writers who convey more information and impressions in the first few pages than you."

Vonnegut learned that from magazine editors.

> You had to do what they told you to do or you couldn't sell them a story. To a great extent they wanted the same thing a good newspaper wants: an arresting lead, lucid prose, an immediate sense of place. When I teach now I frequently get annoyed when I get four paragraphs into a story and still don't know what city, or even what century, the characters are in. I have a right to be annoyed too. A reader has a right, and a need, to learn immediately what sort of people he's encountering, what sort of locale they're in, what they do

for a living, whether they're rich or poor—all of these things make subsequent information that much more marvelous.[276]

So "hooking the reader" means employing an "arresting lead." Not dramatic hyperbole or obfuscation, but arousing curiosity through informing.

One of my beginning students started his first stories with a murder/divorce/arrest, or a kidnapping/drug heist/abortion—you name three or four dramatic events and he had them all there in the opening two paragraphs. The characters were incidental. It turned out he was an avid NYPD fan. Eventually he learned to clue the reader in on who the people were, where they were, and to narrow his focus and build up to a single conflict.

Another opened a novel with the violent death of the narrator's mother. Whether caused by suicide or murder remained unclear until the end of the novel, so the reader was left in the dark throughout, unable to get a grip on the tangled relationships, emotions and motives of the characters.

My own novel's opening suffered as well. I adhered to my character, who wanted to suppress her trauma, at the expense of letting my readers in on what it was she wanted to suppress.

Besides teaching fiction writing for most of my adult life, I've been the fiction editor of *Bellevue Literary Review* for twelve years. *Bellevue Literary Review* publishes semiannually, ten to twelve stories an issue. We receive, on average, 2,000 fiction manuscripts a year; they're divided among first readers, then editors. I have now considered approximately 2,100 stories for publication. I've edited over a hundred. I've learned a lot about writing, being on this editorial side of the fence. One of the most important things is that almost all stories have problems with the setup.

These problems usually entail not furnishing enough information for the reader to easily grasp the who-what-where-when of the situation, using fancy prose that makes the reader stumble, or not getting quickly enough to the central conflict.

Vonnegut's "Creative Writing 101" Rule #8:

> Give your readers as much information as possible as soon
> as possible. To heck with suspense. Readers should have
> such complete understanding of what is going on, where
> and why, that they could finish the story themselves, should
> cockroaches eat the last few pages.[277]

With such an introduction, you will be behaving like "a good
date on a blind date" as Vonnegut suggests you ought to do.[278] You
are inviting your blind date to join you, so that he or she can get in
on the action and understand what's happening and what it means
and experience its impact, instead of being left out in the cold.

———

The last sentences of Rule #8 contradict another major Vonnegut
edict:

> Don't be predictable. End your sentences with something
> unexpected. Keep me awake.[279]

———

Vonnegut applied hyperbole and cockroaches to emphasize the
main point.

Elsewhere in "Creative Writing 101," he says simply,

> Remember my rule number eight? "Give your readers as
> much information as possible as soon as possible"? That's
> so they can play along.[280]

Unlike the people you've been writing for most of your life—
your teachers, other students—editors and general readers are not

required to read what you've written. And they won't, if you don't follow Vonnegut's primary exhortations.

In fact, it's an editor's job to weed out the chaff from the wheat. If something doesn't entice or bewilders, an editor—forced to make many choices for many reasons among many manuscripts—will find relief in having solid reasons to remove a piece from consideration out of her high pile of submissions.

The reverse is also true: when a piece is solid and engaging, an editor will feel relief—and delight—at hitting sure gold.

———

"Throw out the first two pages!" Vonnegut would say over and over in class, responding to a story. Later he converted that into "Creative Writing 101" Rule #5: "Start as close to the end as possible."[281]

"Throw out the first two pages" is better advice, to my mind.

How can you know how close you are to the end if you haven't yet written it?

Both address a penchant people have for warming up to their story—getting their engines going, as it were—and so beginning long before the story quickens. Sometimes doing a first draft, novelists in particular may think they are writing when what they're doing is more akin to composing narrative notes. Sometimes the characters and subject demand emotional fortitude, so the writer eases into tender, painful places with digression and window dressing. Sometimes the writer doesn't quite know what the story is about, and rambles around in search of it.

These discardable "first two pages" may be necessary for the writer in composing the story. They may indeed become expendable. But you do not have to accomplish all the acrobatic tasks required for the beginning when you begin writing the story. Start however you start. The time to worry about perfecting the opening is later, in the revision process. Unless you're a painstaking, sentence-by-sentence "basher" like Vonnegut, and a leathery old cowhand at writing, you're better off throwing out than trying to start perfectly close to the end.

If you've got the hang of narrative and as you gain experience, short story beginnings will start to come more readily. But especially with novels, you may not know what you're truly writing about for many, many pages. Things appear, a new wind stirs up, sailing you in another direction or to a deeper place. It would be impossible, then, to set up a beginning to fit the rest, if you've no idea what the rest will lead to.

Once you do know, then yes, "start as close to the action as you can."

Vonnegut's friend Sidney Offit offers a great example: "I was working at *Fantasy and Science Fiction*. A story came in that was set on Mars but the first three or four pages were about the construction of the space ship. It was good but slow going. When I showed it to the editor there, Anthony Boucher, he said, 'cut it.' . . . The first line for this story is, 'When the space ship landed on Mars.'"[282]

You don't have to build the ship. Just get the ship going.

When that thing lands, something is going to happen. You've snagged the reader's curiosity.

When still a child, I read my mother's original edition of *Gone with the Wind*, and I read it twice more by high school graduation. Its first line is etched on my brain: "Scarlett O'Hara was not beautiful, but men seldom realized it when caught by her charm as the Tarleton twins were."

Men! Not just the Tarleton twins! So a not-beautiful girl could still be a charmer! Capture male attention! What girl or woman would not be hooked? What man wouldn't either?

The next sentences describe Scarlett vividly. Then the first line of the second paragraph provides all the who-what-where-when info the reader needs to play along: "Seated with Stuart and Brent Tarleton in the cool shade of the porch of Tara, her father's plantation, that bright April afternoon of 1861, she made a pretty picture."

No wonder it was an immediate best seller. We are whisked into context, contrast, into place, time, class, and an intriguing character. It's over a thousand pages, and by the third paragraph, we know it's hot outside, Scarlett's rich, charming, young, and eligible; we know she lives on her father's plantation, the name of it, that he owns slaves, and that it's springtime in the slave-holding South, just before the Civil War.[283]

Even in his first published stories and novels, Vonnegut sets the stage right away with information that lends suspense. Here's a sampler of opening paragraphs from the novels, in chronological order by publication date:

Ilium, New York, is divided into three parts.

In the northwest are the managers and engineers and civil servants and a few professional people; in the northeast are the machines; and in the south, across the Iroquois River, is the area known locally as Homestead, where almost all of the people live.[284]

Everyone now knows how to find the meaning of life within himself.

But mankind wasn't always so lucky. Less than a century ago men and women did not have easy access to the puzzle boxes within them.

They could not name even one of the fifty-three portals to the soul.[285]

A sum of money is a leading character in this tale about people, just as a sum of honey might properly be a leading character in a tale about bees.[286]

Here are short story setting-the-stage samples, starting with Vonnegut's first publication:

> Let me begin by saying that I don't know any more about where Professor Arthur Barnhouse is hiding than anyone else does. Save for one short, enigmatic message left in my mailbox on Christmas Eve, I have not heard from him since his disappearance a year and a half ago.[287]

> I don't suppose the oldsters, those of us who weren't born into it, will ever feel quite at home being amphibious— amphibious in the new sense of the word. I still catch myself feeling blue about things that don't matter any more.[288]

> So Pete Crocker, the sheriff of Barnstable County, which was the whole of Cape Cod, came into the Federal Ethical Suicide Parlor in Hyannis one May afternoon—and he told the two six-foot Hostesses there that they weren't to be alarmed, but that a notorious nothinghead named Billy the Poet was believed headed for the Cape.[289]

Concluding his instructions for "Creative Writing 101," Vonnegut makes this pronouncement:

> The greatest American short story writer of my generation was Flannery O'Connor (1925–1964). She broke practically

every one of my rules but the first. Great writers tend to do that.[290]

"The last story in *Dubliners*, 'The Dead,' is not reader-friendly," Kurt told Gail Godwin. "In the first two pages, you've met nine people. You must not do this!"[291]

"One of Kurt's few mantras was 'Never start a story with a question,'" Ronni Sandroff, another former Iowa student, recalls. "Of course I had to give it a try. My story was about a male college student who had wrangled a summer job on the assembly line at a Bronx bread factory, where his pampered piano-playing hands and ego got roughed over. Vonnegut was a total good sport. He told the class he'd found an opening line—'Who's bleeding on the hot cross buns?'—that was a good example of how to break that rule."[292]

Kurt remarked to Gail Godwin a few years later,

> Of course I had students who refused to take my advice. Remember Ronni? She turned in a story whose first sentence was "Listen, you dumb motherfuckers." I said, "Listen, Ronni, you just can't do that." But she did.[293]

"Listen, you dumb motherfuckers," wasn't Ronni's actual line; "Who's bleeding on the hot cross buns?" was. Maybe Vonnegut substituted that phrase because the reason to avoid starting a story with a question is that doing so makes the reader feel like a dumb motherfucker—not knowing who's asking, from where, about what, to whom.

CHAPTER 25

PLOT

What keeps a reader reading?
Howard Campbell, the narrator of *Mother Night*, clues us in:

> I froze.
>> It was not guilt that froze me. . . .
>> It was not a ghastly sense of loss that froze me. . . .
>> It was not a loathing of death that froze me. . . .
>> It was not heartbroken rage against injustice that froze me. . . .
>> It was not the thought that I was so unloved that froze me. . . .
>> It was not the thought that God was cruel that froze me. . . .
>> What froze me was the fact that I had absolutely no reason to move in any direction. *What had made me move through so many dead and pointless years was curiosity* [italics mine].[294]

That's the same thing that keeps a reader reading.

Plot—the very concept, and the structure of any plot—relies on the reader's curiosity.

~

Vonnegut's "Creative Writing 101" Rule #3:

> Every character should want something, even if it is only
> a glass of water.[295]

Wanting something, anything, triggers curiosity. And suspense.
Will the character get what she desires or not?

Kurt told us in class that even a small problem would keep a
reader reading. A nun in our workshop wrote a story in which her
character, also a nun, had a piece of dental floss stuck in her teeth
all day. Would she ever get it out? Kurt was delighted with that.
He used that detail to talk about suspense and plot forever after. I
think he was amazed that his own curiosity about the stuck floss
pulled him along in the story.

> Nobody could read that story without fishing around in
> his mouth with a finger. . . . When you exclude plot, when
> you exclude anyone's wanting anything, you exclude the
> reader, which is a mean-spirited thing to do.[296]

More complex, vital things may be occurring—the nun may be
battling cancer or want to break out of her habit, for example—but
this basic will-she-or-won't-she-get-what-she-wants is the scaffold
upon which those complexities can be built.

Vonnegut says,

> I guarantee you that no modern story scheme, even plot-
> lessness, will give a reader genuine satisfaction, unless one
> of those old-fashioned plots is smuggled in somewhere. I
> don't praise plots as accurate representations of life, but as
> ways to keep readers reading.

Vonnegut gives some examples of "those old-fashioned plots":

> Somebody gets into trouble, and then gets out again;
> somebody loses something and gets it back; somebody is

wronged and gets revenge; Cinderella; somebody hits the skids and just goes down, down, down; people fall in love with each other, and a lot of other people get in the way; a virtuous person is falsely accused of sin; a sinful person is believed to be virtuous; a person faces a challenge bravely, and succeeds or fails; a person lies, a person steals, a person kills, a person commits fornication.[297]

A single, core conflict is at the heart of the structure of a story.

No conflict equals no plot.

Motivation and conflict are the engines that initiate a story, keep it moving, and form its particular shape.

In my first creative writing class at the University of Arkansas, my teacher, the writer William Harrison, drew the shape of a classic short story plot on the blackboard. It consisted of two lines, like the sides of an isosceles triangle: the longer side zigzagged up to a pinnacle, and the shorter side fell straight part way down from that topmost point. Such an illustration can now be found in creative writing texts.

To put it academically: plot consists of exposition, complications or rising action, climax, and denouement.

Exposition plants the conflict. The stakes intensify through complications and obstacles. The turning point or climax happens when the conflict comes to a head: an insight or epiphany occurs, a decision is made, and/or an action takes place that resolves or comes to terms with the basic conflict. The denouement is the final curtain.

A classic short story is like a geometry proof. Or like a sneeze. Ah-ah-Ah-aH-AH-AH-CHOO! with a little spray of recovery at the end. Or orgasm.

The twists and turns take up most of a story.

You can put [the reader] to sleep by never having characters confront each other. . . . It's the writer's job to stage confrontations, so the characters will say surprising and revealing things, and educate and entertain us all. If a writer can't or won't do that, he should withdraw from the trade.[298]

Vonnegut's "Creative Writing 101" Rule #6:

Be a sadist. No matter how sweet and innocent your leading characters, make awful things happen to them—in order that the reader may see what they are made of.[299]

And to lure the reader into turning pages.

"Curiosity killed the cat," my mother used to say. After a pause, she'd add, "But satisfaction brought it back to life again."

Whether gambling, watching a ballgame, or reading a mystery, according to researchers, "people are invested in learning the outcome . . . but they do not wish to learn the outcome too quickly."[300]

___

They also need signposts and reminders.

And you've got to give your reader familiar props along the way. In *Alice in Wonderland*, remember, when she's falling down the hole there are all these familiar, comforting objects along the sides: cupboards and bookshelves and maps. Orange marmalade.[301]

Special attention should be given to the state of good or ill fortune of the focal character or characters *at the beginning* of a tale, and *again at the end*. The *story-teller will customarily help*, will emphasize the high, low, or medium condition of his characters *at crucial points* [italics mine].[302]

Sometimes you need to repeat, by summarizing what's happened already through a character's recollection or some other means, to keep the reader attuned to the stakes, and to up the ante.

According to Sidney Offit, "[Kurt] said the *only* thing you can teach is development. A story has to have a development and change."[303]

That's what the zigs and zags of plot are all about.

The most entertaining and informative discussion of the subject you'll ever see is Vonnegut on YouTube, graphing the shapes of stories.

How that video came about is a story in itself. It has a plot. I hope to tell the story and at the same time to inform more about Vonnegut's plot tactics.

It starts like this: once upon a time, for his master's thesis in 1947 at the University of Chicago (see chapter 3), Vonnegut put forth the theory that a culture's myths are like other anthropological artifacts, and should be considered so by anthropologists. He focused on the formation of new myths during rapid change, specifically North American Indian narratives.

The thesis was rejected. He dropped out and never got the degree.

Nearly twenty years later, in 1965, when first at the University of Iowa, he tried again. Let's say, for this story's motivation's sake, that he wanted a degree more than ever, because in teaching at a university for the first time, surrounded by academics and writers with college degrees, he felt the lack of one more acutely.

All he needed was the thesis. So he wrote another: "Fluctuations Between Good and Ill Fortune in Simple Tales." Its theme is the same as his first, but this time he argues that the shapes of *all* stories can be considered cultural artifacts. It opens with this assertion:

> The tales man tells are among the most intricate and charming and revealing of all his artifacts.

He analyzes a D. H. Lawrence story, "Tickets, Please," to prove his ideas, reproducing it completely. It takes up half his thesis. It "<u>had</u> to be set down in its entirety," he explains. Because "offering only fragments," like chips of a smashed vase, would not have revealed "its <u>form</u>."

> What makes it a cultural treasure is precisely what has been neglected by anthropologists: <u>how the tale is told</u>.

Alluding to the scientific method, he says,

> It is possible . . . to make a . . . useful analysis of any tale's form . . . in such a way that other investigators making independent analyses of the same tale will arrive at conclusions much the same.

He presents a two-line chart. A vertical line is on the left side. A horizontal line starts halfway up the vertical and crosses the page:

The vertical scale represents "degrees of good and ill fortune . . . with good at the top and ill at the bottom, and with a null at its middle, averageness, or perhaps sleep." The horizontal designates a life-as-usual neutral place, upon which Vonnegut illustrates the characters' fortunes fluctuating up and down.

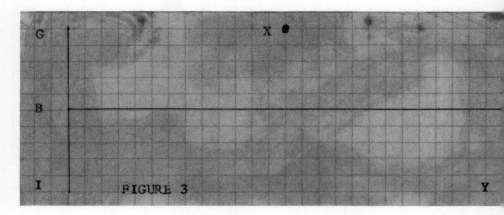

It can be seen now that ... the fluctuations between good and ill fortune in large measure determine form.

For graphic purposes, a tale begins when its focal character or characters experience changes in fortune, and it ends when those fluctuations cease. All else is background.

... A contemporary master story teller cares deeply about the <u>form</u> of his tales because he is obsessed with being <u>entertaining</u>, with not being a <u>bore</u>, with leaving his audience <u>satisfied</u>.

There is a well-known credo for modern tale-tellers who wish to be loved, and I am unable to identify its author, but it goes roughly like this: "A story-teller must tell his story in such a way that the reader will not feel that his time has been <u>wasted</u>."

Within the text, Vonnegut illustrates several classic plots and unusual modern ones. "The Ugly Duckling," "the simplest formula of all," looks like a set of stairs. Kafka's *The Metamorphosis* starts at neutral and plunges below the horizontal line, never to rise above it again.

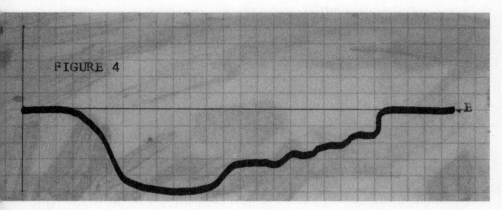

FIGURE 4

The biblical story of Genesis he calls a "remarkably formed artifact":

It begins like nearly all the other creation myths . . . with the "Ugly Duckling" curve. . . . But look at what some tale-telling genius did when he reached the top of the steps in Genesis . . . : He caused Adam and Eve to be expelled from the perfect universe which he had just created for his audience.

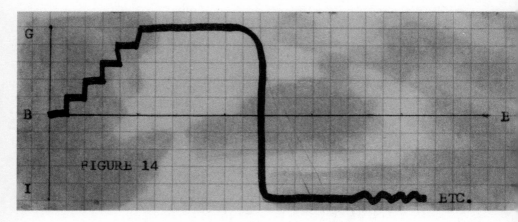

He wraps the thesis up with these fancy remarks:

> The graphic method above brings the skeleton of any tale into the open, where it can, as a skeleton, be examined and discussed with some objectivity. . . .
>   It is my hope that such literary skeletons will be of interest to anthropologists, who are used to working with bare bones.

There's an appendix: "Simple Skeletons of 17 Tales Chosen from Sharply Diverse Sources."[304] It consists of penciled illustrations on cheap, pale-green graph paper. They're kind of thumbing-your-nose hilarious.

Although striving once more to persuade anthropologists that the forms of stories are artifacts as fetching and worthy of examination as any others in a culture, the anthropology department at the University of Chicago rejected his thesis. Again.

Of course they did! Half of it is a reprinted story. The language is informal and nonacademic. The last line is Vonnegut at his whimsical best. Although he does ask provocative questions about stories' cultural implications (such as wondering about editors' insistence in the '50s that stories begin with people "in comfortable circumstances" and conclude with them being "even more comfortable at the end"), this thesis emphasizes the shapes of plot rather than how those shapes are artifacts.

His response at the time to this second rejection: "They can go take a flying fuck at the moooooon."[305]

Meanwhile, at Iowa he was teaching the points he was making about storytelling. Robert Lehrman remembers, "In class, Kurt had annoyed some students by boiling all fiction down to a diagram: 'Get someone in trouble. Get them out!' he would say. 'Man-in-the-hole!'"[306]

Then Vonnegut's fortunes soared. He gained acclaim. Six years after turning his thesis down, the University of Chicago decided *Cat's Cradle* sufficed as a thesis and in 1971 bestowed upon him an honorary degree.

As time went on, he lectured on the shapes of stories, illustrating them as he did in his thesis, but live, in person, on a chalkboard.

To top this success story off, that lecture, based on his rejected thesis, is now the marvelously engaging and instructive one you can see on YouTube.

Vonnegut's gone. But the bare bones of his thesis live on.

End of story.

Talk about desire, disappointment, conflict, surprise, and triumph!

But let's return to that place where a character's fortune takes a decided shift. That turning point or climax can be internal—a character has a change of heart or a realization. It can be external—something happens that forces the conflict to come to a head. It can be both—a character becomes aware or makes an internal decision, then acts upon it.

In this scene from *God Bless You, Mr. Rosewater*, Eliot Rosewater is being questioned by his friend Charley, who thinks he's gone bonkers. Noyes Finnerty, a janitor who's sweeping up nearby, has been eavesdropping.

Noyes Finnerty spoke up. "All he hears is the big click." He came forward for a closer examination of Eliot. . . . "He heard that *click*, man. Man, did he ever hear that *click*."

"What the hell are you talking about?" Charley asked him.

"It's a thing you learn to listen for in prison."

"We're not in prison now."

"It ain't a thing that happens just in prison. In prison, though, you get to listening for things more and more. . . . You get to know a man, and down deep there's something bothering him bad, and maybe you never find out what it is, but it's what makes him do like he does, it's what makes him look like he's got secrets in his eyes. And you tell him, 'Calm down, calm down, take it easy now.' Or you ask him, 'How come you keep doing the same crazy things over and over again, when you know they're just going to get you in trouble again?' Only you know there's no sense arguing with him, on account of it's the thing inside that's making him go. It says, 'Jump,' he jumps. It says, 'Steal,' he steals. It says, 'Cry,' he cries. Unless he dies young, though, or unless he gets everything all his way and nothing big goes wrong, that thing inside of him is going to run down like a wind-up toy. You're working in the prison laundry next to this man. You've known him twenty years. You're working along, and all of a sudden you hear this *click* from him. You turn to look at him. He's stopped working. He's

all calmed down. He looks real dumb. He looks real sweet.
You look in his eyes, and the secrets are gone. He can't even
tell you his own name right then. He goes back to work,
but he'll never be the same. That thing that bothered him
so will never click on again. It's dead, it's *dead*. And that
part of that man's life where he had to be a certain crazy
way, that's *done!*"[307]

The "big click"! What a splendid term for an internal turning
point!

In *Player Piano*, for example, the main character, Paul, ends up in
a jail cell next to his rival. He feels an "exotic emotion" that takes
him a while to understand:

> For the first time in the whole of his orderly life he was
> sharing profound misfortune with another human being.[308]

An external turning point, which doubles as a terrific analysis
of itself, pops up a few pages later:

> Here it was again, the most ancient of roadforks. . . . The
> choice of one course or the other. . . . It was a purely internal
> matter. Every child older than six knew the fork, and knew
> what the good guys did here, and what the bad guys did
> here. The fork was a familiar one in folk tales the world
> over, and the good guys and the bad guys, whether in chaps,
> breechclouts, serapes, leopardskins, or banker's gray pin-
> stripes, all separated here.
> Bad guys turned informer. Good guys didn't.[309]

And so Paul answers his boss Kroner's question about who's the
leader of the Ghost Shirt Society.

But I am beginning to explain, which is a violation of a rule I lay down whenever I teach a class in writing: "All you can do is tell what happened. You will get thrown out of this course if you are arrogant enough to imagine that you can tell me why it happened. You do not know. You cannot know."[310]

"Show, don't tell" is an oft-repeated admonition in fiction teaching and writing. The point it makes is important. Fiction strives to provoke a reader into experiencing what is happening, simulating reality, in which no guide deciphers for you the meaning of what is going on. To explain sabotages that fictional realm. In writing class parlance, "show, don't tell" often implies creating a scene with dialogue rather than narrating a backstory, a character's observations, and so on. As applied to using scenes, the adage can be overused. All writing methods—narration, summary, and scene—make up a story. The whole point of a plot, though, *is* that it "shows." The reader experiences what happens, and what happens makes an impact.

"The thing Kurt seemed to want most in a story," his student Ronni Sandroff recalls, "was to be surprised. He once challenged us to pause before we turned to the next page in a book and try to guess how the sentence we were in the middle of would end. "You'll almost always get it right," he said.

He warned against tiresomeness. He urged originality, freshness.[311]

In *Cat's Cradle*, the chapters are shaped like jokes. Jokes depend on a surprise twist. Those surprise endings keep readers reading as much as the mysteries of plot.

This is the secret of good storytelling: to lie, but to keep the arithmetic sound.[312]

"I don't believe it really happened," Hope objected.

"Makes no difference whether it really did or not," said the General. "Just as long as it's logical."[313]

For a superb example of "arithmetic," investigate Vonnegut's use of the fictional material "ice-nine" in *Cat's Cradle*: check out when he first plants it, how he tantalizes us with increasingly surprising information, then its climactic effect on all the characters' fortunes. You can do the same with the forbidden ritual of "boko-maru." Or any other science fiction bit you choose.

In *Jailbird* he employs the true story of Sacco and Vanzetti in exactly the way you'd plot something fictional. He spreads out their tale to keep the reader enticed and entertained, both by the novel and, more importantly, by Sacco and Vanzetti's history, which he wants so terribly to share.

Sometimes real-life stories such as theirs follow all Vonnegut's suggestions for keeping your reader entertained.

Even then, when retold, the story's "arithmetic" must shape something "sound."

"As for the D. H. Lawrence story, 'Tickets, Please,' I am profoundly reluctant to diagram it," Vonnegut wrote in his thesis, "for it is anything but a simple tale. It is full of horrendous psychological effects, compared to which the plot is nothing. Still and all, let's see what it looks like on the cross."[314]

Hilarious. Yeah, the plot is nothing, he says. Yet let's see how it works on his diagram—the "cross."

He worded an assignment he gave at Iowa similarly (see #2 on the "Form of Fiction" assignment dated March 15, 1966, chapter 14). Kurt was a practical, funny, earnest, ironic man.

———

Consider this passage from *Cat's Cradle*:

> There was a quotation from *The Books of Bokonon* on the page before me. Those words leapt from the page and into my mind, and they were welcomed there.
>
> The words were a paraphrase of the suggestion by Jesus: "Render therefore unto Caesar the things which are Caesar's."
>
> Bokonon's paraphrase was this:
>
> "Pay no attention to Caesar. Caesar doesn't have the slightest idea what's *really* going on."[315]

You might say plot is "Caesar." Plot might not be what's *really* going on, but it's a governing tool, a necessity. It keeps the reader reading. And it may be much more than that, too. What happens, after all, is what happens. And it matters.

———

> Cowboy stories and policeman stories end in shoot-outs . . . because shoot-outs are the most reliable mechanisms for making such stories end. There is nothing like death to say what is always such an artificial thing to say: "The end."[316]

Novices do that also. So many deaths finished off stories in my undergrad Fiction Workshop I classes at Hunter College! Next to beginnings, I have found as an editor, endings need the most touching up and revising. Perhaps because they are artificial, perhaps because exiting is so delicate and can leave such a mark. More than in other parts of a story, attention is drawn to the cadence and the words themselves.

As I approached my fiftieth birthday, I had become more and more enraged and mystified by the idiot decisions made by my countrymen. And then I had come suddenly to pity them, for I understood how innocent and natural it was for them to behave so abominably, and with such abominable results: They were doing their best to live like people invented in story books. This was the reason Americans shot each other so often: It was a convenient literary device for ending short stories and books.[317]

That's the horrible part of being in the short-story business . . . you have to be a real expert on ends. Nothing in real life ends. "Millicent at last understands." Nobody ever understands.[318]

The proper ending for any story about people it seems to me, since life is now a polymer in which the Earth is wrapped so tightly, should be that same abbreviation, which I now write large because I feel like it, which is this one:

And it is in order to acknowledge the continuity of this polymer that I begin so many sentences with "And" and "So," and end so many paragraphs with ". . . and so on."
And so on.[319]

CHAPTER 26

CHARACTER

The "main character" in the skeletal tale of Vonnegut and his theses is not Kurt Vonnegut. The protagonist is Vonnegut-and-his-theses-on-plot-shapes.

Seems fitting, since Vonnegut, as has been said, cared as passionately about the notions his characters conveyed as he did about them as individuals. In *Timequake*, his fictional alter ego explains:

> "If I'd wasted my time creating characters," Trout said, "I would never have gotten around to calling attention to things that really matter: irresistible forces in nature, and cruel inventions, and cockamamie ideals and governments and economies that make heroes and heroines alike feel like something the cat drug in."
>
> Trout might have said, and it can be said of me as well, that he created *caricatures* rather than characters. His animus against so-called *mainstream literature*, moreover, wasn't peculiar to him. It was generic among writers of science fiction.[320]

In *Breakfast of Champions*, the narrator says,

> I agree with Kilgore Trout about realistic novels and their accumulations of nit-picking details. In Trout's novel, *The Pan-Galactic Memory Bank*, the hero is on a space ship two hundred miles long and sixty-two miles in diameter. He gets

a realistic novel out of the branch library in his neighborhood. He reads about sixty pages of it, and then he takes it back.

The librarian asks him why he doesn't like it, and he says to her, "I already know about human beings."[321]

Vonnegut pointed out that Ralph Ellison in *Invisible Man* gave his characters no love interest, nor did Céline in *Journey to the End of the Night*. Nor, for similar reasons, he told an interviewer, did he.

> I try to keep deep love out of my stories because, once that particular subject comes up, it is almost impossible to talk about anything else. Readers don't want to hear about anything else. They go gaga about love. If a lover in a story wins his true love, that's the end of the tale, even if World War III is about to begin, and the sky is black with flying saucers.[322]

There's a priceless, hilarious example of "realistic" marital dialogue in *Player Piano*, showing the sort of arguments that couples find themselves entangled in. I'd like to reproduce the entire knot of it, because not to do so would be like showing only a fragment of a vase. But it's too long. See chapter 18.

Despite disclaimers, Vonnegut possessed a marvelous facility for conjuring up characters, profiling them and employing them in the service of a story. Much can be gleaned from him about trafficking in characters by looking keenly at his.

Granted, Vonnegut may have less expertise developing full-blown characters than a masterful writer of realism. He *said* less about characterization than about plot and beginnings. But he did offer these pointers:

An audience cannot care equally about dozens of characters all at once. It gets confused and then bored, having lost track of who is who. So we give all the important actions and speeches to just a few characters. We create stars. We say in effect to audiences, "Just keep your eyes on the stars, and get to know a little something about them, and you won't miss anything."[323]

Vonnegut's "Creative Writing 101" Rule #2:

Give the reader at least one character he or she can root for.[324]

Here's an example from *The Sirens of Titan*:

"Indianapolis, Indiana," said Constant, "is the first place in the United States of America where a white man was hanged for the murder of an Indian. The kind of people who'll hang a white man for murdering an Indian—" said Constant, "that's the kind of people for me."

I don't know about you, but instantly, I'm rooting for a character who likes that kind of place for those kinds of reasons. That's the kind of character for me.[325]

Characters take their own shape. They can speak and act in alarmingly revealing ways. Vonnegut comments on this in *Breakfast of Champions*.

I had created him, after all. I gave him a name: Harold Newcomb Wilbur. I awarded him the Silver Star, the Bronze Star, the Soldier's Medal, the Good Conduct Medal, and a Purple Heart with two Oak-Leaf Clusters, which made him the second most decorated veteran in Midland City. I put all his medals under his handkerchiefs in a dresser drawer. . . .

And he went on staring at me, even though I wanted to stop him now. *Here was the thing about my control over the characters I created: I could only guide their movements approximately, since they were such big animals* [italics mine]. There was inertia to overcome. It wasn't as though I was connected to them by steel wires. It was more as though I was connected to them by stale rubberbands.[326]

That's the most astonishing and rewarding thing about making characters up. They start to make *you* up, by showing you a thing or two.

———

You do have control—or you can take control—over your attitude toward them, though.

Since Vonnegut was both "a humorist and a serious novelist," he's been likened to Mark Twain, whom he admired enormously. In 1979, he was invited to speak at the one hundredth anniversary of the completion of Twain's house in Hartford, Connecticut.

I now quote a previous owner of this house: "When I find a well-drawn character in fiction or biography, I generally take a warm personal interest in him, for the reason that I have known him before—met him on the river."

I submit to you that this is a profoundly Christian statement, an echo of the Beatitudes.[327]

In the Sermon on the Mount—the Beatitudes—Jesus blesses the multitudes. What Twain meant, Vonnegut goes on to clarify, was that everyone is recognizable, everyone is part of the river.

There's hardly a character Vonnegut created to whom he, as the author, is mean-spirited. He nails characters' flaws. He exposes their guises. He employs some to act and think despicably. But the wide anthropological eye he casts over humanity allows each his or her place in the universe, a position never so simple as purely evil or purely good.

He learned such decency early, particularly from an African American woman employed by his parents as a cook, housekeeper, and general handywoman about the house:

> I was essentially raised by a woman who was Ida Young. . . .
> She was humane and wise and gave me decent moral
> instruction and was exceedingly nice to me. So she was as
> great an influence on me as anybody. . . . The compassionate,
> forgiving aspects of my beliefs came from Ida Young who
> was quite intelligent and from my parents, too.[328]

Roland Weary in *Slaughterhouse-Five* is "stupid and fat and mean." Vonnegut demonstrates Weary's cruel thoughts and actions. "He was always being ditched" by others. He hates being ditched. He wreaks revenge. But Vonnegut tells us Weary is "only eighteen," "at the end of an unhappy childhood," and yearns to belong. He fantasizes of bragging to his loser parents about his war pals (of which there are zero) when he gets home. He is also the one who saves the protagonist, Billy Pilgrim, whose zombie-like response to the war would have made him dead meat over and over without Weary "cursing him, kicking him, slapping him, making him move."[329]

This sort of thing happens over and over in Vonnegut's work—as fate would have it, a repugnant character becomes the catalyst for life-enhancing developments.

While in Kurt's workshop, I wrote a story based on three people I used to wait on at Carnation Ice Cream Parlor in San Diego, where I grew up: a fat, timid middle-aged man and his elderly parents. They appeared at the same time every Sunday after church. They sat in the same booth, took the same seats, ordered the same things. They always left a dime.

They drove me crazy. I felt suffocated looking at them, especially the son. In my story, the waitress plays a trick on him. Her intention was to prod him out of his complacency and collusion with his parents in his own suppression.

Kurt didn't like it. He thought it was mean.

I was rarely mean, even as a kid to other kids. So for me to be so in a story was a stretch and probably a little healthy, psychologically. Nevertheless, dozens of other solutions to release that man could have offered themselves. The effect of Kurt's gentle disapproval impressed upon me that there were kinder alternatives to jump-starting your characters, other human beings, and even yourself.

> There's only one rule that I know of, babies—:
> "God damn it, you've got to be kind."[330]

CONTRAST

In *Sense and Non-sense*, Merleau-Ponty says,

> Every color we perceive in nature elicits the appearance of its complement; and these complementaries heighten one another. To achieve sunlit colors in a picture . . . not only must there be a green—if you are painting grass—but also the complementary red which will make it vibrate.[331]

As in painting, so in storytelling.

The definition of "foil," according to *Webster's*, is "a person or thing that contrasts with and so emphasizes and enhances the qualities of another: *the earthy taste of grilled vegetables is a perfect foil for the tart bite of creamy goat cheese.*"

Billy Pilgrim is pale, shambling, numb. Roland Weary is offensive, gross, outspoken.

Their contrast heightens each other's character.

In the first four chapters of *Mother Night*, prison guards in Israel come on duty successively, all Holocaust survivors. Their divergent responses to that debacle reveal and emphasize their individuality. Collectively, their views depict the horrifying wounds the Nazis inflicted, and the impossibility of escaping those wounds and moral injuries no matter what stance is taken. By juxtaposing these survivors, Vonnegut achieved both an overview and distinct characterization.

In "The Manned Missiles," a story published during the Cold War's space race, two men correspond. They are both fathers of downed astronauts. But one is Russian, the other American.

In "Adam," the tenderest story I believe Kurt ever wrote, two men are in the waiting room of a Chicago lying-in hospital. One, a "gorilla," complains:

> "Seven girls I got now. . . . I can beat the stuffings out of ten men my own size. But, what do I get? Girls." . . .
>
> Sousa turned on Knechtmann. "Some little son of a gun like you, Netman, you want a boy, bing! You got one."

Knechtmann is a thin, slightly hunched survivor of a displaced persons camp, whose German-Jewish relatives all died, it's implied, in the camps. He replies,

> Boy, girl . . . it's all the same, just as long as it lives.[332]

DECEPTION AND COMPLEXITY

Secrets and lies abound in Vonnegut's work.

The contrasts between what a character hides, what they reveal, and the truth enhances characterization all around. It's also a superb device to arouse tension and curiosity.

> Wait was traveling alone. He was prematurely bald and he was pudgy, and his color was bad, like the crust on a pie in a cheap cafeteria, and he was bespectacled, so that he might plausibly claim to be in his fifties, in case he saw some advantage in making such a claim. He wished to seem harmless and shy.[333]

What effects will Wait's deception have? When will this liar be found out?

Secrets and lies can be held by the self without deceiving others purposely. They can be hidden from the self. Partially or completely.

The writer William Harrison, my first creative writing teacher, offered an insight that stayed with me my entire fiction-writing life: "What a character wants and what a character is afraid of are often the same thing."

Conflict within the same character makes that character more complex and compelling. And believable.

Herbert Foster is a guy who works his fool head off in Vonnegut's short story "The Foster Portfolio," even though he's got plenty of money coming in from his investments. The narrator, who works for the investment firm, can't figure out why slope-shouldered Foster endures drudgery and pretends poverty. "The man had maybe seventy-five dollars a day coming in from his securities, and he worked three nights a week to make ends meet!" Turns out, it's in order to act out the surprisingly low-down jazzy side of his personality.[334]

Howard Campbell, the narrator of *Mother Night*, is a double agent for Germany and the US during World War II. Talk about complexity! Conflict! Secrets and lies up the wazoo! Where is the self? What is the truth? Foil upon foil.

The story is told while Campbell's imprisoned in Israel, after the war. If it unfolded during the time he was acting as a double agent, the story would have to lean on plot. But told in retrospect, and in prison, the story centers on character—one forced to account for himself, his duplicity, and the consequence of his actions.

On the opposite end of the spectrum, creating an "innocent" main character—one ignorant of the lay of the land or the problem to be solved—can be a wonderfully natural way to lead your reader into a story. Mystery novels featuring the detective as protagonist do this all the time. Vonnegut often employs this device. In the story mentioned above for example, "The Foster Portfolio," the "innocent" narrator investigates the mystery of Foster's money and work habits. In the novel *Cat's Cradle*, as in any narrative featuring a stranger in a strange land, the protagonist ventures along uncovering the who-what-where-when of the culture and place and people, bringing the reader with him on that journey of discovery, seemingly effortlessly.

REACTIONS

The intensity of good or ill fortune is expressed by the tale-teller, in exposition or in the reactions of characters in his tale. If something seemingly bad or good happens in a tale, *and neither the tale-teller nor his characters are impressed*, then nothing much has really happened.[335]

In *Deadeye Dick*, the twelve-year-old narrator has just been arrested for murdering a pregnant woman, and his father beaten up by the police.

> "Look at your rotten father," [the father] said. "What a worthless man I am." If he was curious about my condition, he gave no sign of it. He was so theatrically absorbed by his own helplessness and worthlessness that I don't think he even noticed that his own son was all covered with ink. Nor did he ever ask me what I had just been through.[336]

What if the son were not "impressed" by what his father says, and gave the reader no clue as to how to decipher it? What if there were only the father's dialogue? "'Look at your rotten father,' he said. 'What a worthless man I am.'"

You wouldn't understand the complexity of either character or, more importantly, the son's comprehension of his father and his neglect. But the son reacts to his father's response. So something has indeed happened.

In the grassroots communal photography project in Manhattan's SoHo that sprang up in response to the September 11, 2001, attack, "Here is New York: A Democracy of Photographs," everyone could contribute two photographs, and these were reproduced, pinned up on walls and on thin wires strung across two small rooms. I volunteered there for months, as the exhibition went on far beyond anyone's expectations. Many, many photographs were of people watching. Many were of people fleeing, crying, numb, people comforting each other. People *reacting*.

The place was hushed. People looked at the photographs. I looked at the faces of the people looking at the photographs.

Billy Pilgrim in *Slaughterhouse-Five* doesn't recall what Dresden looked like after the firebombing. That hell isn't described.

What Pilgrim finally remembers are the Dresden prison guards' faces "in their astonishment and grief" after they peeked out at the firebombed devastation that Dresden had become.

> The guards drew together instinctively, rolled their eyes. They experimented with one expression and then another, said nothing, though their mouths were often open.[337]

It is their response that Vonnegut provides. It conveys awe, speechlessness, a vision beyond the describable.

QUELLING A QUIBBLE

Another, albeit minor, use of a character's or narrator's response is that it can be used to defuse an objection a reader might have. For instance, in the short story "Adam," the reader might protest, "Come on, a man's response to the birth of a seventh child can't possibly equal the response to a firstborn."

When the two fathers have a drink at the bar near the hospital, Sousa gives voice to this objection, saying to Knechtmann, so delighted over his firstborn,

> Wait'll you've racked up seven, Netman. . . . *Then* you come back and tell me about the miracle.[338]

Now it's possible for a reader to root fully for Knechtman's view once again.

In the immensely popular and abominably written 1996 novel *The Bridges of Madison County* by Robert James Waller, there's a passage in which the man says that the way the woman draws off her boot is so sexy and appealing that he hasn't the words to describe it. Or his response.

Well okay, the reader thinks, and lets the writer get away with that laziness.

I was so put off by how badly written the novel was and how taken people were with it that I assigned my fiction-writing students to write a paragraph describing such a thing in the most sensual way possible. In five minutes, all had done that effectively—proven when they read their descriptions aloud and all breaths quickened.

What Waller did do very well, though, was demonstrate this point: if you have a character voice what might be a reader's objection, you can get away with murder, fictionally speaking.

ACTION

Character and action impinge upon one another, in life as in fiction.

A person's inherent character shapes his or her choices. The opposite is also true: character rises out of choice and action.

Interaction between a given personality and a situation of conflict that arises, provoking choice and action—consequently revealing, changing, or deepening a character—is what storytelling is all about.

In *Mother Night*, a woman says to Howard Campbell, the protagonist:

> "You've changed so."
> "People should be changed by world wars," I said, "else what are world wars for?"[339]

Hemingway once counseled his friend Marlene Dietrich, "Never confuse movement for action."[340]

Fiction writers shouldn't either.

Picture a kid in a tantrum, flailing around on the floor. That's movement.

Cops and robbers in a chase. More movement.

True action combines realization—when a character is "impressed"—and acting on it in a way that makes a difference to the character's life or others.

———

CONJURING CHARACTERS

At Iowa, Kurt told us that if we couldn't summon up a character, to base one on a movie star.

This was such workmanlike advice, we were appalled.

Truth is, you can base a character on anyone. Once the juices get going, and the revisions, your character will become individualized. It just takes work.

Sometimes they do come out of thin air. Or so it seems. Vonnegut created oodles of outlandish characters and creatures. The Shah of Bratpuhr of the Kolhouri sect, the Harmoniums, the Tralfamadorians, the Koko-bonos. Even machines become characters—EPICAC, Gokubi, and Mandarax.

How did he do it?

I don't know. But I do know the imagination can be cultivated, by permission and exercise. It's clear Vonnegut let his out to play all the time.

———

Most of Vonnegut's *main* characters, though, are modeled on someone.

In his first unpublished novel, "Basic Training," one central character, the General, "is based on Vonnegut's father's cousin, who had been a captain in the Rainbow Division during World War I and ran his family and farm in the military fashion," according to Kurt's friend Majie Failey.[341]

When *Player Piano* was published, his fellow employees at General Electric were all a-twitter about who in the novel was based on whom at the company. Many characters echoed those he knew, especially the main "character," GM.

His former student, the writer John Casey, asked Vonnegut in an early interview, "Is Winston Niles Rumfoord in *Sirens of Titan* a verbal portrait of FDR?"

> The fact is Roosevelt is the key figure in the book, although the impulse was to write about what FDR had been to me as a young man during the Depression and the Second World War and so forth. Roosevelt took the lead in the book, however, not me.

Roosevelt was President from the time Vonnegut was ten to age twenty-six, and "was one of the biggest figures" in his childhood. The similarity between the character Rumfoord and Roosevelt, Vonnegut told Casey, is that "They both have enormous hope for changing things . . . childish hopes, too."[342]

Here's a quote from the novel:

> [Rumfoord] wished to change the World for the better by means of the great and unforgettable suicide of Mars.[343]

Pressed about other real-life models, Vonnegut answered:

> Well. Eliot Rosewater, for instance, in *God Bless You, Mr. Rosewater*—there really is a man who is that *kind*. Except he's poor, an accountant over a liquor store. We shared an office, and I could hear him comforting people who had very little income, calling everybody "dear" and giving love and understanding instead of money. And I heard him doing marriage counseling, and I asked him about that, and he said that once people told you how little money they'd made they felt they

had to tell you everything. I took this very sweet man and in a book gave him millions and millions to play with.[344]

Dr. Felix Hoenikker, the absent-minded scientist [in *Cat's Cradle*], was a caricature of Dr. Irving Langmuir, the star of the G.E. research laboratory. I knew him some. My brother worked with him. Langmuir was wonderfully absent-minded. He wondered out loud one time whether, when turtles pulled in their heads, their spines buckled or contracted. I put that in the book. One time he left a tip under his plate after his wife served him breakfast at home. I put that in. His most important contribution, though, was the idea for what I called "Ice-9," a form of frozen water that was stable at room temperature. He didn't tell it directly to me. It was a legend around the Laboratory . . . long before my time.[345]

Billy Pilgrim and other characters in *Slaughterhouse-Five* were modeled on Vonnegut's fellow soldiers and prisoners of war. He tells about some of them in the nonfiction first chapter. Another, Gifford Boies Doxsee, imprisoned "in the same Stalag (Stammlager IVB)" as Vonnegut, attests that "The parts of *Slaughterhouse-Five* which describe the historical events of those days are remarkably accurate in terms of my own personal memories of the time though of course Vonnegut has changed names and juxtaposed personalities." An early draft of *Slaughterhouse-Five* uses their actual residence: "We reached Stalag IVB at night."[346]

Vonnegut admittedly based Kilgore Trout on the science fiction writer Theodore Sturgeon:

In fact, it said so in [Sturgeon's] obituary in the [*New York*] *Times*. . . . I was just delighted that it said in the middle of it that he was the inspiration for the Kurt Vonnegut character of Kilgore Trout.[347]

In the story "Long Walk to Forever," Vonnegut uses himself as a model. To anyone who knew him well, it's an accurate self-portrait, insofar as it goes.

> "Could you come for a walk?" he said. He was a shy person, even with Catharine. He covered his shyness by speaking absently, as though what really concerned him were far away—as though he were a secret agent pausing briefly on a mission between beautiful, distant, and sinister points. This manner of speaking had always been Newt's style, even in matters that concerned him desperately.[348]

In the preface to *Between Time and Timbuktu* (the script of a 1972 television production that combined several of his stories), Vonnegut reveals why, after a hiatus of delving into theater and film, he returned to prose:

> I have become an enthusiast for the printed word again. I have to be that, I now understand, because I want to be a character in all of my works. I can do that in print. In a movie, somehow, the author always vanishes. Everything of mine which has been filmed so far has been one character short, and the character is me.
>
> I don't mean that I am a glorious character. I simply mean that, for better or for worse, I have always rigged my stories so as to include myself, and I can't stop now. And I do this so slyly, as do most novelists, that the author *can't* be put on film.[349]

Whether rigging or not, one's self and the myriad aspects of oneself show up in one's characters. The more you are able to encompass and give voice to those aspects, the larger you grow, and the better fiction writer you will be. You'll meet yourself on the river, as it were.

CHAPTER 27
PROSE, THE AUDIAL

It is the premise which shapes each story, yes, but the author must furnish the language and the mood.[350]

L anguid or sharp, voluptuous or minimal: we learn and feel a lot about the time, place, characters, and sense of a piece of writing by the sound of it.

The fiction writer must also furnish dialogue. There's a real art to dialogue. Anyone who's recorded someone speaking and then tried to translate that verbatim into intelligent prose will discover how circular, repetitious, how many hesitations, um's-ah's-and-well's, how dependent on inflection and gesture actual conversation is.

Kurt Vonnegut may have called his Indiana idiom like a "band saw cutting galvanized tin." But he actually had quite an ear.

You probably do too. Cultivate it.

Vonnegut used to read his prose aloud. His grown children remember hearing him in his study in Barnstable. "He rewrote and rewrote and rewrote, muttering whatever he had just written over and over, tilting his head back and forth, gesturing with his hands, changing the pitch and rhythm of the words," his son Mark recalls.[351]

There on the Cape I would indeed talk to myself and I have stopped that, I don't know quite why. Afraid of somebody hearing me and taking me to the crazy house I guess. But as a younger man I did try out all the speeches and indeed tried out sentences to hear what they sounded like and whether they were easily spoken.[352]

Other writers known for their prose style—Grace Paley, for example—did the same. When you read aloud, you hear differently from when you read in your head.

As a fiction writer, you have the oppportunity to experiment with sound. You can imitate different people's speech, play with narrative style, and change tone, according to the story you're telling. Even so, there is your own recognizable voice.

Here's a bit from a letter Kurt wrote to me and my South African classmate and friend, Stephen Gray, in which he offers advice about honoring one's own voice. It was the summer after Kurt left the Iowa workshop, and Stephen and I planned to visit him and his wife Jane on Cape Cod. Stephen, who had a pronounced Johannesburg accent, wrote to Kurt that we couldn't come because he had to have badly needed dental work. In the third paragraph, in the midst of his lovely reply, Kurt included a terrific writing tip. (See opposite page.)

Likewise for you, as for Stephen Gray: try being whoever you are, from wherever you've hailed, and see what happens.

Vonnegut didn't have a lot to say about language, but he has a lot to demonstrate. What follows is a little investigation of his relationship to it and usage, for your erudition and possible adoption.

Kurt Vonnegut was attuned to music. He refers to it often and always as glorious, as evidence of the wonder of life.

KURT VONNEGUT, JR.
SCUDDER'S LANE
WEST BARNSTABLE
MASSACHUSETTS

June 11, 1968

Dear Stephen & Suzanne:

Word of honore we are desolated that you are not coming. We beg you to come at a later time.

I studied anthropology at the University of Chicago for a while, and the physical anthropologists were furious with God for having designed teeth so badly. They last about twenty years — no time at all.

Incidentally, Stephen, your excellent letter is the first indication I have had that you can be comical and loose on paper. Everything else of yours was so solemnly cinematic and French. Try being a South African and see what happens. The New Yorker would love you then, and you'd have money in stacks.

Michael Sissons was introduced to me in London as the hottest agent in town. My impression was that he would have been just as happy and successful selling real estate.

About Chile: When Nelson Algren met Jose Donoso for the first time he looked at Jose gravely and said, "I think it would be nice to come from a country that long and narrow."

My Guggenheim year is drawing to an end. The last check has arrived. I finished my war book during that year, wrote a short movie script and a few xxix articles and reviews. Zip. So much for _that_ year.

Cheers,

Letter from Kurt Vonnegut to Suzanne McConnell and Stephen Gray, June 11, 1968. Courtesy of the author.

If I should ever die, God forbid, let this be my epitaph:
THE ONLY PROOF HE NEEDED
FOR THE EXISTENCE OF GOD
WAS MUSIC[353]

Vonnegut's loveliest creations, I daresay, are the harmoniums in *The Sirens of Titan*. Their "planet Mercury sings like a crystal goblet." They "cling to the singing walls of their caves" and are "nourished by vibrations."[354]

Vonnegut himself played the clarinet and the piano. The teenaged protagonist of "Basic Training," his unpublished early novel, is an aspiring pianist. And in the first published novel, *Player Piano*, what, then, could be a better symbol for the idea of industrialization as dehumanizing than a mechanical piano?

Or in *Mother Night*, the soul murder of the Nazis rendered more acutely than a lullaby sound turned to heart-shattering treachery?

> There was one announcement that was always crooned, like a nursery rhyme. Many times a day it came. It was the call for the Sonderkommando.[355]

And in *Galápagos*, when burying the dead, employing this black-humored phrase as comfort?

> Oh, well—he wasn't going to write Beethoven's Ninth Symphony anyway.[356]

———

> Music . . . makes practically everybody fonder of life than he or she would be without it. Even military bands, although I am a pacifist, always cheer me up. . . . The priceless gift that African Americans gave the whole world when they were still in slavery was . . . the blues. All pop music . . . is derived from the blues.

A gift to the world? One of the best rhythm-and-blues combos I ever heard was three guys and a girl from Finland playing in a club in Krakow, Poland.[357]

Vonnegut makes a lot of references in his fiction to the jazz he loved as a teenager. In *Hocus Pocus*, the protagonist declares:

what I would really like to have been, given a perfect world, is a jazz pianist.

Instead, he plays

the Lutz Carillon, the great family of bells at the top of the tower of the college library. . . . The happiest moments in my life, without question, were when I played the Lutz Carillon at the start and end of every day.[358]

In *Welcome to the Monkey House*, there's this description of a pianist:

Suddenly he struck, and a spasm of dirty, low-down, gorgeous jazz shook the air, a hot, clanging wraith of the twenties.[359]

This is the point:

Language is a kind of music. Silence at play with sound. Cadence, beats, accents, and tone.

The vocal cords, throat, tongue, nose, lips: our amazing apparatus for speech is the same as for singing.

Out of "galvanized tin," Kurt Vonnegut created his own ragtime, rhythm and blues, jazz. He made up charming music for the ears by translating sounds into onomatopoetic "words." He fabricated languages, snazzy words, and fanciful, insightful definitions.

> Paul paused for a moment to listen to the music of Building 58. . . . The lathe groups, the tenors: *"Furrazz-ow-ow-ow-ow-ow-ak! ting! Furr-azz-ow-ow . . ."* The welders, the baritones: *"Vaaaaaaa-zuzip! Vaaaaaaa-zuzip!"* And, with the basement as a resonating chamber, the punch presses, the basses: *"Aw-grumph! tonka-tonka. Aw-grump! tonka-tonka."*[360]

> *"Puka pala koko, puku ebo koko, nibo aki koko,"* said the Shah.
> "What's the foreign gentleman after?" asked Homer Bigley, proprietor of the barber shop.
> "He wants a little off the sides, a little off the back, and leave the top alone," mumbled Khashdrahr Miasma, under a steaming towel in the barber chair next to the Shah's.[361]

Vonnegut versified, goofily. Here are two from *Cat's Cradle* and *Jailbird*:

> If you wish to study a *granfalloon*,
> Just remove the skin of a toy balloon.[362]

> *Don't care if I do die,*
> *Do die, do die!*
> *Like to make the juice fly,*
> *Juice fly, juice fly!*[363]

Half the fun and wisdom of *Cat's Cradle* is delivered through the guru-dictator Bokonon's frolicking religious vocabulary. "Karass," "granfalloon," "wrang-wrang," "stuppa," "duffle," "pool-pah."
Bokonon-ist oom-pah-pahs!

"Sometimes the *pool-pah*," Bokonon tells us, "exceeds the power of humans to comment." Bokonon translates *pool-pah* at one point in *The Books of Bokonon* as "shit storm" and at another point as "wrath of God."[364]

—————

Though music and language go hand in hand in brotherly love, Vonnegut's reverence for language surpassed even his love of music.

In the 1980s Vonnegut and his wife, the photographer Jill Krementz, attended a requiem written circa 1570, with a "new musical setting" by the composer Andrew Lloyd Webber of *Jesus Christ Superstar* and *Cats* fame.

"Nobody seemed to know or care what the Latin words meant or where they came from. We were all there for the music." But the English translation in the program notes caught Vonnegut's eye. "They were terrible!" They promised "a Paradise indistinguishable from the Spanish Inquisition."[365]

So he rewrote the words. Here's a comparison of an original verse and Vonnegut's:

> My prayers are not worthy;
> but Thou, of Thy goodness, deal generously with me,
> that I burn not in the everlasting fire.

> My prayers are unheard,
> but Thy sublime indifference will ensure
> that I burn not in some everlasting fire.[366]

Vonnegut searched for a Latin scholar to translate his English to Latin, a composer to create the music, musicians to produce it, and a place in which to perform it. On jury duty he met a composer, Edgar Grana, who spent a year composing music for Vonnegut's new words.

I would say the music was sort of a postmodern, multiple-crossover, semi-classical bebop lemon marmalade.

Three years after hearing the original, on March 13, 1988, in Buffalo, "the best Unitarian Universalist choir in the country," according to Vonnegut, performed his revised requiem.

> When it was all over, though, I hadn't heard a single word distinctly. That is how overwhelming the music was. . . . The composer and the performers had a stunning success. . . . I alone was disappointed, a crank who cared about the language.
>
> . . . The point I had tried to make by writing new language rather than new music for a mass for the dead: In the beginning was the word.[367]

Vonnegut wrote in *God Bless You, Mr. Rosewater*:

> The thing was that Earth was the only place in the whole known Universe where language was used. It was a unique Earthling invention.
>
> Everybody else used mental telepathy, so Earthlings could get pretty good jobs as language teachers just about anywhere they went.
>
> The reason creatures wanted to use language instead of mental telepathy was that they found out they could get so much more *done* with language. Language made them so much more *active*. Mental telepathy, with everybody constantly telling everybody everything, produced a sort of generalized indifference to *all* information. But language, with its slow, narrow meanings, made it possible to think about one thing at a time—to start thinking in terms of *projects*.[368]

Throughout his work, Vonnegut conjured and indicated words.

> [Dr. Ed Brown] coined a new word for Sylvia's disease, *"Samaritrophia,"* which he said meant, *"hysterical indifference to the troubles of those less fortunate than oneself."*[369]

> The Germans and the dog were engaged in a military operation which had an amusingly self-explanatory name, a human enterprise which is seldom described in detail, whose name alone, when reported as news or history, gives many war enthusiasts a sort of post-coital satisfaction. It is, in the imagination of combat's fans, the divinely listless loveplay that follows the orgasm of victory. It is called "mopping up."[370]

He attended to *le mot juste.*

Choosing the right word does not mean merely picking one with the most accurate definition. Duke Ellington was right: "It don't mean a thing if it ain't got that swing." Here's one of Vonnegut's fancier cadences:

> The gun made a ripping sound like the opening of the zipper on the fly of God Almighty.[371]

Here are some terrific word choices:

> [Rudy Hertz] popped a nickel into the player piano.[372]

Listen to that alliteration: *p* and *p p*! Hear how "popped" pops!

> There are all these people bragging about how they're

survivors, as though that's something very special. But the only kind of person who can't say that is a corpse.[373]

Landing on "corpse" with the rhythm of "is a" leading up to it—that long drawn-out "corrrr" with the end lisp-spit—that's what gives the zing.

Le mot juste is the one that hits the nail on the head with sense/sound/cadence all together.

———

And about "hitting the nail on the head": remember Vonnegut's adage in the section on plot about including familiar props to comfort the reader while taking them on the spree of your story? Vonnegut offers such comfort in prose by using clichés and familiar quotations.

In *Mother Night*, he presents as code for identifying the double agent "a song often sung by an idealistic American girls' organization called 'The Brownies.'

> Make new friends,
> But keep the old.
> One is si-il-ver,
> The o-ther's gold.[374]

In *Galápagos'* voyage into the bewildering future, the translation machine Mandarax spits out recognizable quotations.

> *For of all sad words of tongue or pen,*
> *The saddest are these: "It might have been!"*
> John Greenleaf Whittier (1807–1892)[375]

> *All is well that ends well.*
> John Heywood (1497?–1580?)[376]

Kurt Vonnegut uses an awful lot of biblical references for an atheist, as his Christian friend Dan Wakefield points out. The Bible was once well known to a general audience, and we are historically and presently a predominantly Christian nation. He directs readers to its most soul-enhancing values.[377]

He has Mandarax in *Galápagos* offer:

> *Greater love hath no man than this, that a man lay down his life for his friends.*
> —St. John (4 B.C.?–30?)[378]

He opens *Breakfast of Champions* with this epigraph:

> *When he hath tried me,*
> *I shall come forth as gold.*
> —Job

He riffs on the Biblically familiar in *The Sirens of Titan*:

> In the beginning, God became the Heaven and the Earth. . . . And God said, "Let Me be light," and He was light.
> —*The Winston Niles Rumfoord Authorized Revised Bible*[379]

How do you name characters?

Vonnegut often uses similar names for his characters. Why? According to him,

> [It's] only a perversity to not look in a former book. I don't look in a former book. And it's just a perversity that comes from having written so long, I guess. Just fuck it, it doesn't really matter what their names are. You look at old copies

of the *Writer's Digest*; there's article after article on how to pick names for characters.[380]

It's obvious, though, that he selected Billy Pilgrim's name in *Slaughterhouse-Five* carefully. He'd chosen many others in earlier drafts. "Billy" is quite American. It's a nickname, a boy's name. What other country has pilgrims in their history? We grow up in elementary school drawing them along with turkeys, we remember them every Thanksgiving. And "Pilgrim" means pilgrim.

Other Vonnegut characters also have names that impart a sound-sense. "Rosewater" of *God Bless You, Mr. Rosewater* conjures up the notion of looking through rose-colored glasses and of ladies in a gentler time dabbing themselves with rosewater. "Rumfoord" in *The Sirens of Titan* has an old wealthy Dutch ring to it, like "Roosevelt." "Mary O'Looney" in *Jailbird* sounds looney. And so on.

In choosing names, follow Vonnegut's lead. Select names that convey the associations you want your reader to make, consciously or unconsciously, and those appropriate for your character's background, status, century, and so on. In other words, find the visual and audial *mot juste*.

Sometimes Vonnegut plays around with the names of people he knew. Many writers do. "Starbuck," for example, was the surname of the head of the Writers' Workshop, the poet George Starbuck, at the time Vonnegut was there.

In *Galápagos*, he uses thinly disguised names of friends and acquaintances, and also of the famous: Mrs. Onassis is Mrs. Onassis; Dr. Teodoro Donoso has the surname and qualities of his friend José Donoso, the Chilean writer who taught at the workshop; "Private Geraldo Delgado" is hairbreadth close to Geraldo Rivera, his former son-in-law; and "Mary Hepburn" rings of Katharine

Hepburn as well as the Marys he's known whose names he's used before, his war buddy's wife Mary O'Hare, and his student Mary Kathleen O'Donnell.

As he became well known, he could tease his readers with inside info. He created his own world, recycling his characters' names so they seem familiar.

After you've written many novels and become famous, you can do that too.

———————

At a slumber party in junior high, my friend and I sneaked her parents' sex manual into her bedroom and read parts aloud. "This will give you exquisite pleasure," it said, after describing the sexual act. We giggled nervously. We turned the page. It described another position. "This will give you exquisite pleasure," the book said. Another page, another act. "This will give you exquisite pleasure."

Our nervous giggles became directed at the text. Between us for the rest of our lives, saying "This will give you exquisite pleasure" or even "exquisite" would evoke Vesuvius-like eruptions of laughter.

Avoiding repetition is a fundamental rule of good writing. It's a cliché of the writing trades.

———————

On the flip side Richard Yates told us in class that he once read a newspaper article about bananas. There's not much substitute for the word "banana." A banana is a banana. So, Yates said, the journalist repeated it and repeated it—"banana" this and "banana" that—and then, at the very end, wrote "this long yellow fruit."

———————

Usually, it's indeed tiresome to read the same word or phrase, however exquisite, over and over. It's evidence of laziness; it becomes ridiculous.

Repetition can also be incredibly effective, used deliberately.

In *Slaughterhouse-Five*, the protagonist is on a German transport train, along with other soldiers just taken prisoner of war.

> Most of the privates on Billy's car were very young—at the end of childhood. But crammed into the corner with Billy was a former hobo who was forty years old.
>
> "I been hungrier than this," the hobo told Billy. "I been in worse places than this. This ain't so bad." . . .
>
> "This ain't bad," the hobo told Billy on the second day. "This ain't nothing at all."[381]

"This ain't bad," the hobo says again on Christmas Day, on the eighth day, the ninth. The reader begins to cringe when the hobo appears: he's going to say it again. Each time it becomes more heartbreaking.

Repeating something can reinforce themes. "Little did they know," Vonnegut's narrator states again and again in *Galápagos*. He alludes to "the blue tunnel into the Afterlife" often as well. Without opening a page of that novel, you know something about it from these refrains.

Such repetition can make the reader feel comfortable, expectant, and like a participant with the text.

"So it goes."

How many times does that phrase occur in *Slaughterhouse-Five*? Take a guess. So many that it's become a catchword, like "Catch-22"; so many that innumerable books about and references to Vonnegut's work include it in the title; so many that if you google the phrase, tattoos, songs, and a magazine pop up.

It's a phrase already common in the English language. It accumulates gravitas by repetition alone.

In fact, it *reverses* meaning by repetition.

Originally Billy Pilgrim explains that by using those words, he's adopted the Tralfamadorians' response to death:

> When a person dies he only *appears* to die. He is still very much alive in the past. . . . All moments, past, present, and future, always have existed, always will exist. . . .
>
> When a Tralfamadorian sees a corpse, all he thinks is that the dead person is in bad condition in that particular moment, but that the person is just fine in plenty of other moments. Now, when I myself hear that somebody is dead, I simply shrug and say what the Tralfamadorians say about dead people, which is "So it goes."[382]

This attitude toward death is the most important thing he learns on the planet Tralfamadore, Billy says. But since "so it goes" is repeated every time someone dies while its Tralfamadorian interpretation is presented only once, the phrase takes on the doomsday weight of the grim reaper, it seems to me, rather than the incredible lightness about being that the Tralfamadorians taught.

Sounds and cadence themselves can impart meaning, and their repetition even more so.

"So it goes": a trip of the tongue in three steps. The third drops and draws out a smidgen, as in resignation, or so it sounds.

The chant of the snare drum to soldiers marching in *The Sirens of Titan* works on the ear, surpassing word-logic.

> Rented a tent, a tent, a tent;
> Rented a tent, a tent, a tent.
> Rented a tent!
> Rented a tent!
> Rented a, rented a tent.[383]

This snare drum chant opens the chapter "Tent Rentals" and is repeated four times in nine paperback pages. As the critic Jerome Klinkowitz wrote, "By the end of the chapter this nonsense makes a perfectly sensible statement about freedom and bondage more powerfully than any oration."[384]

The Harmoniums' limited vocabulary, in the same novel, works an opposite magic on the ear, with a singsong repetition:

> They have only two possible messages. The first is an automatic response to the second, and the second is an automatic response to the first.
>
> The first is, *"Here I am, here I am, here I am."*
>
> The second is, *"So glad you are, so glad you are, so glad you are."*[385]

If their utterances were restricted to single phrases, "Here I am" and "So glad you are," they would not possess their charming, musical, meaningful, nursery-rhyme impact.

———

> Trout . . . shaped . . . a story [in *Breakfast of Champions*] . . . about a planet where the language kept turning into pure music, because the creatures there were so enchanted by sounds. Words became musical notes. Sentences became melodies. They were useless as conveyors of information, because nobody knew or cared what the meanings of words were anymore.
>
> So leaders in government and commerce, in order to function, had to invent new and much uglier vocabularies and sentence structures all the time, which would resist being transmuted to music.[386]

CHAPTER 28

PROSE, THE VISUAL

Written language is one of the visual arts.

Visual devices that we call punctuation direct the reader when to pause, or stop. They alert you to what's more important (and less). Quotation marks let you know someone is speaking, paragraphing that a new thought-cluster is occurring, and a line skipped after a paragraph that there's a change coming in subject, time, or point of view.

Et cetera.

If you read unpunctuated or non-paragraphed print, you quickly realize how much visual cues assist in deciphering the text.

The pictorial aspect of prose was impressed upon me when I taught remedial writing and discovered that if reading their essays aloud, students did not necessarily read what they had actually written. They read what they had *intended*, self-correcting like spellcheck, as they read. They did not see what was actually on the page.

Check *this* out, for further evidence of the visual:

TYPOGLYCEMIA

I cdnuolt blveiee that I cluod aulaclty uesdnatnrd what I was rdanieg. The phaonmneal pweor of the human mind. Aoccdrnig to a rescheearch at Cmabrigde Uinervtisy, it deosn't matter inwaht order the ltteers in a wrod are, the olny iprmoatnt thing is that the frist and lsat ltteer be in the rghit pclae. The rset can be a taotl mses and you can still raed it wouthit a porbelm. This is bcuseae the human mind deos not raed ervey leter by istlef, but the word as a whlohe. Amzanig, huh?

———

Kurt Vonnegut doodled during class at the Writers' Workshop. His father and grandfather were architects, his sister a gifted artist, his daughters are painters, and his son, the doctor-writer, paints too. Kurt's early childhood home, designed by his father, is a singularly beautiful house. It's a no-brainer: Vonnegut was tuned and trained to the visual, as well as the audial.

Vonnegut revealed his style in *Slaughterhouse-Five*, via the fictional Tralfamadorians:

> Billy couldn't read Tralfamadorian, of course, but he could at least see how the books were laid out—in brief clumps of symbols separated by stars. Billy commented that the clumps might be telegrams.
>
> "Exactly," said the voice.
>
> "They *are* telegrams?"
>
> "There are no telegrams on Tralfamadore. But you're right: each clump of symbols is a brief, urgent message—describing a situation, a scene."[387]

In an interview, Vonnegut explained how he arrived at that style:

> The people who were senior to me at the *Sun* [Cornell University's newspaper] were full of advice. . . . The theory was that large, sprawling paragraphs tended to discourage readers and make the paper appear ugly. Their strategy was primarily visual—that is, short paragraphs, often one-sentence paragraphs. It seems to work very well, seemed to serve both me and the readers, so I stayed with it when I decided to make a living as a fiction writer.[388]

Like any other writer or artist, Vonnegut's style evolved.

Yours will too.

In his unpublished first novel, "Basic Training" (now published with another previously unpublished novella under the title *You Are What You Pretend to Be*), only occasional idiosyncratic bits of prose hint of his future style. In his next, his first two published novels, he conjures up worlds, words, inserts verse, chants, and plays in the middle of the prose.

But it's not until his third book, *Mother Night*, that each chapter telegraphs a "brief, urgent message."

Kurt told us in class that *Cat's Cradle* was composed in the form of jokes. One could say a joke, a telegram, and a poem have a lot in common.

Shapes of text are like clothing: they're what content wears. Advertisers know this.

As a teenager, Vonnegut worked in advertising. He wrote

> copy for ads about teenage clothes. I had to wear the clothes
> I praised. That was part of the job.[389]

Kurt, though a rumply dresser, knew the importance of appearance. The protagonist in *Mother Night* talks about it:

> Howard W. Campbell, Jr., now discussed the uniform of
> the American enlisted in World War Two: *Every other army*
> *in history, prosperous or not, has attempted to clothe even its*
> *lowliest soldiers so as to make them impressive to themselves and*
> *others as stylish experts in drinking and copulation and looting*
> *and sudden death.*[390]

At a Prague Communist cultural history museum in the 1980s, I viewed a Nazi officer's uniform on display and understood instantly something I never had before: how compellingly "impressive to themselves and others" the Nazis knew how to make their soldiers feel.

By contrast, Billy Pilgrim in *Slaughterhouse-Five* is dressed this way when captured:

> He had no helmet, no overcoat, no weapon, and no boots. On his feet were cheap, low-cut civilian shoes. . . . Billy had lost a heel, which made him bob up-and-down, up-and-down. . . .
>
> He didn't look like a soldier at all. He looked like a filthy flamingo.[391]

Here's what the fictional Englishman, who has been a prisoner of war in Dresden for months before Billy arrives, advises him and the other newcomers about survival:

> "If you stop taking pride in your appearance, you will very soon die." He said that he had seen several men die in the following way: "They ceased to stand up straight, then ceased to shave or wash, then ceased to get out of bed, then ceased to talk, then died."[392]

The text of "How to Write with Style," the piece written as part of the series sponsored by the International Paper Company and published in the *New York Times*, whose prescriptions appear in chapter 1 of this book, was reproduced in Vonnegut's collection of essays *Palm Sunday* word for word. But the graphics weren't. They are reprinted for the first time here as this book's endsheets.

Without them, it's not nearly as entertaining.

When they aren't parsed between columns, numbers, indents, boldface, cartoons, photos, Vonnegut's writing tips don't make nearly the impact. They do no song and dance for the eyes.

Ironically, "How to Write with Style" was reproduced without its visual style.

To sum up:
Appearance counts. On the page as on the body.

Vonnegut often broke up blocks of narrative with some alternative print configuration—plays, poems, quotes. The shape shift as well as the change in sound-sense brings a reader relief. They act as pacing devices.

> I experimented with putting recipes in *Deadeye Dick* which is an extremely gloomy book; it just suddenly struck me as a very funny idea. I already had the character, a very good cook, and experimenting with him I had him tell a recipe of something he was particularly proud of and it looked very funny on the page, also it looked very appetizing. I realized that this worked as well as music often does in some dramatic production, it's lovely to hear the melody and relief, and have the recipe work in the same way because almost everybody is crazy about food.[393]

Vonnegut cavorted all over the page with drawings in some of his books, notably *Breakfast of Champions*. He employed more sedate graphics in others.

> For one reason or another I found it very congenial to write short episodes, short essays, and separate these by some typographical device.[394]

"_____" and "❋ ❋ ❋", for example.

He capitalizes certain lowercase words in *Hocus Pocus* and decides to "let numbers stand for themselves," using "2" for example, instead of the word "two." He spells out years—e.g., "Nineteen-hundred and Seventy-five"—in *Jailbird*. He places asterisks beside characters doomed to die within *Galápagos*.

All these aim for "melody and relief" and how it looks "on the page."

> Also, I am fond of jokes and so my books have tended to be mosaics, being comic novels rather than tragic ones.[395]

———

Some readers find the reiteration of "so it goes" irritating.
Some react similarly to these graphic shenanigans.
Occasionally, I have too.

———

Critics have sometimes underestimated Vonnegut's work because of these maneuvers, and because of his readability. Not only critics, but ordinary readers. People sometimes say they read Vonnegut in college or high school, as if only then would one take him seriously. In response to one literary critic, John Irving asserted in the *New Republic* that "Vonnegut's lucidity is hard and brave work," skewering the absurd notion that "if the work is tortured and a ghastly effort to read, it must be serious."

Vonnegut's playfulness can also lead to the misperception that Vonnegut is careless about grammar and punctuation. A Columbia University graduate student suggested that to me last week. To the contrary. He is a master of both.

He could play around so much because he had the mechanics and architecture of language and writing firmly under his belt. Freedom to fool around comes with mastery.

Vonnegut's Iowa student Barry Kaplan handed in a three-page story consisting of a single sentence: "a mathematical formula about statistical probability. Vonnegut asked if I had been a math major. I told him I'd made up the formula because I just wanted to see how long a sentence I could write and have it make grammatical sense. Vonnegut liked that."

One could do an entire study on the effectiveness of Vonnegut's paragraph breaks. Someone probably has.

The space a paragraph break takes is just enough for the eye and brain to pause, thereby subtly emphasizing the last sentence of the previous paragraph and the introductory one of the next. Check these out, in this passage from *Hocus Pocus*:

> In the folder was a report by a private detective hired by Wilder to investigate my sex life. . . . He didn't miss a thing Zuzu and I did during the second semester. There was only 1 misunderstood incident: when I went up into the loft of the stable, where the Lutz Carillon had been stored before there was a tower and where Tex Johnson was crucified 2 years ago. I went up with the aunt of a student. She was an architect who wanted to see the pegged post-and-beam joinery up there. The operative assumed we made love up there. We hadn't.
>
> We made love much later that afternoon, in a toolshed by the stable, in the shadow of Musket Mountain when the Sun goes down.[396]

Vonnegut explains the surprising loveliness of the chapter on har-moniums in *The Sirens of Titan* in terms of pacing. They served as a way to "lighten it up for a while," he told John Casey in an interview, saying that he used to think about "things like that."

> Well, I don't think that way anymore. There was a time when I was a very earnest student writer and had a teacher, Kenneth Littauer, an old-time magazine editor, agent, and splendid old gentleman. And we would talk about things like that, that is, after dark passages you have a light one . . . and use sentences with short words when people are running, and long sentences and long words when people are sleeping. Those things are all true, the things I learned from Littauer about pace and point of view, things that are discussed in *Writer's Digest*, decent and honorable things to know.[397]

The evidence is that he did keep "thinking that way," possibly without having to think. Vonnegut was so practiced, he moved between light and dark, between the rhythms of the audial and the visual, instinctively.

Dialogue is the most pictorial component of ordinary prose.[*]
Even veteran writers have to work on the mechanics of dialogue.

A good conversation on the page can look like a tennis match. One swings. The other swings back.

No speaker attributions. Just the ball of dialogue going back and forth.

The trick is to make clear who's who with the least interference.

---

[*] For a lesson in its graphics, just so you know, in case you don't already, see my website.

Vonnegut says in *Bagombo Snuff Box*:

> Here is a lesson in creative writing.
> First rule: Do not use semicolons. They are transvestite hermaphrodites representing absolutely nothing. All they do is show you've been to college.[398]

Please note these two nicely placed semicolons on the first page of *Player Piano*, penned by none other than Kurt Vonnegut:

> In the northwest are the managers and engineers and civil servants and a few professional people; in the northeast are the machines; and in the south, across the Iroquois River, is the area known locally as Homestead, where almost all of the people live.[399]

What's the matter with transvestite hermaphrodites, anyway? They're exceptional.
They're fine.
As long as they know their place.

CHAPTER 29
THE JOKE BIZ

An advantage of a writer's having a joke-making capability is that he or she can be really funny in case something really is funny.[400]

As the youngest kid, Kurt discovered he could get the attention of his family by being funny. He had an inclination for the comic and motivation to develop it. If you do, too, then these chapters may be particularly valuable for you. At any rate, a book on Vonnegut's writing advice wouldn't be complete without investigating how he creates humor, and what he says about it.

Besides being admittedly better "than most people in my trade at making jokes on paper," Vonnegut was better than most people at joking off the cuff.[401] Sidney Offit tells about a time he and Kurt decided to go to a popular porn movie one afternoon, to see what all the fuss was about. It opened with an orgy. After about a half hour of it, Kurt got up and walked out. Sidney followed. "Too much of a good thing," Kurt murmured.

***

I'm in the business of making jokes; it's a minor art form. I've had some natural talent for it. It's like a mousetrap. You build the trap, you cock it, you trip it, and then bang! My books are essentially mosaics made up of a whole bunch of tiny little chips; and each chip is a joke. They may be five lines long or eleven lines long. . . . One reason I write so slowly is that I try to make each joke work. You really have to or the books are lost.[402]

How do you concoct a mousetrap?

A bait-and-switch surprise is one tactic Vonnegut uses. Please refer to the paragraph-break example from *Hocus Pocus* in the last chapter. The initial one-liner about the narrator's sex life being investigated sets you up to expect something deliciously salacious. The paragraph leads you on. Like the investigator, you expect the womanizing narrator and the woman architect he was showing around in the loft to have made love. But it ends, "We hadn't."

That's an eye stopper. And sort of a disappointment.

Then comes the switch-and-surprise, the punch line: "We made love much later that afternoon." Starting a new paragraph with that is scrumptious in terms of emphasis—and comic.

Here's a more elaborate trap, a 21-liner. The protagonist, Eliot Rosewater, is talking with his father, the Senator, in *God Bless You, Mr. Rosewater*:

> "You know—" said Eliot, "Kilgore Trout once wrote a whole book about a country that was devoted to fighting odors. That was the national purpose. There wasn't any disease, and there wasn't any crime, and there wasn't any war, so they went after odors." . . .
>
> "This country," said Eliot, "had tremendous research projects devoted to fighting odors. . . . But then the hero, who was also the country's dictator, made a wonderful scientific breakthrough, even though he wasn't a scientist, and they didn't need the projects any more. He went right to the root of the problem."
>
> "Uh huh," said the Senator. He couldn't stand stories by Kilgore Trout, was embarrassed for his son. "He found one chemical that would eliminate all odors?" he suggested, to hasten the tale to a conclusion.

"No. As I say, the hero was dictator, and he simply eliminated noses."[403]

———

Besides in jokes, humor abounds in bits and single lines throughout Vonnegut's work, like little glimpses of reality fractured through his comic lens.

He deconstructs and plays around with visual and linguistic metaphors.

> He visualized the notion of man and wife as one flesh—a physical monstrosity, pathetic, curious, and helpless Siamese twins.[404]

> "The girl there."
> "That's not a girl. That's a piece of paper."
> "Looks like a girl to *me*." Fred Rosewater leered.
> "Then you're easily fooled," said Harry. "It's done with ink on a piece of paper. That girl isn't lying there on the counter. She's thousands of miles away, doesn't even know we're alive."[405]

"Rest eternal grant them, O Lord, and let light perpetual shine upon them," the requiem that Vonnegut revised begins. He comments parenthetically,

> A credulous and literal-minded person might conclude from this that Huxley and Kennedy and Céline and Hemingway and my sister and my first wife Jane and all the rest of the dead are now trying to get some sleep with the lights on.[406]

What language is *actually* saying jolts a reader out of the accepted metaphor and into the ludicrous of the literal.

Another one-liner method of Vonnegut's, part and parcel of his education in chemistry and anthropology, is a kind of scientific-anthropological personification of things:

> One end of the garter of the sock in the shoe on the wash-basin was in the water. It had saturated itself and its sock, too, through the magic of capillary action.[407]

> Dwayne's bad chemicals made him take a loaded thirty-eight caliber revolver from under his pillow and stick it in his mouth. This was a tool whose only purpose was to make holes in human beings.[408]

> All of us were stuck to the surface of a ball, incidentally. The planet was ball-shaped. Nobody knew why we didn't fall off, even though everybody pretended to kind of understand it.
> The really smart people understood that one of the best ways to get rich was to own a part of the surface people had to stick to.[409]

Kurt and his sister Alice shared a fondness for slapstick. He told George Plimpton in the *Paris Reivew* interview:

> We loved Laurel and Hardy. But the thing my sister and I loved best was when somebody in a movie would tell everybody off, and then make a grand exit into the coat closet. He had to come out again, of course, all tangled in coathangers and scarves.[410]

In *Jailbird*, Vonnegut bases a relationship on two people whose intimacy is tied to silly question-and-answer jokes. Sarah, a nurse, is the narrator Walter's girlfriend—his first—for seven years. Years later, Walter reminisces:

> What tender memories did I have of Sarah? Much talk about human suffering and what could be done about it—and then infantile silliness for relief. We collected jokes for each other, to use when it was time for relief. We became addicted to talking to each other on the telephone for hours. Those talks were the most agreeable narcotic I have ever known. We became disembodied—like free-floating souls on the planet Vicuna. If there was a long silence, one or the other of us would end it with the start of a joke.
>
> "What is the difference between an enzyme and a hormone?" she might ask me.
>
> "I don't know," I would say.
>
> "You can't hear an enzyme," she would say, and the silly jokes would go on and on—even though she had probably seen something horrible at the hospital that day.[411]

Decades pass. They rediscover each other—both over sixty—soon after Walter is freed from prison. Their first conversation is on the phone. They exchange news for a bit, and laugh over a recollection.

> She said that it was good that we could still laugh, despite all we had been through. "At least we still have our sense of humor," she said. . . .
>
> "Yes—at least that," I agreed.
>
> "Waiter," she said, "what's this fly doing in my soup?"
>
> "What?" I said.
>
> "What's this fly doing in my soup?" she persisted.
>
> And then it came back to me: This was the opening line in a daisychain of jokes we used to tell each other on the

telephone. I closed my eyes. I gave the answering line, and
the telephone became a time machine for me. It allowed me
to escape from Nineteen-hundred and Seventy-seven and
into the fourth dimension.

"I believe that's the backstroke, madam," I said.

"Waiter," she said, "there's also a needle in my soup."

"I'm sorry, madam," I said, "that's a typographical error.
That should have been a noodle."[412]

And so the litany of such call-and-response jokes goes, for over
three pages.

To use these hackneyed jokes successfully in a novel takes a real
impresario. Vonnegut gets away with it because he uses them as
fodder for Sarah and Walter's relationship.

Not only that, he honors this tie with his sister and provides
his reader with a similar kind of comfort, pleasure, and bonding.

Vonnegut remarks on the durability of old jokes at the same time
that he cracks them in the following examples:

Yes, and there in my padded cell I told myself a joke I
had read in *The Harvard Lampoon* when a freshman. It had
amazed me back then because it seemed so dirty. When I
became the President's special advisor on youth affairs, and
had to read college humor again, I discovered that the joke
was still being published many times a year—unchanged.
This was it:

SHE: How dare you kiss me like that?

HE: I was just trying to find out who ate all the macaroons.[413]

Wits throughout the county poised themselves to tell
a tired and untruthful joke about Fire Chief Charley

Warmergran, who had an insurance office next to the fire-house: "Must have scared Charley Warmergran half out of his secretary."[414]

———

Vonnegut grew up under the influence of Kin Hubbard,

an Indianapolis humorist who wrote a joke a day for news-papers when I was young.[415]

In my opinion, Kin Hubbard was as witty as Oscar Wilde.[416]

Vonnegut pays homage to his most famous joke in *God Bless You, Mr. Rosewater* and again in *Slaughterhouse-Five*.
"Well," said one at last, "it ain't no disgrace to be poor." This line was the first half of a fine old joke by the Hoosier humorist, Kin Hubbard.
"No," said another man, completing the joke, "but it might as well be."[417]

America is the wealthiest nation on Earth, but its people are mainly poor, and poor Americans are urged to hate themselves. To quote the American humorist Kin Hubbard, "It ain't no disgrace to be poor, but it might as well be."[418]

In *Timequake*, he cites this one:

"The Indianapolis humorist Kin Hubbard said about Prohibition that it was "better than no liquor at all."[419]

Hubbard quips have become part of our collective cultural wisdom. I first heard both these lines from my father, who was a teenager during Prohibition, and who as a young man rode the rails looking for farmwork during the Great Depression. I never knew where they originated until I read Vonnegut's work.

Mark Twain cast a similar eye over the American landscape in his time, and provided a similar balm and wit to the American people. Vonnegut admired Twain so much that he named his son after him.

No doubt there's a child or grown-up named after Kurt in America now.

CHAPTER 30
BLACK HUMOR

I had made her so unhappy that she had developed a sense of humor, which she certainly didn't have when I married her.[420]

This line from *Bluebeard*'s narrator remarks on another kind of humor, the black humor Vonnegut is best known for. Its source is helplessness and despair. He explains:

Laughter or crying is what a human being does when there's nothing else he can do.[421]

A scene in *Cat's Cradle* illustrates it as well as any in Vonnegut's oeuvre. The character Phillip Castle is telling another about a catastrophic shipwreck off the fictional island of San Lorenzo. It washed a load of people onshore.

"At Father's hospital, we had fourteen hundred deaths inside of ten days. Have you ever seen anyone die of bubonic plague?"' [He describes blackened bodies, swollen glands, "stacks of dead."] . . .

". . . Father worked without sleep for days, worked not only without sleep but without saving many lives, either." . . .

". . . Anyway, one sleepless night I stayed up with Father while he worked. It was all we could do to find a live patient to treat. In bed after bed after bed we found dead people.

"And Father started giggling," Castle continued.

"He couldn't stop. He walked out into the night with his flashlight. He was still giggling. He was making the flashlight beam dance over all the dead people stacked outside. He put his hand on my head, and do you know what that marvelous man said to me?" asked Castle.

"Nope."

"'Son,' my father said to me, 'someday this will all be yours.'"[422]

———

This quintessential Vonnegut mousetrap—dark as pitch, funny as hell—is well known to Vonnegut fans. Let me tell you how one of those fans employs it.

Like Jon Stewart, who said, when introducing Kurt on *The Daily Show*, that "as an adolescent he made my life bearable," Joshua confided, at a fledgling Vonnegut book club in New York, that Vonnegut's books had saved him as a teenager. When he discovered that Vonnegut had majored in anthropology, he did too.

What has he done with that degree?

Worked all over the globe for NGOs, starting in Sri Lanka during their civil war, first working for an organization that assisted victims of one side of the conflict, then for an organization that assisted the other side. A very Vonnegut-like thing to do indeed! Kurt would have loved that. He'd be proud. He'd laugh.

At that moment, Joshua was working to rebuild houses of people hit hard by Hurricane Sandy.

A year or so later, he sent me the following e-mail:

I'm writing from the disputed Ukrainian/Russian border. I am working for the Danish Refugee Council, leading the planning and implementation of shelter for Ukrainian refugees displaced by the conflict. . . .

I thought of you today when I quoted Vonnegut. I was

orienting a new aid worker. I told him, "Someday this could all be yours."

———

The term "black humor" was coined by writer Bruce Jay Friedman, who compiled an anthology of contemporary writers in 1965 entitled *Black Humor*. Vonnegut objected to that classification at first, since the writers were a diverse lot. Eventually he had quite a lot to say about it.

> In the Modern Library edition of *The Works of Freud*, you'll find a section on humor in which he talks about middle-European "gallows humor," and so it happens that what Friedman calls "black humor" is very much like German-Austrian-Polish "gallows humor." . . . One of the examples Freud gives is a man about to be hanged, and the hangman says, "Do you have anything to say?" The condemned man replies, "Not at this time."

> "This country has made one tremendous contribution to 'gallows humor,' and it took place in Cook County Jail." Kurt reported that Nelson Algren told him this incident. "A man was strapped into the electric chair, and he said to the witnesses, 'This will certainly teach me a lesson.'"[423]

> Laughter is a response to frustration, just as tears are, and it solves nothing, just as tears solve nothing. . . . The example [Freud] gives is of the dog who can't get through a gate to bite a person or fight another dog. So he digs dirt. It doesn't solve anything, but he has to do *something*. Crying or laughing is what a human being does instead. . . . My peak funniness came when I was at Notre Dame, at a literary festival there. It was in a huge auditorium and the

audience was so tightly tuned that everything I said was funny. All I had to do was cough or clear my throat and the whole place would break up. . . . Martin Luther King had been shot two days before. . . . There was an enormous need to either laugh or cry as the only possible adjustment. There was nothing you could do to bring King back. So the biggest laughs are based on the biggest disappointments and the biggest fears. . . .

One of my favorite cartoons—I think it was by Shel Silverstein—shows a couple of guys chained to an eighteen-foot cell wall, hung by their wrists, and their ankles are chained, too. Above them is a tiny barred window that a mouse couldn't crawl through. And one of the guys is saying to the other, "Now here's my plan. . . ." It goes against the American storytelling grain to have someone in a situation he can't get out of, but I think this is very usual in life. . . . And it strikes me as gruesome and comical that in our culture we have an expectation that a man can always solve his problems. There is that implication that if you just have a little more energy, a little more fight, the problem can always be solved. This is so untrue that it makes me want to cry—or laugh.[424]

———

Jim Siegelman, a "nugget," the term Vonnegut's Harvard students gave themselves, tells this anecdote about Kurt's humor:

Kurt taught us death was the world's biggest joke, the ultimate punch line, the last laugh, so to speak. I wrote a story that was a parody of *Love Story*, which was all the rage then, and presented it in class. The hero, Sidney, a Harvard freshman, falls in love with a svelte Radcliffe senior, Leslie, who comes down with a terminal case of mercury poisoning.

But the real punch line of my story was this one, which took place during a moment of post-coital reflection:

"There's just no communication between me and my parents," said Sidney.

"Whose fault is that?" asked Leslie.

"It's nobody's fault really," he said. "They're both dead."

Siegelman says, "That broke Kurt up. I never saw anybody laugh so hard."[425]

At the Iowa workshop, sometimes Vonnegut tried out jokes on us in class. One day he told us that the crucifixion story didn't teach compassion. What the story really illustrated was that it was okay to murder somebody: just be sure he's not well connected. He laughed until he wheezed when he told us. We laughed hard too.

In a revised, more moral story, he said, a nobody would be crucified. Just before he died, God would adopt him. *That* story would teach that any nobody could be the son of God. Our response let him know we thought the joke and the idea superb.

And there it is, in chapter 5 of *Slaughterhouse-Five*.

One thing Kurt never tried on us was his own wit at our expense. If something irritated or angered him, he was direct and outspoken about it.

The fact that we're animals conscious of ourselves as alive and simultaneously of our impending demise makes fecund soil for gallows humor. Talk about helplessness! The tragic! Sure, Kurt found death the world's biggest joke.

He jokes about it even in the unlikeliest places. In *Cat's Cradle*, a man is working on a huge mosaic of a beautiful woman. The narrator wants to take the artist's picture. But he doesn't have his camera. The artist replies,

"Well, for Christ's sake, get it! You're not one of those people who trusts his memory, are you?"

"I don't think I'll forget that face you're working on very soon."

"You'll forget it when you're dead, and so will I. When I'm dead, I'm going to forget everything—and I advise you to do the same."[426]

Vonnegut told a graduating class in 2004,

I am, incidentally, honorary president of the American Humanist Association. . . . We Humanists behave as honorably as we can without any expectations of rewards or punishments in an afterlife. We serve as best we can the only abstraction with which we have any real familiarity, which is our community. . . .

If I should ever die, . . . God forbid, I hope some of you will say, "Kurt's up in Heaven now." That's my favorite joke.[427]

In *Timequake*, written when he was closer than ever to the heaven he didn't believe in, Vonnegut applies the phrase several times.

O'Hare [his war buddy Bernard O'Hare], having become a lawyer for both the prosecution and the defense in later life, is up in Heaven now.[428]

A boyhood friend of mine, William H. C. "Skip" Failey, who died four months ago . . . is up in Heaven now.[429]

⌒

The nicotine habit plagued Vonnegut all his life.

In *Jailbird*, the narrator, Walter, confesses that he used to smoke "four packs of unfiltered Pall Malls a day." But he quit. The day he's released from prison, tobacco-free for years, he has a nightmare.

> In the dream my damp, innocent pink lungs shriveled into two black raisins. Bitter brown tar seeped from my ears and nostrils.
> But worst of all was the *shame*.[430]

Vonnegut himself quit smoking a few times. Never for long.

He considered smoking a form of suicide, as he says in the preface to *Welcome to the Monkey House*. Late in his life, he turned this lifelong struggle and self-accusation against committing suicide by tobacco into a joke.

> I am going to sue the Brown & Williamson Tobacco Company, manufacturers of Pall Mall cigarettes, for a billion bucks! Starting when I was only twelve years old, I have never chain-smoked anything but unfiltered Pall Malls. And for many years now, right on the package, Brown and Williamson have promised to kill me.
> But I am now eighty-two. Thanks a lot, you dirty rats.[431]

He didn't get off scot-free, though. He suffered from emphysema, guilt, and was once hospitalized for smoke inhalation from a fire caused by his cigarettes.

How do you acquire the knack for the blackly comic? Again, it's partly a native talent. According to his daughter Edie, even when he was a youngster, Kurt displayed that sensibility.

It can also be cultivated. All you have to do is take a look around through that lens. As I write, we're in the middle of a political campaign that's enough to make you cry—or laugh.

As I edit this manuscript months later, we're in the middle of a presidential administration that threatens to turn most citizens of our nation into black humorists. It has succeeded in provoking superlative *Saturday Night Live* sketches, as well as jokes from John Oliver, Stephen Colbert, and other comedians.

You don't have to endure catastrophe or a war. But it might help. The following anecdote may illustrate that.

Biafra was a fledgling nation of the Ibo people—the writer Chinua Achebe among them—which for many reasons declared independence from Nigeria in 1967. War ensued. A blockade caused massive starvation. Images of the starving created a cause célèbre in the US. Miriam Reik, daughter of the famous psychoanalyst Theodore Reik, invited Kurt Vonnegut and Vance Bourjaily, both World War II veterans, to go there as witnesses in 1970 as the nation was falling, and to write about it.

"It was like a free trip to Auschwitz when the ovens were still going full blast," Kurt reported.[432]

> The worst sufferers there were the children of refugees. . . . At the end, a very common diet was water and thin air.
>
> So the children came down with kwashiorkor [a rare disease caused by a lack of protein]. . . .
>
> The child's hair turned red. His skin split like the skin of a ripe tomato. His rectum protruded. His arms and legs were like lollipop sticks.
>
> Vance and Miriam and I waded through shoals of children like those at Awo-Omama. We discovered that if we let our hands dangle down among the children, a child would grasp each finger or thumb—five children to a hand. A finger from a stranger, miraculously, would allow a child to stop crying for a while. . . .
>
> . . . When little children took hold of his fingers and stopped crying, Vance burst into tears.[433]

The three of us spent an hour with him [the Biafran president, General Odumegwu Ojukwu]. He shook our hands at the end. He thanked us for coming. "If we go forward, we die," he said. "If we go backward, we die. So we go forward." . . .

His humor was gallows humor, since everything was falling apart around his charisma and air of quiet confidence. His humor was superb.

"Later, when we met his second-in-command, General Philip Effiong, he, too, turned out to be a gallows humorist. Vance said this: "Effiong *should* be the number-two man. He's the second funniest man in Biafra."[434]

They're all up in heaven now: Kurt, Vance, Miriam. Ojukwu and Effiong.

In Biafra, Vonnegut noted,

Miriam was annoyed by my conversation at one point, and she said scornfully, "You won't open your mouth unless you can make a joke." It was true. Joking was my response to misery I couldn't do anything about.[435]

Kurt mentioned Miriam's comment in person, ruefully. He couldn't stop himself there, he said, from making jokes.

The worst thing about a writer's having a joke-making capability, of course, as James Thurber of Columbus, Ohio, pointed out in an essay years ago, is this: No matter what is being discussed, the jokester is going to head for a punch line every time.

Some smart young critic will soon quote that line above against me, imagining that I am . . . too dense to know that I have accidentally put my finger on what is awfully wrong with me.[436]

What *is* "awfully wrong" about that? In terms of writing, Vonnegut says it's this:

But joking is so much a part of my life adjustment that I would begin to work on a story on any subject and I'd find funny things in it or I would stop.[437]

The problem is that jokes deal so efficiently with ideas that there is little more to be said after the punch line has been spoken. It is time to come up with a new idea—and another good joke.[438]

A therapist might say that to joke relentlessly is to avoid your real feelings, and that acceptance and expression of your authentic feelings is a primary goal to self-actualization.

For whatever reason, American humorists or satirists or whatever you want to call them, those who choose to laugh rather than weep about demoralizing information, become intolerably unfunny pessimists if they live past a certain age.[439]

It's true. Kurt became more pessimistic and less prone to joking about everything as he aged.

Why?

Maybe this is one reason: aging is all it's cracked up to be.

According to his doctor-son, Mark, damaged brain chemistry was the cause.

Here's Kurt's explanation, speaking in 1979 as a late-middle-aged man:

> Religious skeptics often become very bitter toward the end, as did Mark Twain, I do not propose to guess now as to why he became so bitter. I know why I will become bitter. I will finally realize that I have had it right all along: that I will not see God, that there is no heaven or Judgment Day.[440]

Whatever the complexity of causes, Vonnegut's later novel *Hocus Pocus* features this sober jokester:

> Everything, and I mean everything, was a joke to him, or so he said. His favorite expression right up to the end was, "I had to laugh like hell." If Lieutenant Colonel Patton is in Heaven, and I don't think many truly professional soldiers have ever expected to wind up there, at least not recently, he might at this very moment be telling about how his life suddenly stopped in Hué, and then adding, without even smiling, "I had to laugh like hell." That was the thing: Patton would tell about some supposedly serious or beautiful or dangerous or holy event during which he had had to laugh like hell, but he hadn't really laughed. He kept a straight face, too, when he told about it afterward. In all his life, *I don't think anybody ever heard him do what he said he had to do all the time, which was laugh like hell* [italics mine].[441]

CHAPTER 31

MUCH BETTER STORIES: RE-VISION AND REVISION

References about revision pop up everywhere in Vonnegut's work. They have appeared throughout this book. Yet revision is so colossally germane to writing and Vonnegut's advice on writing that it deserves a dedicated chapter.

The narrator says in *Slapstick*:

> The story of "The Ugly Duckling" was about a baby bird that was raised by ducks, who thought it was the funniest-looking duck they'd ever seen. But then it turned out to be a swan when it grew up.
>
> Eliza, I remember, said she thought it would have been a much better story if the little bird had . . . turned into a rhinoceros.[442]

"I am such a barbarous technocrat," Vonnegut declared, "that I believe [stories] can be tinkered with like Model T Fords."[443]

Vonnegut wrote in the preface to *Wampeters, Foma & Granfalloons*,

> The *Playboy* Interview with me in this book is what I *should* have said, not what I *really* said. *Playboy* showed me a typescript of what I had said into their tape recorder, and it was obvious to me that I had at least one thing in common with Joseph Conrad: English was my second language. Unlike

279

Conrad, I had no first language, so I went to work on the transcript with pen and pencil and scissors and paste, to make it appear that speaking my native tongue and thinking about important matters came very easily to me.[444]

Similarly, Vonnegut's *Paris Review* interview is prefaced with this instructive confession:

This interview with Kurt Vonnegut was originally a composite of four interviews done with the author over the past decade. The composite has gone through an extensive working over by the subject himself, who looks upon his own spoken words on the page with considerable misgiving . . . indeed, what follows can be considered an interview conducted with himself, by himself.[445]

When reproduced as a chapter in his nonfiction book *Palm Sunday*, Vonnegut entitled it "Self-Interview."

This is what I find most encouraging about the writing trades. They allow mediocre people who are patient and industrious *to revise* [italics mine] their stupidity, to edit themselves into something like intelligence. They also allow lunatics to seem saner than sane.[446]

These quotes reveal beliefs Vonnegut held dear: that what stories say are of the utmost importance to people and a culture, and that smart, effective writing results from the sweat equity of revision.

"His novels, speeches, short stories, and even dust-jacket comments are very carefully crafted," his son Mark Vonnegut attests. "Anyone who thinks that Kurt's jokes or essays came easily or were written off the cuff hasn't tried to write."[447]

At a writing conference panel on writing humorously about painful experiences, Dr. Harrison Scott Key read from his memoir about his abusive father, *The World's Largest Man*, and believe it or not, we in the audience were laughing our heads off. In the Q and A, someone asked, "Does your stuff start out funny in the first draft?"

He answered with a joke. Everyone laughed. Then he asked for the microphone back. "The third draft. Seriously." He said the first was anguished, the least funny. Each draft gave him more distance and he applied more craft, which meant, for him—as for Vonnegut—more humor.

TWO HATS

As a writer, you're required to be your own editor.

This is when the Third Player—those outside voices—and your own critical voice come in handy, and are, in fact, indispensable.

According to my midwife-niece, "The neocortex is the front part of our brain that we use to talk and make decisions. When the neocortex is in use, it decreases the helpful hormones of labor. This is why most female mammals find a dark, quiet spot alone to labor and have their babies."

But after labor and birth comes caretaking. That requires many decisions and assistance. It takes a village.

The village starts with you.

Put aside the newborn draft. Let it rest for as long as it takes to be able to see it anew. Hours, days, weeks, months, even years. Postpartum rest is imperative.

Then:

Read with fresh eyes, as if it's not your own child.

Assess.

Revise.

Do these three steps again and again until you've got the piece as ready as you can. Then call in the editorial assistants for feedback: your peer writing group, a friend you trust to give honest responses, a teacher or former teacher, an editor.

Consider the feedback. Revise accordingly until you're satisfied it's finished.

Whether you're a "swooper"—Vonnegut's moniker for a writer who drafts a piece all the way through before revising—or a "basher," as he claimed to be, revising close to composing, the steps above apply.

Sidney Offit observed, "[Kurt] wrote most of the day and sometimes into the night. He was also a streak writer. He would get it going and keep at it. I know he was a perfectionist because his waste basket was constantly overflowing."[448]

***

RE-VISION

Let's classify the word "revision" into two sorts.

The first is a true re-visioning, seeing anew, an "aha"—gained by grueling experimentation or sudden insight—of how material may be dealt with quite differently from what you've thought or got already. It's about the big picture. Here are two examples of that transformative process.

"After *Slaughterhouse-Five*," Richard Todd reported in the *New York Times Magazine* in January 1971,

> Vonnegut began work on a novel called *Breakfast of Champions*, about a world in which everyone but a single man, the narrator, is a robot. He gave it up, however, and it remains unfinished. I asked him why, and he said, "Because it was a piece of —." Later I mentioned "that book that wasn't going well," and he said: "It was going fine. It was a piece of —, that's all. It would have sold a lot of copies, been a Book-of-the-Month. People would have loved it."
>
> As if he were asking for a contrary opinion, Vonnegut read a section of the novel to a Harvard audience this fall,

with the same sort of disclaimer: "It's never coming out; it bores me stiff." The passage began: "I am an experiment by the creator of the universe." It described the moment when the voice of the book perceived that all around him were people who could not help doing what they were doing (Jesus Christ: "He was a robot who died for my sins").[449]

If you've read *Breakfast of Champions*, you know it's not the same book he read to that Harvard audience. A month after the article's appearance, and several after that fall 1970 reading, Kurt wrote to his publisher:

February 26, 1971
New York City
TO SAM LAWRENCE

... It is true that I have started working on *Breakfast of Champions* again, slowly and painfully, from the very beginning. It takes me so long to find out what my books are about, so I can write them. If I had pressed onward with the book before, and finished it willy nilly, it would have been an enormous fake. It probably would have made us a fortune. [. . .]

Come see me soon. [. . .] I've stopped horsing around so much. I have now met George Plimpton, so I've reached the peak of my career as a social butterfly. Back to work.
Cheers,
Kurt Vonnegut, Jr.[450]

In 1973, soon after *Breakfast of Champions* was published, he told a *Playboy* interviewer:

Slaughterhouse and *Breakfast* used to be one book. But they just separated completely. It was like a pousse-café, like oil and water—they simply were not mixable. So I was able to decant *Slaughterhouse-Five*, and what was left was *Breakfast of Champions*.[451]

———

As you may discern, this last remark oversimplifies a great deal.

———

The following comes from an early draft of a scene for Vonnegut's novel on Dresden, describing captured soldiers being transported in a boxcar.

As for repose: it was necessary that we take turns lying down. There were so many of us, and there was so little floor. The sleepers nestled, xxxxxxxxxx while the legs of the wakers were like so many fenceposts driven into an earth composed of huge and squirming, sighing, farting, nestling spoons. Some people were good at nestling, and others weren't. So it soon became a matter of desperation to seek an ideal sandwich, xxxx and, having found it, to recreate it every sleeping time. Xx Any person who was discontented with his place in xxxxx previous sandwiches faced an ever-growing aggregate of those who knew exactly where they should be. In time, there was an unbreakable and complacent mass of those who nestled well, who found xx outsiders and experimenters intolerable, and there was a frantic minority of outsiders, bad nestlers, thrashers, howlers, rollers, punchers, kickers, teeth-grinders, who had the choice of being wakers all around the clock, or of nestling with those who, exactly like themselves, could xxxxxxxxxxxxxxxxx not lie still. I have forgotten so much, but I remember still how my particular sandwich was made in my particular corner of my particular boxcar. My mind apparently xxxxxx still regards that information as valuable, xxxxxxxxxxxxxxxx suspects that I may have to lie down x in that boxcar again. There was a xxxxxxxxxxxxxxx cook named Newbold Sayles in front of me, and an anti-tank gunner named Robert Shamil behind me. "Lucky Pierre," you may say. It was said many times on the boxcar, before we all lost interest in speech. I still get Christmas cards from Sayles.[452]

The passage goes on about the nestlers Sayles and Shamil in the present and their takes on the past for another full page, unbroken by paragraphing.

In his final version, *Slaughterhouse-Five*, Vonnegut strews the boxcar experience episodically over two chapters. He lodges it in character, enhances it with comparison and concrete detail, and enriches the spooning relationships by zeroing in on one that is particularly heartbreaking. It starts like this:

Billy Pilgrim was packed into a boxcar with many other privates. He and Roland Weary were separated. Weary was packed into another car in the same train.

There were narrow ventilators at the corners of the car, under the eaves. Billy stood by one of these, and, as the crowd pressed against him, he climbed part way up a diagonal corner brace to make more room. This placed his eyes on a level with the ventilator, so he could see another train about ten yards away.

What Billy sees is the guards' boxcar, a far cry—cozy and candlelit—from the prisoners'. At the chapter's end, the prisoners' boxcar is viewed from Vonnegut's uniquely anthropological perspective, landing lightly again on Billy's experience:

Even though Billy's train wasn't moving, its boxcars were kept locked tight. Nobody was to get off until the final destination. To the guards who walked up and down outside, each car became a single organism which ate and drank and excreted through its ventilators. It talked or sometimes yelled through its ventilators, too. In went water and loaves of blackbread and sausage and cheese, and out came shit and piss and language.

Human beings in there were excreting into steel helmets which were passed to the people at the ventilators, who dumped them. Billy was a dumper. The human beings also passed canteens, which guards would fill with water. When food came in, the human beings were quiet and trusting and beautiful. They shared.

. . .

Human beings in there took turns standing or lying down. The legs of those who stood were like fence posts driven into a warm, squirming, farting, sighing earth. The queer earth was a mosaic of sleepers who nestled like spoons.

Now the train began to creep eastward.

Somewhere in there was Christmas. Billy Pilgrim nestled like a spoon with the hobo on Christmas night, and he fell asleep, and he traveled in time to 1967 again—to the night he was kidnapped by a flying saucer from Tralfamadore.[453]

REVISION

The second use of the term "revision" refers to the close-up detail of line editing. That means reworking the puzzle of the sound and sense of sentences.

Every sentence must do one of two things—reveal character or advance the action.[454]

That's Vonnegut's "Creative Writing 101" Rule #4. It's intended for the economical form of the short story.

This could stop you dead in your tracks if you considered it every time you composed a sentence.

Every sentence has to fight for its life, but you have to know the life it's fighting for. When you know what your story is truly about, you'll know better what to keep, to perfect, or discard.

Then, attend to the finer points of line editing:

Revise for clarity.

Revise for words that are more accurate, concrete, and alive.

Revise sentences so their sound and structure yield the most bang for the buck you intend.

Proofread for glitches of punctuation, typos, misspellings, and so on.

These fine-tuning exhortations appear in most books about writing and elsewhere from Vonnegut in this one. That's because they're tried and true. And so bear repeating.

Vonnegut wrote his friend Knox Burger, then an editor, in 1954:

> Have you read Aristotle's *Poetics*? I just did, and found in there everything any editor or writer ever told me about putting a story together. I couldn't think of a single amendment based on discoveries since 322 B.C. It's clear, and it isn't very long—and you might well recommend it to promising youngsters. Like me.[455]

HAVE THE GUTS TO SPILL THEM

When a story is puzzling to readers or there's an imbalance or something not full enough about it or the characters, it's sometimes because the writer has skirted or withheld the tough emotional part. Even though transmuting your experience into a changeling through the medium of fiction, you need to tap into autobiographical sources, the core well of your truth, and draw from it. Vonnegut clearly did that. How else do you become passionate about a subject, Vonnegut's prime advice, if not through what has touched you?

Even as a fictionalized changeling, truth can be scary.

Suck your thumb or hold someone's hand for help, but spill it.

———

HAVE THE GUTS TO CUT

Deadwood:

* unnecessary words, passages, characters, scenes, events
* those that slow and obscure the most important words and deeds

"Your deadwood is my foliage," a private writing client, Jay Greenfield, once said to me.

True, it can be hard to tell the difference, especially if it's your own. Foliage is beautiful and enhances blossoms. Deadwood is excessive, unnecessary, and blurring.

To cut to the punch: Foliage enhances. Deadwood obscures.

Discerning the difference is one of the most important editorial skills required of any writer, as Vonnegut points out in his article "How to Write with Style." How is it acquired? The same way, as the old joke goes, you get to Carnegie Hall: practice.

It's easier to gut great stuff if you tell yourself you're going to write other great stuff. Don't be cheap on yourself! There's more where that came from!

Remind yourself that this trim is in service of the whole!

Two of the "most important lessons I learned from Kurt Vonnegut," Dan Gleason, an Iowa student of Vonnegut's, wrote, "were 1) Take out all the parts that people don't like to read 2) Keep readers turning the pages fast."[456] Deadwood is all the parts people don't like to read. Without it, readers *will* turn the pages faster.

Look at this marvelous chapter, nowhere to be found in the published *Cat's Cradle*. I would not have had the courage to delete this, if it were mine (so help me God). But—does it further the plot or characterization? Obviously, Vonnegut didn't think so.

277

Chapter 120

                                   daintily untying
I fell asleep, was awakened by someone ~~gentlyxtakingxoff~~ my shoes.

It was my heavenly Mona. "Boko-maru?" she whispered.

"Why not?" I said.

And we did the thing. And she was as filled with rapture as before. I must say, for me, Boko-maru was still very nice, but it had definitely lost some of its blam.

I was thinking while we did it, which was a mistake. The charm of boko-maru is its brainlessness. "When done properly," Bokonon tells us, "boko-maru should leave a ~~prxxxt~~ participant absolutely mystified as to whether ten seconds, ten minutes, ten hours, or ten days have passed."

~~Bxxxyxxxxxxd~~

I found myself counting every second. "Think of nothing but your feet," Bokonon tells us, "and then forget your feet." I could not forget my feet. And, as time clanked by, I couldn't even concentrate of my feet. "Mona -- ?" I said.

She paid ~~texxxxxxxt~~ no attention.

"Mona -- listen to me," I said.

She was deaf, dumb, blind and drunk on boko-maru.

I pulled my feet away. "Mona!" I said sharply.

"Yes?" she said dazedly.

"I don't want to murder time right now," I said.

"Murder?" she said.

"So much has happened," I said. "I've got to talk, to think — "

"Wouldn't you rather do <u>boko-maru?</u>" she said.

"I don't see that that would <u>solve</u> anything," I said.

"Wouldn't you rather do <u>boko-maru?</u>" she said.

"Or get drunk?" I said. This was irony, a form of protest
with which she was unfamiliar.

"<u>Boko-maru</u> is cheaper," she said earnestly, "and there is no
hangover."

"Mona," I said, "if you're going to be my wife, and be reasonably
happy at it, xxxtxx and if I'm going to be the next President of
San Lorenzo, you're going to have to be tolerant when I get unhappy
and wordy and inquisitive
and confused/from time to time."

"Oh sure," she said.

"Oh sure?" I said.

"Oh sure," she said. tWit "We will hak do <u>boko-maru</u> all the time."

"Life can't be <u>boko-maru</u> all the time," I said, "especially for
a chief executive."

"Sometimes I will play the xylophone," she said.

"I hate to tell you — " I said, "but your xylophone is in Davy
Jones' Locker."

"I know," she said. "But the next President of San Lorenzo will
get me a new one, a better one, with two more octaves."

I shrugged. "I suppose I will," I said.

"You?" she said. She shook her head. "You will not be the
next President of San Lorenzo. It is in the Books of Bokonon who
the next President will be. Not you."

"Who then?" I said.

She recited the verse:

"I think I hear an old man moaning.

It is the great president-hater, old man Bokonon.

Why does he have the blues?

God Almighty gave him the bad news:

The next president is the president-hater, ~~Bokonox~~ the president-baiter,
(very old)
Old man Bokonon."

Drafts from *Cat's Cradle.* **Courtesy of the Lilly Library, Indiana University,
Bloomington, Indiana.**

Cat's Cradle, by the way, was once entitled *Cat's Call*. It took ten years. In a 1962 letter, he refers to it this way:

> The thing I did for Dell took me ten years to do, though it wasn't worth anything like ten years.

Some "thing"! Some less-than-worthwhile ten years![457]

THIRD-PLAYER FEEDBACK

Vonnegut attended to people's responses. Here is some evidence from a variety of sources: readers, critics, actors, and an editor.

He was asked in 1974, "What about this different ending to *Breakfast*—at what point did you change that?"

> Well, I was working on it and working on it and working on it and finally said all right, that's *it*. . . . And there was a lot of messenger work, as these days I live about six blocks from my publisher. So I'd send them pieces of that manuscript, and they'd send proof back and forth, hand-carried by people. And a couple of young people in the production department—I'm sorry I don't know their names—showed up with some part of the script, I forget what, and one of them said, "I didn't like the ending." And I said, "What's the matter with it?" And they said, "We don't like it; that's not the way we think it should end; we just thought we should say so." And I said, "Okay, I'll think about it," and thanked them. And I should know their names because— they were right![458]

In the early stages of his play *Happy Birthday, Wanda June*, Vonnegut wrote later, "there were about 60 didactic speeches."

Critics noticed his preaching. "So we knocked out half an hour."

> We learned to trust the audience. We've had so much suc-
> cess with cuts that we thought of writing a disappearing
> play. Every night, we'd take another word out until all the
> actors would do is come out for a curtain call.[459]

A senior editor at Vonnegut's publishing house sent him ten pages of notes regarding the manuscript of *Deadeye Dick*, divided into "General" and Specific": two single-spaced pages with six suggestions on characterization and plot, and eight pages with 115 line edits. All but five of the line edits have a checkmark; evidently Kurt checked each off after he dealt with it.

But on the editor's comments regarding amplifying or playing down certain characters or aspects of the plot, only two marks of Vonnegut's pen underscore his editor's critique. Here is one, about the prose: "The device of using the theater pieces—scenes written as scenes from a play—is a fairly dramatic or radical one stylistically. I must confess when I first read these scenes I was sort of jarred and put off by them. Upon reflection I'm of two minds: . . . What I thought you might consider is rewriting some of the scenes done in this style as directly narrated, dramatized, straight scenes and just keeping a couple of the theater pieces. It might make the ones you keep more effective."[460]

The finished novel shows Vonnegut addressed that criticism. There remain only three instances in which he has the playwright narrator render what might be prose into script form, and before the first one, he explains why he does it. Still, out of the editor's six substantive suggestions, Vonnegut apparently ignored four.

This is to say, from Vonnegut's example: You do not have to take anyone's suggestions. You are the final editor.

If you adhere to every voice offering suggestions, pandering to one and then the other, you may find yourself so far off course that you're out at sea. Especially beware of a hidden promise of fame or success ("If you change this so it's more like the best seller so-and-so"). You may realize one day that you are no longer writing the book that you yourself wanted to write. You may no longer even be enjoying the process of writing. So be careful. You have to listen to the third parties. You also must listen, most closely, to yourself.

Here's a letter Kurt wrote to me in which he's emphatic about satisfying one's own—in this case, my—artistic vision. The "slit-my-throat" line was thrilling, boosting my confidence at a time when it was pretty wobbly.

228 E 48 10017
Nov 1 1980

Dearest of all possible Suzannes —

I got your manuscripts this Saturday morning, and I read them at once with a great deal of admiration and satisfaction, and now I am returning them. You know this town as well as I do by now. We both know that there are practically no magazines left that will publish serious and madly idiosyncratic stories like your CHAMBERS STREET. On top of everything else, it's a poem. Too much! At the same time, I would rather slit my throat than tell you to write more commercially. CHAMBERS STREET does exactly what it is supposed to do.

As for the piece from the novel: Keep it up. I reads good, organic and sexy. Maybe I suggested this before, but I wish you would go have a talk about writing as a business with my friend Elaine Markson, a feminist agent at 44 Greenwich Avenue, practically in the same zipcode with you.

Love —

Kurt Vonnegut

HAVE THE GUTS TO QUIT

Vonnegut did.

"I have thrown away whole books," he says in a documentary film.[461]

In *Jailbird*'s prologue, he says,

> I tried to write a story about a reunion between my father
> and myself in heaven one time. An early draft of [*Deadeye
> Dick*] in fact began that way. I hoped in the story to become
> a really good friend of his. But the story turned out per-
> versely, as stories about real people we have known often
> do. It seemed that in heaven people could be any age they
> liked, just so long as they had experienced that age on
> Earth. . . . As author of the story, I was dismayed that my
> father in heaven chose to be only nine years old.
>
> He turned out to be a "strange little boy," and quite
> demanding. "It insisted on being a very unfriendly story,
> so I quit writing it."[462]

Sometimes quitting means laying a piece aside, maybe for years.
Perceiving it in those terms can be a useful way to permit yourself
to stop if something isn't working. And maybe that, in fact, will
be the truth. Sometimes it means that whatever is on your mind
will find another avenue of expression. Sometimes it is a goodbye.

Keep your drafts! It's tricky, viewing your work with a clear eye.
One day what you consider genius will look, on another day, like
idiocy. What you decide one night is utter dreck, you may realize
the next morning is eloquent.

Sticky issue, whether letting go or going on is the thing to do. If you're wondering, check your mental health. If it's going downhill, give what you're working on a rest. Write something else entirely.

HAVE THE GUTS TO KEEP ON TRUCKIN'

After a breather, take a look at the manuscript you were stuck on. See how you feel, how it reads. It may be that you simply got too close or burned out momentarily. Reread what Kurt Vonnegut wrote to José Donoso in chapter 8. Get some advice about yourself and the manuscript from other writers you respect, people who know you and the work.

Then decide. Commit yourself to your decision.

Either way, giving up or going on, it takes guts.

Either way, you're further along in your writing practice.

The following is from *Cat's Cradle*:

> "Father needs some kind of book to read to people who are dying or in terrible pain. I don't suppose you've written anything like that."
>
> "Not yet."
>
> "I think there'd be money in it. There's another valuable tip for you."
>
> "I suppose I could overhaul the 'Twenty-third Psalm,' switch it around a little so nobody would realize it wasn't original with me."
>
> "Bokonon tried to overhaul it," he told me. "Bokonon found out he couldn't change a word."[463]

CHAPTER 32
EENY-MEENY-MINY-MOE
OR CHOICE

In the *Paris Review* interview, Vonnegut reveals a revolutionary realization he had once in conversation with his sister Alice:

> [Alice] could have been a remarkable sculptor. . . . I bawled her out one time for not doing more with the talents she had. She replied that having talent doesn't carry with it the obligation that something has to be done with it. This was startling news to me. I thought people were supposed to grab their talents and run as far and fast as they could.

"What do you think now?" the interviewer inquired.

> Well—what my sister said now seems a peculiarly feminine sort of wisdom. I have two daughters who are as talented as she was, and both of them are damned if they are going to lose their poise and senses of humor by snatching up their talents and desperately running as far and as fast as they can. They saw me run as far and as fast as I could—and it must have looked like quite a crazy performance to them. And this is the worst possible metaphor, for what they actually saw was a man sitting still for decades.

"At a typewriter," the interviewer says.

"Yes, and smoking his fool head off."⁴⁶⁴

Although he *felt* compelled, he concludes here, in actuality, as Alice points out, he had a choice. You *don't* have to make something of your talent. You *don't* have to run with it. Any more than you must strive to be an Olympic swimmer if you're a talented swimmer, or a zoologist if you love animals, and so on.

Vonnegut mentions this revelatory exchange with his sister several times. He toys with the idea of purposefulness throughout his fiction.

A character says in *Slapstick*:

> We could have raised chickens. We could have had a little vegetable garden. And we could have amused ourselves with our ever-increasing wisdom, caring nothing for its possible usefulness.⁴⁶⁵

On the other hand, free will—even the choice to be a writer—is always suspect in Vonnegut's oeuvre.

The biggest familial influence on Vonnegut as a writer was his mother, Edith Lieber Vonnegut, a well-educated, intelligent, cultivated woman. When his parents lost their fortune through investing in a Ponzi scheme during the Great Depression, she tried earning money by writing for magazines.

> She was a good writer, it turned out, but she had no talent for the vulgarity the slick magazines required. Fortunately, I was loaded with vulgarity, so, when I grew up, I was able to make her dream come true. Writing for *Collier's* and *The Saturday Evening Post* and *Cosmopolitan* and *Ladies' Home Journal* and so on was as easy as falling off a log for me. I only wish she'd lived to see it. I only wish she'd lived to see all her grandchildren. She has ten. She didn't even get to see

the first one. I made another one of her dreams come true: I lived on Cape Cod for many years. She always wanted to live on Cape Cod. *It's probably very common for sons to try to make their mothers' impossible dreams come true* [italics mine]. I adopted my sister's sons after she died, and it's spooky to watch them try to make her impossible dreams come true.[466]

Even his sister's decision *not* to use her talent may be more constricted than it appears, he remarks in *Fates Worse than Death*:

Alice was just a girl . . . and . . . she was traumatized mainly by having every piece of sculpture or picture she made celebrated by Father as though it were Michelangelo's *Pietà* or the ceiling of the Sistine Chapel. In later life (which was going to last only until she was forty-one) this made her a lazy artist. (I have often quoted her elsewhere as saying, "Just because people have talent, that doesn't mean they have to *do* something with it.")[467]

"The main business of humanity is to do a good job of being human beings . . . not to serve as appendages to machines, institutions, and systems," the protagonist, Paul, says in *Player Piano*.[468]

Caught up in the competitive, collective tunnel-vision focus of the writing life—MFA programs, conferences, online forums, peer groups, the endeavor to publish—one can easily forget that writing is simply one among many possible expressions of your sensibilities. Here is an anecdote of my own such revelation, for what it's worth:

When I left the University of Iowa Writers' Workshop in 1968, after two and a half years, I taught full-time. For the first time in my life, I was gainfully employed while doing something I'd discovered I loved, that engaged me thoroughly, and that wholly involved me in writing and literature but from a completely different angle than writing itself. One weekend, after not having been in the hothouse of the workshop for over a year, I returned to Iowa City for a visit, and went into the Iowa Book and Supply, the university's bookstore. There on the shelf was a novel by an acquaintance, Tom, with a lively psychedelic-looking picture of him and his wife Janyce on the white cover. I had introduced them my first year in Iowa City, and they had fallen in love and married. I read the book jacket. The novel was based on their romance. I checked the price. I began to laugh.

So being a writer is just putting together your experience between fancy eye-catching covers and selling it for $7.95!

It seemed hilarious. After a year of teaching working-class students and vets in a segregated Saginaw, Michigan, with a Dow Chemical plant in nearby Midland manufacturing napalm while the Vietnam War was raging, this endeavor—writing—taken so seriously that many of us measured our self-worth solely in terms of it, seemed absurd, ridiculous, comic!

Tom's novel didn't center on gripping societal issues, nor did it intend to. Still, whatever life it was about was now compressed in static print between covers.

I was in the midst of this epiphany when another friend from the workshop walked in, Howard McMillan. He had come in to the Iowa Book and Supply to view his own novel on the shelf. He asked what I was laughing about. I explained. He looked quizzical. He checked Tom's sales with the clerk. He located his book. Checked his own sales. We each departed.

I would never forget this.

On the other hand, I would forget it again and again.

It behooves you to keep remembering that you have choices.

> Trout was petrified there on Forty-second Street. I [the fictional author] had given [Trout] a life not worth living, but I had also given him an iron will to live. This was a common combination on the planet Earth.[469]

Consider slacking up on the iron will to write, if it gives you a life not worth living.

Caught up in the writing life—and the idea of being "a writer"—the reasons you began writing in the first place may dim.

Consider slacking up on that involvement, if that happens. Do something else that's compelling to you.

Come back, after a break. Retreat to the basics with regard to writing: the passion and pleasure of spilling and shaping what it is you have to say.

"Like his books, Kurt's words caused me to fall head over heels in love with my imagination," Jim Siegelman, Kurt's student at Harvard, recalls. "Yet at the end of the term I told him that, from everything I had heard, I didn't think I would like the life of a writer. His reply wasn't exactly a hard sell:

"Don't be a writer," [Kurt] said, "if you possibly can't."[470]

In *Breakfast of Champions*, the narrator offers marvelous bird's-eye perspectives on life. Here are two:

"I can't tell if you're serious or not," said the driver.

"I won't know myself until I find out whether *life* is serious or not," said Trout. "It's *dangerous*, I know, and it can hurt a lot. That doesn't necessarily mean it's *serious*, too."[471]

I daydreamed at Celia's funeral. There was no reason to expect that anything truly exciting or consoling would be said. Not even the minister, the Reverend Charles Harrell, believed in heaven or hell. Not even the minister thought that every life had a meaning, and that every death could startle us into learning something important, and so on. The corpse was a mediocrity who had broken down after a while. The mourners were mediocrities who would break down after a while.

The city itself was breaking down. . . .

The planet itself was breaking down. . . .

There in the back of the church, I daydreamed a theory of what life was all about. I told myself that Mother and Felix and the Reverend Harrell and Dwayne Hoover and so on were cells in what was supposed to be one great big animal. There was no reason to take us seriously as individuals. Celia in her casket there, all shot through with Drano and amphetamine, might have been a dead cell sloughed off by a pancreas the size of the Milky Way.

How comical that I, a single cell, should take my life so seriously![472]

CHAPTER 33
MAKING A LIVING

PART A: FROM WRITING

> I used to teach a writers' workshop . . . and I would say at the start of every semester, "The role model for this course is Vincent Van Gogh—who sold two paintings to his brother."[473]

The toughest, most fundamental question for a serious writer or artist of any kind, if you're not born with a silver spoon in your mouth, is how to support your habit.

Not only must the habit be supported. Like everyone else, the artist must first make the means to eat, clothe, and shelter him- or herself and dependents. So the artist has two major tasks. And one (which may entail several) has to bring in the bacon.

Asked what advice he would give to new young authors interested in pursuing a writing career, Vonnegut answered:

> It is much harder for young writers to start now . . . it is much harder for young a lot of things to start now. . . . It's too bad there is no way for a poor person to make a beginning as a writer now.[474]

Vonnegut said that in 1973! What has changed in over forty-five years? It's gotten even harder to earn money by writing. And forget making a living at it. The statistics reflect the general income disparity: there's a tiny group of financially successful writers, a "1 percent," and then everyone else. This cuts across genres.

Do a quick Internet search about writers' earnings, and the following headlines will pop up: "Don't Quit Your Day Job—The Financial Reality of Writing Science Fiction and Fantasy,"[475] "What Writers Earn: A Cultural Myth,"[476] "My Amazon Bestseller Made Me Nothing:"[477] The last one, by Patrick Wensick, spells out the upshot most starkly:

> Even when there's money in writing, there's not much money. . . .
>
> This is what it's like, financially, to have the indie book publicity story of the year and be near the top of the bestseller list.
>
> Drum roll.
>
> $12,000. . . .
>
> The book sold plus or minus 4,000 copies.

Why is this so? Vonnegut sums it up:

> There is no shortage of wonderful writers. What we lack is a dependable mass of readers.[478]

According to a Pew Research Center survey, adult Americans read an average of twelve books a year, heavily weighted on either end of the age spectrum.[479] How many read fiction? God only knows.

For perspective, consider this:

> Bill Styron pointed out one time, in a lecture I was privileged to hear, that the great Russian novels—which were more of an influence on American writers than Hawthorne or Twain or any American writer you'd want to name—were

written for very small audiences because the literate population was very small, amid an enormous empire of illiterate
people.[480]

———

Kurt Vonnegut began writing short stories *in order* to make money.
Imagine doing that now!

I had a family and wasn't making nearly enough money
to support the family so I started writing short stories on
weekends and there was an enormous magazine industry
at that time which paid very high prices for the stories and
they needed lots of them.[481]

October 28, 1949
Dear Pop:
    I sold my first story to Collier's. Received my check ($750
minus a 10% agent's commission) yesterday noon. It now
appears that two more of my works have a good chance of
being sold in the near future.
    I think I'm on my way. I've deposited my first check in
a savings account and, as and if I sell more, will continue
to do so until I have the equivalent of one year's pay at
GE. Four more stories will do it nicely, with cash to spare
(something we never had before). I will then quit this goddamn nightmare job, and never take another one so long
as I live, so help me God.
    I'm happier than I've been for a good many years.
    Love.
    K[482]

The equivalent of that $750 today: $7,481.
Two years later, in 1951, he quit his day job.

Then Vonnegut had to scramble, and scramble he did. His family expanded. His earning situation reversed: now he had to supplement his writing income with other jobs to make ends meet. He taught, he tried selling Saabs. He came up with cockamamie schemes.

He pitched one to his friend Miller Harris—fellow vet, reporter for the Cornell *Sun*, and aspiring writer who had just published a story in *Harper's* and was working in his family's shirt-making business:

> February 28, 1950
> Alplaus, NY
> Dear Miller:
> O.K., so people who want to write for a living are doomed to failure. I have other angles, about which this letter is.
> This letter is to Harris the shirtmaker. I have a proposition for a man who can manufacture and market bowties. Can you? I know nothing about the garment trade, so perhaps the whole thing is preposterous.
> Anyway, I have an idea for a bowtie. If you heard this idea, I think you would agree that it would be a sensational teen-ager fad for a few wild, lucrative weeks.
> Does this sort of thing interest you? The tie would cost virtually nothing to make—no mechanical gadgets, no wires, no electronic tubes. It's just a plain, ordinary bowtie (no, it doesn't glow in the dark, dammit), put together like any other bowtie. But there is one thing about it that would make it a natural for promotion.
> Are you interested? If you are, and if the idea is any good, how will you reward me?

Writing novels paid little compared to short stories.

"Doubleday wants me to expand 'Barnhouse' into a full novel.

That way, I could make another $750," he wrote ironically to Harris.

Yet it was only in the novel form that he could be free from the strictures of the popular magazine market to have his own say.

"I have a pitch, which I think will pay off," he confides in the same letter. "I hope to build a reputation as a science-fiction writer."[483]

———

Vonnegut's conflict between taking the risk of doing what he wanted to do, on the one hand, and his obligation as the family breadwinner and his dislike of the corporate grind, on the other, surface in his fiction during those years, notably in the story "Deer in the Works" and the novel *Player Piano*.

He wasn't alone with these conflicts. Many returning World War II veterans were dismayed to find themselves in suburbia, working in corporations. In the mid-'50s, *The Organization Man* by William H. Whyte and the novel *The Man in the Gray Flannel Suit* by Sloan Wilson, both critical of the corporate world's conformist mentality, were best sellers.

———

The main point: things have changed and things have stayed the same, essentially. Yes, Vonnegut made money writing stories and cut his fiction writer's eyeteeth on them at the same time, impossible to do now. But even though he quit his GE job to write full-time, basically he'd traded one full-time job for several others. Most of the time, though learning how to construct a darn good saleable story, he was not writing what he wanted to write.

Today, you can learn how to write well while writing whatever you really want to write. You just can't make money at it. In fact, it's likely you will pay to learn how. But the conflict between free-lancing and the reliable nine-to-five remains.

Psychologically, Kilgore Trout is what I thought I might become once I noticed how poor science fiction writers were and I was one of them at the time and I was as poor as any of them.[484]

"When I was ten," Mark Vonnegut recalls, "Kurt asked if he could borrow the three hundred dollars I had saved up from my paper route."[485]

> "I only wish Kilgore Trout were here," said Eliot [in *God Bless You, Mr. Rosewater*], "so I could shake his hand and tell him that he is the greatest writer alive today. I have just been told that he could not come because he could not afford to leave his job! And what job does this society give its greatest prophet?" Eliot choked up, and, for a few moments, he couldn't make himself name Trout's job. "They have made him a stock clerk in a trading stamp redemption center in Hyannis!"[486]

The Good News:

Vonnegut struggled. If you are a writer, you will probably struggle financially as well. But struggle isn't bad. Struggle means you're engaged, you're learning, striving. What *really* sucks is listlessness, indifference, purposelessness.

Listen to this: the toughest part of Kurt's life economically was also the most productive.

> The bulk of my work was written on Cape Cod where I lived from 1950–1970 . . . probably was the shank of my creative life. . . . I would have been quite content to have created what I did by 1970 when I finally left Cape Cod. I used to walk on the great salt marshes there and geese would fly up ahead of me and I would come home from a four-hour walk feeling healthy and happy.[487]

PART B: ABOUT YOUR DAY JOB

When a child of the Great Depression loses a job, it is sort of like losing a billfold or a key to the front door. You go get another one.[488]

Sometimes going to "get another one" produces startling results. "Kurt Vonnegut once wrote that 'only nut cases want to be president.' But he helped me become a White House speechwriter," Robert Lehrman began an article he wrote in the *New York Times*. "In 1965, Vonnegut was my adviser at the University of Iowa Writers' Workshop, where I was studying fiction. One day, he said he could get me an assistantship, but I'd have to teach speech.

"'I know nothing about speech,' I said.

"He said something like: 'Learn. It's 1,800 bucks.'"[489]

So Bob did. He discovered he loved the art of speaking. He was, as I recall, vitally involved in the anti-war movement and was often on soapboxes. The appeal of politics coalesced with his growing expertise at writing speeches, and eventually he landed a position as the chief speechwriter for Vice President Al Gore from 1993 to 1995. While working full-time as a speechwriter, he also published four novels and a hundred nonfiction articles. Washington politics became fuel for short stories, and his life-long "day job" for a well-received book about it, *The Political Speechwriter's Companion: A Guide for Writers and Speakers*, 2009. He still teaches speech, and continues to be in high demand as a commentator and speechwriter.

The *ideal* "day job" is one you enjoy, that fosters your fiction, and pays decently. Something that satisfies other aspects of yourself than writing—the physical, for example, or the collaborative or interactive. Better yet, one that entails unusual expertise, situations or environments that pique readers' curiosity, and in itself provides fodder for stories. The practices of medicine and law have yielded up notable writers who've used them as subjects.

If you're young and starting out, you might consider choosing another profession that's satisfying and lucrative, as your first goal toward writing. If highly motivated and disciplined, with supportive family circumstances and abundant energy, you will write. Perhaps you can work part-time or will delay writing until you've amassed enough money to quit.

If the stories don't come, at least you're earning a living and having adventures doing something you value.

———

On the other hand, you may not choose or want, for many reasons, to have two full-time professions. Or you may not have available to you the "ifs" listed above that two professions require. Most people don't. No worries. That's not who you are, or what your circumstances are, or your style.

———

The way to handle jobs you aren't particularly partial to: find *something* about the job that you *do* care about.

Vonnegut cared a great deal about the guys he worked with at G.E., for example. Several remained friends throughout his life.

In *God Bless You, Mr. Rosewater*, he writes about an insurance salesman who practices what might be called "obligatory caring":

> Poor, lugubrious Fred spent his mornings seeking insurance prospects in the drugstore, which was the coffee house of the rich, and the news store, which was the coffee house of the poor. He was the only man in town who had coffee in *both* places. . . .
>
> Poor Fred worked like hell for the few dollars he brought

home once in a while. He was working now, beaming at the carpenter and the two plumbers in the news store.

He engages them in conversation about their wives.

"I've done what I can for [my wife]," Fred declared. "God knows it isn't enough. Nothing could be enough." There was a real lump in his throat. *He knew that lump had to be there and it had to be real, or he wouldn't sell any insurance* [italics mine]. "[Insurance is] something, though, something even a poor man can do for his bride."[490]

I discovered "obligatory caring" this way: Writing biographical prefaces for the Franklin Library Publishing Company freelance, I once got blocked when assigned what I considered a mediocre novel, until a veteran freelancer advised that instead of trying to fake it, I find something I cared about and latch onto that. I admired the author, John Hersey, just not that novel. That admiration carried me through.

In spite of Vonnegut's hating the GE job, it provided him with the subject of his first novel and the passion to write it, as well as valuable instruction in public relations.

All jobs are gold mines for fiction.

Vonnegut encouraged us to write about work. People don't write enough about it, he said. Most people spend a lot of time at their jobs, and the workplace holds a wealth of potential for conflict, characterization, and societal comment.

Nonprofessional jobs allow you avenues into experiencing class, power, and the inner mechanisms and underbelly of the workplace, less emotionally accessible otherwise.[491]

"It's a tremendous advantage to be on the edge if you're an artist of any kind, because you can make a better commentary than someone at the center could," Vonnegut said.[492]

He was a private in World War II, not an officer.

———

Kurt told us one day about a writer friend of his who decided to paint houses, thinking that he could paint all day mechanically while his mind focused on writing. But what happened, Vonnegut said, erupting into his wheezing laughter, is that his friend just painted all day.

Similarly, I waitressed at a jazz club in the '70s, figuring I could both earn money and listen to music. It turned out that most of the customers were other jazz musicians, too poor to tip well, and that you can't attend to customers and listen to music simultaneously. It was also dangerous on the subway in the middle of the night. But that was fodder for a great bit in a short story.

Moral: Your job is your job. Ya gotta be present for it.

———

In a 1983 documentary, Kurt reported:

> I get up at 7:30 and work four hours a day. Nine to twelve in the morning, five to six in the evening. Businessmen would achieve better results if they studied human metabolism. No one works well eight hours a day. No one ought to work more than four hours.[493]

It's easy to resent the time your job takes, to think that only if you had more time, you could write a blue streak. A novelist acquaintance, who worked full-time in the letters department of a weekly magazine, quit when her first novel sold successfully, and confided a few years afterward, "You have no idea how much I resented *Newsweek*." What she'd discovered, though, was that having all the time in the world did not change her relationship to writing nearly as substantially as she'd thought it would.

To have ample time to let your own rhythms guide you, to be free of feeling your writing squeezed between necessities is marvelous. The gift of time is no joke. It matters. But the use and quality of the time matters more.

In fact, the pressure of that squeeze can make your writing time more sacred and productive.[494]

———

Here's what Vonnegut says about the notion that hack-writing jobs cripple talent:

> That's romance—that work of that sort damages a writer's soul. At Iowa, Dick Yates and I used to give a lecture each year on the writer and the free enterprise system. The students hated it. We would talk about all the hack jobs writers could take in case they found themselves starving to death, or in case they wanted to accumulate enough capital to finance the writing of a book. Since publishers aren't putting money into first novels anymore, and since the magazines have died, and since television isn't buying from young freelancers anymore, and since the foundations give grants only to old poops like me, young writers are going to have to support themselves as shameless hacks. Otherwise, we are soon going to find ourselves without a contemporary literature. There is only one genuinely ghastly thing hack jobs do to writers, and that is to waste their precious time.[495]

This student didn't hate that lecture. I appreciated it. I felt as if someone, finally, was actually worried about us and our futures, in a fundamental way. I had just begun to worry about it myself.

As I recall, it was Kurt who engineered that forum. It wasn't part of the curriculum. It was a surprise, a gift.

In that hard-nosed lecture, he and Yates invited us to open our mental doors to wage-earning possibilities. Technical writing, medical writing, grant writing, industrial film writing—all kinds of avenues were proposed. They suggested the advertising industry as a possible wage maker. I could hardly believe my ears. Advertising, at the heart of the heart of the establishment, was repudiated in those antiestablishment '60s years. Talk about selling out!

To show how far out that suggestion was at the time, here's an invite to a surprise gathering with Allen Ginsberg that circled around that same May:

Flyer for *Gentle Thursday*, which took place on May 11, 1967, at the University of Iowa. Courtesy of the author.

Vonnegut knew about others' contempt in the face of necessity.

> When I was supporting myself as a freelance writer doing stories for the *Saturday Evening Post* and *Collier's*, I was *scorned*! I mean, there was a time when to be a slick writer was a disgusting thing to be, as though it were prostitution. The people who did not write for the slicks obviously did not need the money. I would have liked very much to have been that sort of person, but I wasn't. I was the head of a family, supporting the damn thing in what seemed—to me, at least—an honorable way.[496]

If Kurt Vonnegut had been too touchy or precious about work, he might not have become successful. He could have disdained reviewing *The Random House Unabridged Dictionary* for the *New York Times*—the one that caught his future publisher Sam Lawrence's eye. "On the face of it," his biographer Charles Shields observed, "reviewing a dictionary was a pretty awful assignment," a "bone from the feast" of that year's plum reviewing jobs. Furthermore, he could have been affronted by the copy of the book he was sent.[497] He showed it to Barry Jay Kaplan, his graduate assistant at Iowa. Barry reports they'd sent a salesman's copy. It was only A's and B's. But thick. Kurt wasn't angry. He thought it was hilarious.

Check out the review in *Welcome to the Monkey House*. It's a marvel. Vonnegut manages to be colloquial, imaginative, informative, and also to set forth his political agendas, praising writers he loves and advocating certain social and political attitudes, all in the examination of a humble dictionary.

Whatever writing you do increases your skill in tangling with words.

Another "ghastly thing" about hack-writing jobs: they replicate the confines of writing. Who wants to stare at a computer screen after staring at one already for hours? Or play with words for yourself after arranging them for hours for your paycheck?

To circumvent that duplication, you might write by hand, or in snatches of time, or in a bar—anywhere distinctly different and more playful than your day job requires.

~

Kurt concluded the lecture about jobs and how to get ahead in this way:

"Use us," he said, bluntly.

Meaning the veteran writers who were our teachers.

I've a vivid recollection of *how* he said it. He looked straight at us, then dropped his eyes and let the words slide out of his mouth. This, he seemed to me to be conveying, was necessity's bottom line.

Vonnegut's student Ronni Sandroff tells an anecdote about this notion:

> I wrote a story called "The Frump Queen" about a home-coming parade in Iowa City. Vonnegut liked "The Frump Queen" and offered to send it to *Redbook* magazine for me, but I refused. Please mother, I'd rather do it myself. The story was accepted—my first paid publication—and it wasn't until more than a decade later that I learned that Vonnegut had sent *Redbook* a letter asking them to keep an eye out for the story, and the editors were super-excited to have heard from him. That was embarrassing. For years I had been telling people I was living proof that you could sell a story from the slush pile. It was something I wanted to believe, that the world was merit, not connection, based.
>
> By the time *Party Party and Girlfriends*, my first book of two novellas, was ready for publication I was willing to look unfairness in the face and ask Vonnegut for a quote. "Strong, imaginative, spookily candid," he wrote. He compared me to J. D. Salinger, too, but the editor left out that part.

Out of twenty students in a class anywhere in the country, Vonnegut told an interviewer, six will be "startlingly talented" and two might actually publish something. What distinguishes the two who get published from the others equally talented?

They will have something other than literature itself on their minds. They will probably be hustlers, too. I mean that they won't want to wait passively for somebody to discover them. They will insist on being read.[498]

Vonnegut admired a certain kind of chutzpah.

"Winter, 1967," the writer Dan Gleason recounts, "and I was shivering in one of those flimsy old tin-roof Quontset huts . . . waiting impatiently for my first and only class with the great Kurt Vonnegut." He was an undergrad journalism student, unregistered for the class, hoping to audit. But it was standing room only. Vonnegut told him to come see him before the next semester and he could enroll.

I was actually going to comply but when the class met again . . . I swiped a chair from another hut and carried it into Vonnegut's class and plopped down. . . . When I caught his eye, he did a double take and asked if I was supposed to be in the class.

I said, "Yeah, you don't remember me from last class?"

He shot me a puzzled look, paused a couple beats and nodded. "Oh, yeah . . . okay then."

Weeks later, he spotted me in the Student Union and said to sit. "Didn't you hand in a story about three teenage boys who hide out at some whorehouse?"

I said I did.

"I really like that story," he said. "But level with me. You aren't supposed to be in that class, are you?"

"I don't guess I am."

A grin big as a watermelon slice creased his face. "Hell, I knew that. But I let you stay because I liked your moxie. You don't get far in this world without moxie."

The [third] most important lesson I learned from Vonnegut: Moxie will open doors.[499]

————

Writers who think cynically that connections are the sole key to publishing are naïve.

Publishers are in business. They want their business to thrive. They are not going to publish something they don't think will sell or have some future promise, or that will damage their reputations. *Redbook* wouldn't have bought Sandroff's story if it were poorly written or didn't serve their readers.

When connections work, it's because the "project," as they say in the publishing industry, is a good fit. All things being equal, the endorsement of a well-connected person may certainly boost a piece of work into being chosen over a competitor. Same thing is true about jobs. So yes, connections can be helpful. Sometimes instrumental. Sometimes detrimental. With or without them, you have to do your best work.

Here are two examples from Vonnegut's career: Kurt met Knox Burger at Cornell, and reconnected when he submitted a story to *Collier's* magazine, where Knox worked as an assistant editor. Knox rejected the story, commenting, "This is a little sententious for us."

Eventually, Knox Burger became instrumental in Vonnegut's early publishing career as an editor and friend, publishing Vonnegut's first short story and as an editor at a publishing house, his first short story collection, *Canary in a Cat House*, and editing *Mother Night*.[500]

The publisher Sam Lawrence was swayed by Vonnegut's dictionary review to pursue Kurt Vonnegut with a three-book contract.[501]

Thank you for sending us the accompanying
manuscript. We have read it carefully and
regret that it does not meet the present needs
of Collier's.

We shall be glad to receive other
contributions which you think suitable to
Collier's and promise a thorough reading
and a prompt decision.

.   Sincerely,

THE EDITORS

*This is a little
sententious for
us. You're not the Kurt Vonnegut
who worked on the Cornell Sun
in 1942, are you?*

Knox Burger

Collier's rejection letter to Kurt Vonnegut. Courtesy of the Lilly Library,
Indiana University, Bloomington, Indiana.

Possibly it helped that Vonnegut happened to mention Bennett Cerf, Lawrence's former boss, in the review—though that isn't in the realm of "connection" or even intention, but the Fairy Godmother's "if the accident will." If Kurt's review had been clunky, referring to Cerf would have signified nothing.

In the literary magazine world, the same thing holds true. We at the *Bellevue Literary Review* avoid that kind of impropriety like the plague, sometimes to our detriment. Significant prize money was withdrawn after we did not publish a piece by the famous, wealthy sponsor of it. We have even rejected a submission by someone who had been a contest judge for us. All that matters to us as editors is the piece of writing and the balance in the current issue under consideration.

Moxie has limits. So does being well connected.

The playwright-narrator of Vonnegut's novel *Mother Night* is slipped a question in the prison yard from Adolf Eichmann.

"Do you think a literary agent is absolutely necessary?" The note was signed by Eichmann.
My reply was this: "For book club and movie sales in the United States of America, absolutely."[502]

Ten years after borrowing his paper route money, Mark Vonnegut writes, his father "went from being poor to being famous and rich in the blink of an eye."[503] During the blink, Kurt told an interviewer,

I am frankly embarrassed by the money. Success makes you feel the world has gone mad. When you are successful, you discover that you can publish almost anything, and the response to that is to simply stop writing. That is why I'm looking for a new line of work.[504]

Catapulting from relative obscurity to limelight's blinding blaze was certainly disconcerting. Fame is destabilizing. Kurt confided his worry about John Irving at the time Irving was becoming well known, in the early '80s. "At least when it happened to me, I was already in my forties," Kurt said.

People confuse your personhood with your persona. They fear you, demand things of you, project and expect.

At a party honoring Vonnegut after a reading at a university, no one, he told me at about the same time, came up and spoke to him or his wife Jill. Everyone was too timid.

Joseph Shipley, an Indianapolis native, related this anecdote as I was assisting the Kurt Vonnegut Museum and Library table at the Brooklyn Book Festival one recent September. As a sophomore in high school, just after reading *Cat's Cradle* and *Slaughterhouse-Five*, he passed Kurt Vonnegut himself on the street one fall day in downtown Indianapolis.

"I know you!" Joe blurted.

"No, you don't," Kurt replied.

A few years later Kurt rocketed from shame-faced classroom confession about trying to be urbane to joining the company of other renowned writers invited to the White House.

Such a propulsion is hard on friends and family. Your dad, husband, uncle—even your teacher—is suddenly someone else, someone exalted, someone fans think they know, someone who has much less time for you.

"I grew up thinking everything would be perfect if we just had a little more money. Instead the money just blew everything apart," according to Mark. "Once he was famous, people gathered around my father like hungry guppies around a piece of bread. There was never enough Kurt to go around."[505]

It took quite a bit of getting used to, by all parties.

———

Later in his life, Kurt told Mark that he was proud of restoring the family fortune.

In doing so, Kurt made his mother's biggest dream come true.[506]

———

Success enabled Vonnegut to expand creatively. It allowed him to participate in and influence society in ways impossible without the power of that position—giving speeches, lending his voice to social causes. He achieved his goal of being a good citizen, and then some.

———

Don't worry. You probably won't have to endure the downsides of fame and fortune.

But you can emulate the upsides.

CHAPTER 34

CARING FOR YOUR PIECE
IN THE GAME

That is my principal objection to life, I think: It is too easy, when alive, to make perfectly horrible mistakes.[507]

Your well-being is primary. Your mind and body—you—are what you inhabit and what you employ in this cosmic game. You are, as a writer, your equipment. So attention must be paid to your health and upkeep.

"Here are two things that ruined my earlier life: life insurance and envy," Vonnegut told interviewers. Quitting GE to become a full-time writer, he said, was "an alarming thing to do."

It frightened me so much what could happen to my family that I bought a perfect bruiser of a life insurance policy. Every nickel I made went into this until it was obvious I could make a hell of a lot of money by merely dying. I became obsessed with this idea.[508]

He asked a metallurgist friend how much life insurance he had. The friend had none at all. He didn't worry about what would happen after he was dead, he told Kurt, because he'd be dead. Kurt let his policy lapse.[509] Consequently, he advises:

You should have some scientists among your friends—they think straight.

On envy, well, I was nearly consumed with it, like being shot full of sulfuric acid. I have beaten it pretty well.[510]

We witnessed an outburst generated at least in part by his envy during a workshop. A student, David Milch, presented a story that ridiculed businessmen. The generation gap and "Don't trust anyone over 30" was then prime-time, as well as rage at the military-industrial complex, corporations, and the men who ran them. It wasn't unusual to scoff at businessmen.

But Kurt lashed out at Milch. "Those men are my peers! I worked with men like them!" They supported families, they were hard-working, he said, and they deserved respect.

David Milch was charismatic and fresh out of Yale, where he'd graduated summa cum laude, won a prestigious literary prize, and been a protégé of the writer Robert Penn Warren.

"Vonnegut didn't like the Ivy League or where I was coming from," Milch recalls. He was "defiantly philistine. My credentials disqualified me." Other literary Ivy Leaguers were among us, however. It had become clear in class even before this scene that Vonnegut had a bug in his bonnet about Milch.

The dispute softened, Milch says, through Richard Yates's interceding, David's friendship with Kurt's daughter Edie, and because both Kurt and David "enjoyed their cocktails" at Donnelly's, one of the bars in town.

Ironically, Milch left the teaching job he got at Yale after getting his MFA to write in LA for television's *Hill Street Blues*, then went on to create *NYPD Blue* and *Deadwood*, far from the hallowed halls of literature.

Such honest emotional responses distinguished our writer-teachers, especially Kurt, from most instructors, and afforded growth. Milch learned from the incident that "The divide was much more pronounced between student and teacher and people of different backgrounds than I'd realized." I myself learned, in spite of my allegiance to Kurt's writing-from-passionate-response-to-life view rather than response-to-literature, that *that* stance could be unfair, that envy from perceived disenfranchisement could be destructive to the innocently successful.

Much has been written about the green-eyed monster. "Sulfuric acid" it is. It shrink-wraps your soul. It feels like shit. It's ungenerous. It invites you to shirk responsibility for your choices, to look askance rather than keeping your eyes on your own prize. It assumes that you know the state of another's soul and fate. It negates your own.

Everyone experiences it.

Later in Vonnegut's life, after he'd had fame and fortune and been around others in that exalted boat the same length of time as he'd been poor, this line appears in *Hocus Pocus*:

> I agree with the great Socialist writer George Orwell, who felt that rich people were poor people with money.[511]

In 1997 he told a graduating class,

> We may never dissuade leaders of our nation or any other nation from responding vengefully, violently, to every insult or injury. . . . But in our personal lives, our inner lives, at least, we can learn to live without the sick excitement, without the kick of having scores to settle with this particular person, or that bunch of people, or that particular institution or race or nation. And we can then reasonably ask forgiveness for our trespasses, since we forgive those who trespass against us.[512]

Kurt Vonnegut struggled with depression. This did not come across in his lively, responsive teaching. I was unaware of it until I remarked to Andre Dubus's wife Pat how much I adored Vonnegut, and she replied, "Yes, but I wouldn't want to be married to him."

"Why not?" I asked.

"He's too depressed."

Then I pictured him at home writing *Slaughterhouse-Five*, burdened with that tale and the writing of it for years, along with family responsibilities of which I was then only dimly aware.

———

Dr. Nancy Andreasen at the University of Iowa Medical Center has spent her life investigating, in Vonnegut's words, "whether or not our neuroses were indistinguishable from those of the general population."

Kurt wrote in *Palm Sunday*:

> The psychiatric department of the University of Iowa's hospital . . . has taken advantage of the large numbers of reputable writers who come to Iowa City. . . . So they have questioned us about our mental health and about that of our ancestors and siblings, too. It is apparent to them, I am told, that . . . overwhelmingly, we are depressed, and are descended from those who, psychologically speaking, spent more time than anyone in his or her right mind would want to spend in gloom.[513]

If that is true, and I have grave doubts, then circumstances contribute. Here are some, in chronological order.

———

> Writing means working in solitude, sitting still day after day. Occasionally I say to myself, "This is a damn insult to life."[514]

Vonnegut told an interviewer, in regard to this physical drawback:

> My friend Vance Bourjaily worked up a scheme which makes sense to me. He wants to build an enormous type-writer keyboard with each key about the size of a dinner plate, and he would mount these keys on the wall of the study. Each morning he would get up, take a shower, eat Wheaties, Breakfast of Champions, and, in a sweatsuit and a pair of boxing gloves, he would spend all morning slugging these keys. He would lose weight, his blood would circulate beautifully, and he could eat a big lunch and feel in great shape. He proposed this as a joke, but it didn't seem very funny to him and it didn't seem very funny to me. I think one of us will build this gadget. [laugh][515]

Today lots of people suffer from sitting still day after day. What's more, we're using devices that don't involve much muscle. Try a manual typewriter, and you'll discover how engaged your shoulders, arms, and fingers must be!

If you're going to keep writing, without pain, you *must* tend to ergonomics.

Create an ergonomic workstation. Do all the things health experts suggest: get up and move often, stretch, exercise. Well-Being 101: take care of your bod.

In the short story "Unready to Wear," Kurt solves the human condition of physicality altogether. It starts:

> I just think it's a dirty shame what [human beings] have to do to take care of their bodies.[516]

Kurt hunched his long body over a typewriter on a low-set table, violating every basic rule of good posture.

———

As for being alone, Kurt wrote to José Donoso:

> I have met a lot of writers by now, and they all carry twenty
> acres of Sahara Desert with them wherever they go. I have
> no idea what the explanation for this is, other than the
> necessary smallness of their organizations.[517]

It is indeed a heavy weight to carry the entire vision and execution, all by yourself, of a long work of art that no one else sees
or quite understands for years on end.

In most other arts, the work is more communal or at least more
apparent. Dancers, actors, playwrights, architects, and musicians
interact. Visual artists' work, even in progress, can be readily
viewed, and to that extent, shared.

The flip side: the whole organization—including its lovely, protective privacy—is yours.

"I have been into films and plays and TV," Kurt wrote to Gail
Godwin in 1971, "and now understand that other people can't help
much with what I do. So it's back to books and stories."[518]

———

Uncertainty. Rejection. Those can certainly lend themselves to
making a person feel periodically down in the dumps.

In a 1951 letter to his friend Miller Harris, Kurt enclosed a *New
Yorker* rejection slip:

> Dear Miller:
>   I've had several hundred of these things bound into
> scratch pads.[519]

Here's a beauty from his archives:

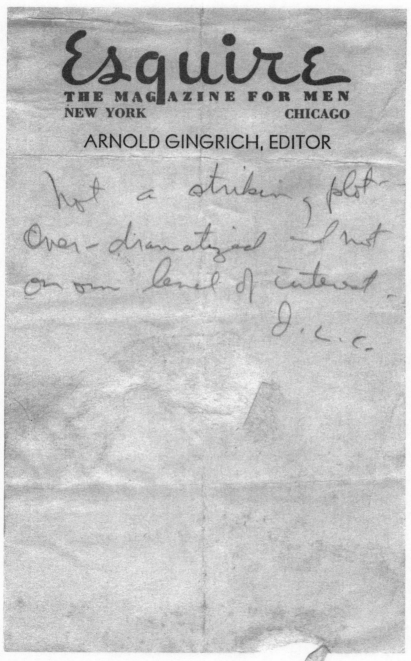

Rejection letter from *Esquire* magazine to Kurt
Vonnegut. Courtesy of the Lilly Library, Indiana
University, Bloomington, Indiana.

Even after a work is accepted, chances are it falls short of one's original vision. Vonnegut asked in the preface to *Breakfast of Champions.*

> What do I myself think of this particular book? I feel lousy about it, but I always feel lousy about my books. My friend Knox Burger said one time that a certain cumbersome novel ". . . read as though it had been written by Philboyd Studge." That's who I think I am when I write what I am seemingly programmed to write.

How did the beginning writer Vonnegut handle the pressure of sitting still, isolation, uncertainty, rejection, and economic difficulty?

In the winter of 1953 on Cape Cod, when things got too sticky, thirty-year-old Kurt wrote to his friend and champion Knox Burger in New York City and asked for help.

> Sport:
> Things are getting somewhat sticky with me mentally, and I would appreciate any words you might have picked up down there in the city with respect to treatment.
> The nut of the matter is that I can't write anymore, and I'm not very nice to my family anymore either. [. . .]
> [. . .] So, be a good chap, will you, and tell me if you ever knew anybody who got any good out of psychotherapy. Case histories of writers would be most to the point.
> Kurt[520]

Soon after, he wrote to Knox again:

> I had my eighty-foot driveway shoveled out by two

ten-year-olds so I could go have my head examined by a psychiatrist in S. Dennis. Are people supposed to keep stuff like that a secret?[521]

———

I myself appealed to Vonnegut, again, when my writerly spirits were in the abyss. After a year's abstinence while getting married, building a loft with my husband, and teaching, I'd returned to writing my novel in despair over any evidence of its worth. I sent Kurt a letter beseeching, "Don't give up on me." He replied:

228 E 48 10017 July 10 88

Dearest Suzanne --

   Give up on you? Never even considered it. You had a lot of native wisdom when I first met you. Now you've drunk deeply of life, and, my goodness, what a swell husband you got for yourself! You know how much I admired his knotted pipes. I am now astonished by what else he does. You'll wow him right back, Honeybunch, when you finish that book.

Love as always --

Letter from Kurt Vonnegut to Suzanne McConnell, July 10, 1988.
Courtesy of the author.

The word "depression" is often used for what might be called a siege of the blues. The mental illness called "depression" is quite another animal. It's a debilitating disease.

Vonnegut would wrestle throughout his life and writing with understanding mental illness, since he and so many family members—his mother, wife, son—were affected by it.

> Long before Mark [Vonnegut's son] went crazy, I thought mental illness was caused by chemicals, and said so in my stories. I've never in a story had an event or another person drive a character crazy. I thought madness had a chemical basis even when I was a boy, because a close friend of our family, a wise and kind and wryly sad man named Dr. Walter Bruetsch, who was head of the State's huge and scary hospital for the insane, used to say that his patients' problems were chemical, that little could be done for them until that chemistry was better understood.[522]

It took some time before Kurt comprehended that this idea of chemicals applied to his own states of mind. The *Playboy* interviewer, inquiring about his depression, asks, "Have drugs been a solution for you?"

> No—although I did get into the prescribed-amphetamines thing because I was sleeping a lot. . . . It's a common response to depression. I was taking these enormous naps and I decided it was a waste of time. So I talked to a doctor about it and she prescribed Ritalin. It worked. It really impressed me. I wasn't taking a whole lot of it, but it puzzled me so much that I could be depressed and just by taking this damn little thing about the size of a

pinhead, I would feel much better. I used to think that I was responding to Attica or to the mining of Haiphong. But I wasn't. I was obviously responding to internal chemistry. All I had to do was take one of those little pills. I've stopped, but I was so interested that my mood could be changed by a pill. . . .

Until recently, about every twenty days, I blew my cork. I thought for a long time that I had perfectly good reasons for these periodic blowups; I thought people around me had it coming to them. But only recently have I realized that this has been happening regularly since I've been six years old. There wasn't much the people around me could do about it. They could probably throw me off a day or so, but it was really a pretty steady schedule. . . . I've been going to a doctor once a week. It isn't psychoanalysis: It's a more superficial sort of thing. I'm talking to her about depression, trying to understand its nature. And an awful lot of it is physiological. In this book I've just finished, *Breakfast of Champions*, the motives of all the characters are explained in terms of body chemistry.[523]

In *Galápagos*, published twelve years later, set in a future after the environmental crisis has surpassed the breaking point, Vonnegut tackles brain chemistry again. This time the brain nearly becomes a character itself.

Just about every adult human being back then had a brain weighing about three kilograms! . . . This was a very innocent planet, except for those great big brains.[524]

To the credit of humanity as it used to be: More and more

people were saying that their brains were irresponsible, unreliable, hideously dangerous, wholly unrealistic—were simply no damn good.[525]

Apologies for momentary brain failures were the staple of everybody's conversations: "Whoops," "Excuse me," "I hope you're not hurt," "I can't believe I did that," "It happened so fast I didn't have time to think," "I have insurance against this kind of a thing," and "How can I ever forgive myself?" and "I didn't know it was loaded" and on and on.[526]

He shows our brains acting like a collective nincompoop. Cultural disasters result.

About that mystifying enthusiasm a million years ago for turning over as many human activities as possible to machinery: What could that have been but yet another acknowledgement by people that their brains were no damn good?[527]

His characters exhibit preposterous glitches in common sense. Mary Hepburn, once a biology teacher who'd believed that "the human brain was the most admirable survival device yet produced by evolution," is now tortured by her brain's urging her to commit suicide.[528]

[Private Geraldo Delgado] was only 18 years old, and was a paranoid schizophrenic. He should never have been issued live ammunition.

His big brain was telling him all sorts of things that were not true. . . . [He] thought his big problem was enemies with little radios.[529]

The narrator confesses that he often

received advice from my own big brain which, in terms of
my own survival, or the survival of the human race, for that
matter, can be charitably described as questionable.[530]

Kurt Vonnegut, *There Is a Ceiling*, June 8, 1980.
Courtesy of Nanette Vonnegut.

⎯⎯⎯

Researchers, by the way, have discovered that the human microbi-
ome—"the assemblage of microbes" that inhabit our body—functionally
act as another organ, and what's more, equal the brain in weight. Our
bugs rival our big brains' weight. Think of that![531]

⎯⎯⎯

Current investigators into the brain's mechanisms back up some of
Vonnegut's contributions on the subject. They've begun to pinpoint
the precise locations causing such mental states as depression and
bipolar disorder, and are discovering how to alleviate suffering,
sometimes by methods akin to rewiring.[532]

⎯⎯⎯

The body and mind are spectacular, but they can go temporarily
awry even if they are not diseased. Assistance, Vonnegut suggests
by example, is helpful. Because in any life, shit happens. The protagonist of *Hocus Pocus* says:

> This library is full of stories of supposed triumphs, which
> makes me very suspicious of it. It's misleading for people to
> read about great successes, since even for middle-class and
> upper-class white people, in my experience, failure is the
> norm. It is unfair to youngsters particularly to leave them
> wholly unprepared for monster screw-ups and starring
> roles in Keystone Kop comedies and much, much worse.[533]

"Did the experience of being interned—and bombed—in Dresden
change you in any way?" the *Playboy* interviewer asked.

No. I suppose you'd think so, because that's the cliché. The importance of Dresden in my life has been considerably exaggerated because my book about it became a best seller. If the book hadn't been a best seller, it would seem like a very minor experience in my life. And I don't think people's lives are changed by short-term events like that. Dresden was astonishing, but experiences can be astonishing without changing you.[534]

He would affirm later:

Being present at the destruction of Dresden has affected my character far less than the death of my mother, the adopting of my sister's children, the sudden realization that those children and my own were no longer dependent on me, the breakup of my marriage, and on and on.[535]

Indeed, shit happens to entire societies. Or to put it another way, entire societies make God-awful mistakes.

In an address to the American Psychiatric Association, Kurt comments:

Like most writers, I have at home the beginnings of many books which would not allow themselves to be written. . . . [One] was to be called *SS Psychiatrist*. This was about an MD who had been psychoanalyzed, and he was stationed at Auschwitz. His job was to treat the depression of those members of the staff who did not like what they were doing there. . . .

My point was, and maybe I can make it today without having to finish that book, that workers in the field of mental health at various times in different parts of the world must find themselves asked to make healthy people happier in cultures and societies which have gone insane.

Let me hasten to say that the situation in our own country is nowhere near that dire. The goal here right now, it seems to me, is to train intelligent, well-educated people to speak stupidly so that they can be more popular.[536]

When printed in *Fates Worse than Death*, Vonnegut introduced this address by saying it was given "at the time of the disgraceful Bush vs. Dukakis campaign for the Presidency of the United States of America." For a well-considered supposition of what he'd say now that we've Trumped ourselves, see *The Vonnegut Encyclopedia* author Marc Leeds's essay "What Would Kurt Vonnegut Think of Donald Trump?"[537]

———

Vonnegut offers a lot of wisdom on personal and societal addiction.

"Just because something feels better than anything else," [Boaz] said in his thoughts, "that don't mean it's good for you."[538]

The late British philosopher Bertrand Russell said he lost friends to one of three addictions: alcohol or religion or chess. Kilgore Trout was hooked on making idiosyncratic arrangements in horizontal lines, with ink. . . .

. . . Both my wives, Jane and now Jill, have said on occasion that I am much like Trout in that regard.

My mother was addicted to being rich, to servants and unlimited charge accounts, to giving lavish dinner parties, to taking frequent first-class trips to Europe. So one might say she was tormented by withdrawal symptoms all through the Great Depression.[539]

I am, of course, notoriously hooked on cigarettes. I keep

hoping the things will kill me. A fire at one end and a fool at the other.

But I'll tell you one thing: I once had a high that not even crack cocaine could match. That was when I got my first driver's license—look out, world, here comes Kurt Vonnegut!

And my car back then ... was powered, as are almost all means of transportation and other machinery today, and electric power plants and furnaces, by the most abused, addictive, and destructive drugs of all: fossil fuels.

... Here's what I think the truth is: we are all addicts of fossil fuels in a state of denial. And like so many addicts about to face cold turkey, our leaders are now committing violent crimes to get what little is left of what we're hooked on.[540]

What has been America's most nurturing contribution to the culture of this planet so far? Many would say jazz. I, who love jazz, will say this instead: Alcoholics Anonymous.

... The AA scheme ... is the first to have any measurable success in dealing with the tendency of some human beings, perhaps ten percent of any population sample anyone might care to choose, to become addicted to substances that give them brief spasms of pleasure but in the long term transmute their lives and the lives of those around them into ultimate ghastliness.

... I am persuaded that there are among us people who are tragically hooked on preparations for war.

... If Western Civilization were a person, we would be directing it to the nearest meeting of War Preparers Anonymous.[541]

In his address to the American Psychiatric Association, Vonnegut cited the research at the University of Iowa regarding writers' mental health, and drew this conclusion:

> Most of us, myself included, proved to be depressives from families of depressives.[542]
>
> From that study I extrapolate this rough rule, a very approximate rule, to be sure: You cannot be a good writer of serious fiction if you are not depressed.

Was Vonnegut joking? Or did he actually believe that because it was his own experience (i.e., was "methodologism" at work)? The evidence is he may have been tempted to believe it, but knew the logic was suspect. Because he also points out another such idea that's bit the dust:

> A rule we used to be able to extrapolate from cultural history, *one which doesn't seem to work anymore* [italics mine], is that an American writer had to be an alcoholic in order to win a Nobel Prize—Sinclair Lewis, Eugene O'Neill, John Steinbeck, the suicide Ernest Hemingway.[543]

The lore of alcohol as necessary creative fuel may have been tied to other cultural concepts, and perhaps male identity. It didn't seem to apply to women. After quitting drinking, Raymond Carver and other artistic recovering alcoholics debunked the myth of alcohol as the elixir of creativity. But this romantic fable dies hard.[544]

Likewise, the notion of madness and depression associated with creativity may be a cultural myth.

In 2014, forty-five years after Vonnegut was interviewed, Dr. Andreasen published an article in the *Atlantic Monthly* about her lifelong investigation of the creative brain, this time including scientists among her subjects.[545] She claims that higher rates of mental illness among creative people do occur, although admits that they share "a personality style" which may impact that assertion:

> They take risks. . . . They have to confront doubt and rejection. And yet they have to persist in spite of that, because they believe strongly in the value of what they do. This can lead to psychic pain, which may manifest itself as depression or anxiety, or lead people to attempt to reduce their discomfort by turning to pain relievers such as alcohol.

"Particularly in science," she writes, "the best work tends to occur in new frontiers. (As a popular saying among scientists goes: 'When you work at the cutting edge, you are likely to bleed.')"[546]

A comparable line appears among writers: "There's nothing to writing. All you have to do is sit down at a typewriter, open a vein, and bleed."

Which comes first? The chicken or the egg?

Wrangling at length and in depth over issues of concern—growing your soul—is not for the fainthearted. It demands quite a bit of balance to keep all the wheels spinning in any creative person's life. More, perhaps, than for most people.

I'm unconvinced that the creative are inherently more prone to mental illness than others. But if true, Dr. Andreasen offers booby prizes. She learned incidentally that "creative people work much harder than the average person—and usually that's because they love their work." Paradoxically, "though many of them suffer from mood and anxiety disorders, they associate their gifts with strong feelings of joy and excitement."[547]

Cleaving to the idea that creativity is coupled with mental illness is troubling. It behooves us to be well. Disease is dis-ease—neither fruitful nor romantic. As Vonnegut counseled in *Mother Night*:

> We are what we pretend to be, so we must be careful about what we pretend to be.

For daily well-being, here are three Vonnegut-based guidelines:
  First: Be compassionate to your mind-body, and to others'.

> "I can't help it," I said. "My soul knows my meat is doing
> bad things, and is embarrassed. But my meat just keeps
> right on doing bad, dumb things."
>   "Your what and your what?" he said.
>   "My soul and my meat," I said.
>   "They're separate?" he said.
>   "I sure hope they are," I said. I laughed. "I would hate
> to be responsible for what my meat does."
>   I told him, only half joking, about how I imagined the
> soul of each person, myself included, as being a sort of
> flexible neon tube inside. All the tube could do was receive
> news about what was happening with the meat, over which
> it had no control.[548]

Second: When in troubled waters, be sweet to yourself. Adopt
the self-nurturing embrace that Vonnegut's narrator in *Jailbird*,
recently released from prison, discovers.

> There was something odd about the position of my arms
> in my reflection. I pondered it. I appeared to be cradling a
> baby. And then I understood that this was harmonious with
> my mood, that I was actually carrying what little future I
> thought I had as though it were a baby. I showed the baby the
> tops of the Empire State Building and the Chrysler Building,
> the lions in front of the Public Library. I carried it into an
> entrance to Grand Central Station, where, if we tired of the
> city, we could buy a ticket to simply anywhere.[549]

Third: Practice the pause of appreciation.

Every graduation pep talk I've ever given has ended with words about my father's kid brother, Alex Vonnegut, a Harvard educated insurance agent in Indianapolis, who was well-read and wise.

. . . One of the things he found objectionable about human beings was that they so rarely noticed it when they were happy. He himself did his best to acknowledge it when times were sweet. We could be drinking lemonade in the shade of an apple tree in the summertime, and Uncle Alex would interrupt the conversation to say, "If this isn't nice, what is?"

So I hope that you will do the same for the rest of your lives. When things are going sweetly and peacefully, please pause a moment, and then say out loud, "If this isn't nice, what is?"[550]

CHAPTER 35

FARTING AROUND IN
LIFE AND ART

B esides counseling to take stock of dangers to one's health as a writer, Vonnegut provides some awfully good advice on how to maintain well-being.

Maintenance is, probably, the most important thing a person can do.

Think of the advice in the rest of this book as housekeeping tips for the body and soul, to ward off dust-devil demons like writer's block, the humdrums, and fear, and to keep your writerly and human engine humming.

How beautiful it is to get up and go out and do something. We are here on Earth to fart around. Don't let anybody tell you any different.[551]

Vonnegut liked to play tennis and was avid for Ping-Pong. He did the crossword puzzles, played chess, swam. He loved to have a good time. Whatever *you* like to do for a good time, do it.

Playing around in other arts is one of the most soul-replenishing, exhilarating ways to fart around. Banging on drums, shaping clay, acting—any art can revitalize you and your writing. And you may discover, as Vonnegut did, an avocation that allows another part of your soul self-expression.

Freedom from professional criticism—yours and others—is one reason doing other arts can be invigorating. It's humbling to be an amateur or a beginner, though, so in order to do it, you must insist on your right to be amateurish and a beginner.

"You've said that a problem for new performers is that they're competing with the best in the world," an interviewer said to Vonnegut.

> They are. That's dismaying, too. You take my home town of Indianapolis. We used to have our own boxers, our own wrestlers, our own songwriters, singers, and painters. Now it's all got to be from out of town. You think you're funny? You're not funny. We're going to get Bob Hope. . . .
>
> It makes life a lot less fun. I remember dancing. I was dancing with my first wife one time on Cape Cod and having a great time and some mean kid was playing the drums, and he said, "Man, you can really jitterbug," and he said it with a sneer, and I wanted to wade right in and beat the shit out of him. [Laughter] I didn't dance well enough for him, and he was going to deprive me of the joy of dancing.[552]

Kurt Vonnegut liked to work with his hands. He even proposed an article on it. (See opposite page.)

"The days my father got his hands dirty were happier days," his daughter Nanny recalls, than the usual ones, rat-a-tat-tat-ting on the typewriter.[553] Once Kurt chiseled the final words from Molly Bloom's soliloquy in Joyce's *Ulysses* into marble stepping-stones behind their Barnstable house (". . . yes, I said yes yes I will Yes."). He shoveled, built, carved.

In *Mother Night*, the despondent main character gets some of his mojo back that way:

> And then one day in 1958, after thirteen years of living

The READER'S DIGEST *Pleasantville, N.Y.*

Editors • DE WITT WALLACE • LILA ACHESON WALLACE

Executive Editor • KENNETH W. PAYNE

August 20, 1948

Dear Mr. Vonnegut:

The satisfaction of working with one's hands is a subject we have approached in several ways over the years, one of the most recent efforts being O. K. Armstrong's article, "Let Them Learn With Their Hands," in October, '47. It is a topic of timeless appeal, but I feel that this treatment does not contribute quite enough fresh material in the way of anecdotes or observations to warrant our using it. Many thanks, nonetheless, for the opportunity of reading it.

You may be sure that in the event of an opening on the staff, we shall be glad to keep your promising qualifications very much in mind.

With best wishes,

Sincerely yours,

[signature]

Mr. Kurt Vonnegut
Alplaus, New York

Letter from DeWitt Wallace to Kurt Vonnegut, August 20, 1948. Courtesy of the Lilly Library, Indiana University, Bloomington, Indiana.

like that [as a despondent recluse], I bought a war-surplus wood-carving set. . . .

When I got it home, I started to carve up my broom handle to no particular purpose. And it suddenly occurred to me to make a chess set.

I speak of suddenness here, because I was startled to

find myself with an enthusiasm. I was so enthusiastic that I carved for twelve hours straight, sank sharp tools into the palm of my left hand a dozen times, and still would not stop. I was an elated, gory mess when I was finished. I had a handsome set of chessmen to show for my labors.

And yet another strange impulse came upon me.

I felt compelled to show somebody, somebody still among the living, the marvelous thing I had made.

So, made boisterous by both creativity and drink, I went downstairs and banged on the door of my neighbor, not even knowing who my neighbor was.[554]

The neighbor turned out to be a painter. They played chess with the narrator's newly carved set right then, and every day for the next year.

Vonnegut farted around in class and on the page by doodling.

Vonnegut's incessant doodling found its way onto his published pages as illustrations, first in *Slaughterhouse-Five* and then in *Breakfast of Champions*.[555] Check out the nose on the left side of the page above the torso from this draft page from the early '60s. At a certain point he decided to take himself more seriously as an artist. In the 1980s, he drew on large pieces of acetate, and in 1993 he began collaborating with the artist Joe Petro II, who converted the drawings to silk-screened prints. What did he draw? Mainly faces.

"The human face is the most interesting of all forms," he told an interviewer. "Because that's how we go through life, reading faces very quickly."

Thirty were exhibited in 1983 in a one-man show at the Margo Feiden Gallery in New York. Another exhibition occurred there posthumously in 2014 to celebrate the publication of *Kurt Vonnegut's Drawings*, a beautiful book introduced and compiled by his daughter Nanny, and another took place in September 2015

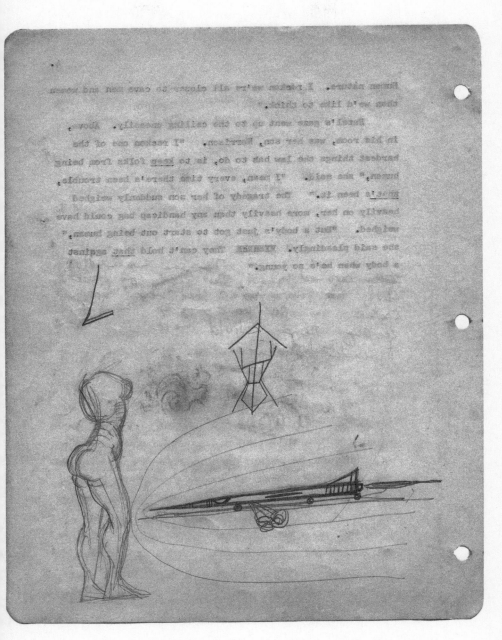

Doodle on draft of short story "Harrison Bergeron." Courtesy of the Lilly Library, Indiana University, Bloomington, Indiana.

at the Herbert F. Johnson Museum of Art at Cornell University. His equipment? Colored felt tip pens.

"Oil is such a commitment," he said.[556]

What do they look like? Realistic? Not on your life. They're whimsical, sometimes a little horrifying. Surprise!

Intriguingly, in light of Vonnegut's graphs of plots, Peter Reed says in *Kurt Vonnegut's Drawings*, "When I watched Vonnegut draw, he began with a vertical line, and then a horizontal one. It was almost as if he were about to draw a graph."[557] Maybe Vonnegut approached faces as plots.

In 2017, the National Veterans Art Museum in Chicago, which houses more than 2,500 works by veterans, acquired thirty-one of Vonnegut's screen prints, on exhibit from January to May of that year.[558]

While at the Writers' Workshop, a painter classmate gave me Henry Miller's small book *To Paint Is to Love Again*, in which he waxes exuberantly upon the sheer pleasure of mucking around with color and in another art. "Every artist worth his salt has his [hobby]," he wrote. "It's the norm, not the exception."[559] The creators of the workshop were wise to the value of exploring other mediums: the MFA *required* taking another art.

All the arts involve the creative process. Yet each is distinct. Besides just giving you a kick, delving into another form's practice can give you a kick in the butt, a shockingly fresh view, and insight. You are yourself no matter what medium you use, as Vonnegut's drawings evidence.

Vonnegut, like Miller, turned to painting when the writing wasn't going well, in order for the well to fill again, especially while wrangling with his last novels, *Hocus Pocus* and *Timequake*. Writing itself is labor, the reward coming with completion, Vonnegut said, whereas the painter "gets his rocks off while actually doing the painting."[560]

Vance Bourjaily invited workshop people to jam sessions in his studio at the Bourjailys' Red Bird Farm. Kurt would bring his clarinet. Vance would be on his trumpet. Vance confessed one night at such a session that if he were really good at it, he'd prefer to be a trumpeter.

"Virtually every writer I know would rather be a musician," Kurt wrote, years later. "Because music gives pleasure as we never can."[561]

Perhaps he underestimated the pleasure people get from words. As with painting, though, playing music is immediate and physical.

In New York, Kurt occasionally jammed with Woody Allen at Allen's Dixieland pub gig. His friend and lawyer, Don Farber, said Vonnegut was a "remarkably skilled" musician. "Not many people knew he played a mean piano too."[562]

Mark Vonnegut remarked offhandedly that his father was even better on the piano than on the clarinet, as he was showing me around his house, filled with his own paintings, furniture he'd made, and a piano we were passing. All Vonnegut's children embraced their father's belief in the arts. Dabblers as well as serious artists, each is devoted to one form and investigates others. I once attended a terrific musical in Barnstable that Edie Vonnegut—first and foremost a painter—wrote, directed, acted in, and, I believe, costumed. When Vonnegut exhorts that making art is good for the soul, there is nothing more convincing of his sincerity than the legacy he provided his own brood.

"Since I took up carpentry," Mark the pediatrician avows, "I measure children much more carefully, sometimes to 1/32 of an inch."[563]

A former student at Iowa, Dick Cummins, recalls the last class of his first semester with Vonnegut, expecting a final exam:

It was January and . . . the wind was whipping a fine powder of snow around the door of our Quonset [hut]. . . . At a quarter past the door flew open and [Vonnegut] strode in, snow swirling behind him. He pushed the door closed with his foot and put the purple box and the 78-record sheath he was cradling down on the desk. We could see it was a child's portable phonograph as he unclipped the hinged side speakers. Without making eye contact he untied the chin laces that lashed down the thick ear flaps of his Chinese Communist infantry winter cap, slapping off the snow against his desk. Then, sliding a 78 record out of the dust cover he wriggled it onto the spindle and spun the volume knob all the way up. Finally, he lifted the tone arm up and lowered it onto the record. There was a nickel Scotch-taped to the top to keep it from skipping.

. . . "If you want to make a living as a writer you'll have to top this!" he shouted over the blaring phonograph. Pressing the fur cap down hard against his head, he escaped back out into the snow, leaving the door open. It was the 1812 Overture, turned so loud it rattled and buzzed the speakers.

Finally a fellow named Herb in the front row reached over and turned it off.

On the way out into the storm we grumbled about what kind of grade we could possibly get.

. . . When we checked our grades at the beginning of the second semester, it turned out Vonnegut had given us all As.[564]

No matter how corrupt, greedy, and heartless our government, our corporations, our media, and our religious and charitable institutions may become, the music will still be wonderful.[565]

So too will be the sublime act of going out and farting around in any of the arts.

CHAPTER 36

LOVE, MARRIAGE, AND BABY CARRIAGE

Jane Vonnegut and Maria Pilar Donoso (the writer José Donoso's wife) were standing on the sidewalk one day having an intense conversation outside where I lived in Iowa City, Black's Gaslight Village, adjacent to the Vonneguts'. When I came across them, I paused. They explained they were discussing men and marriage. Jane declared, "The thing is, you can't live with them, and you can't live without them."

This encounter jarred my youthful inclination to deem being married a more enviable state than being single. The truth is, each has advantages and disadvantages.

But if you're going to "live with them," and you're a writer or an artist, Vonnegut offers some wisdom and examples.

———

Advice on choosing a partner serves as the epigraph of *Palm Sunday*.

> Whoever entertains liberal views and chooses a consort that is captured by superstition risks his liberty and his happiness.

It's taken

from a thin book, *Instruction in Morals*, published in 1900

353

and written by my Free Thinker great-grandfather Clemens
Vonnegut, then seventy-six years old.[566]

If you're a writer or an artist—besides picking someone who's somewhere in the same ballpark on fundamental issues, as this quote suggests, and all the other considerations in marrying—you need a partner who, at the very least, respects what you do, and at best actively
supports it, in whatever ways that may mean to you. Kurt Vonnegut
was married twice, to two very different women at two very different
times in his life. Both, though in distinct ways, fortified him as a writer.

Kurt and Jane Cox met in kindergarten. As Dan Wakefield notes
in his introduction to Vonnegut's *Letters*, not only was it a wife's duty,
pre–women's lib, to be the housekeeper and children's caretaker, but a
writer's wife was expected to serve as the equivalent of a combination
editorial assistant and public relations expert. Jane graduated Phi
Beta Kappa from Swarthmore. She thought her husband a genius.
She did all she could to support him, except his typing.

If she had not been willing to risk the economic precariousness
he took in quitting GE to become a full-time writer, or to take on
the primary care of raising not only their three children but their
adopted nephews, Kurt's writing would likely have been derailed.
Certainly, he wouldn't have been able to carve out the protected
time she enabled him to have. They built his career together, something he "readily acknowledged."[567]

Kurt and Jill Krementz met in 1971 as his and Jane's marriage was
foundering and he was on the crest of fame. They married in 1979.
Nearly two decades younger, an ambitious photographer already
well known and established in New York, as Kurt's wife, Jill continued her commitment to her own career, but also arranged and fielded
his social commitments and kept the calendar going. Her captivating
portraits of him enhanced his book jackets and other publicity. They
adopted a child, Lily, and so again, Vonnegut became a parent.

I never knew a writer's wife who wasn't beautiful.[568]

I stayed with Kurt and Jane on Cape Cod in 1969, and I remember Jane pausing, as she swept through the living room gathering up whatever didn't belong in it on her way out to the garage to drive to Boston to take one of the kids shopping, to tell me her theory of housekeeping. It's the Swiss-cheese idea, she explained: deal with any "hole" you come across as you come across it.

Jane Vonnegut, Barnstable Bay, Massachusetts, 1969.
Photo by the author.

One of my own theories about marriage is a roommate idea: a huge part of marriage entails working out the same kinds of things you'd work out with a roommate. Your spouse *is* your roommate. It's useful to separate "roommate" problems from other issues. That's what Kurt's doing in his contract epistle to Jane (see chapter 1).

My mates have often been angered by how much attention I pay to paper and how little attention I pay to them.

I can only reply that the secret to success in every human endeavor is total concentration. Ask any great athlete.

To be fair to his mates, and honest, he adds:

To put it another way: Sometimes I don't consider myself very good at life, so I hide in my profession.

But to be fair to himself as a writer, he then adds:

I know what Delilah really did to Samson to make him as weak as a baby. She didn't have to cut his hair off. All she had to do was break his concentration.[569]

Kurt Vonnegut had a separate study on Cape Cod and New York in which to write. If you don't, you can find privacy via public spaces that protect you from domestic interference, such as coffee shops, writers' rooms, libraries. Even with a room of your own, people can open the door, look over your shoulder, interrupt. But no one is a mind reader. Setting the parameters of your working needs is up to you. Let your mate—your roommate— know what those are. Here's when consideration for your work is truly put to the test: during the process, in the most mundane everyday way.[570]

"I have had some experiences with love, or think I have, anyway," Vonnegut writes in his 1976 introduction to *Slapstick*,

> although the ones I have liked best could easily be described as "common decency." I treated somebody well for a little while, or maybe even for a tremendously long time, and that person treated me well in turn. Love need not have had anything to do with it.
>
> Also: I cannot distinguish between the love I have for people and the love I have for dogs.
>
> Love is where you find it. I think it is foolish to go looking for it, and I think it can often be poisonous.
>
> I wish that people who are conventionally supposed to love each other would say to each other, when they fight, "Please—a little less love, and a little more common decency."
>
> My longest experience with common decency, surely, has been with my older brother, my only brother, Bernard, who is an atmospheric scientist in the State University of New York at Albany.

Even in Vonnegut's unpublished first novel "Basic Training," he questions assumptions about "love" covering all the complexities of a relationship. The General—who went away to war when his daughter was a baby, so they haven't had "much time to get to know each other"—says to her,

> "You don't like me because you think I'm a bully, that it's fun for me to push other people around."
>
> "Noooo," objected Hope, tearfully. "I love you, Daddy, really I do."
>
> "Don't doubt it. Never did. That's an entirely different matter."[571]

In *Bluebeard*, his characters discuss what it means to be *in* love:

> "People think we're in love," I said to her on a walk one day.
>   And she said, "They're right."
> "You know what I mean," I said.
> "What do you think love is anyway?" she said.
> "I guess I don't know," I said.
> "You know the best part—" she said, "walking around like this and feeling good about everything. If you missed the rest of it, I certainly wouldn't cry for you."[572]

Often Vonnegut depicts the roles society has traditionally shaped for men and women, and shows how they affect marriage. They also affect writers.

In *Galápagos*, just as a guy who's terrified of dogs is proposing marriage, one comes out barking. The man dashes up a tree. He's treed for an hour. As a result, he tells the woman:

> I am not a man. I am simply not a man. I will of course never bother you again. I will never bother any woman ever again.[573]

In *Hocus Pocus*, the narrator, home from the Vietnam War, complains about his wife and mother-in-law:

> That mother-daughter team treated me like some sort of boring but necessary electrical appliance like a vacuum cleaner.[574]

In *Player Piano*, the wife is trying to stand her ground with two men. One retorts that if she doesn't show more respect for men's privacy, he'll design a machine that's everything you are and *does* show respect. . . . Stainless steel, covered with sponge rubber, and heated electrically to 98.6 degrees.[575]

Patty Keene [in *Breakfast of Champions*] was stupid on purpose, which was the case with most women in Midland City. The women all had big minds . . . but they did not use them much for this reason: unusual ideas could make enemies, and the women, if they were going to achieve any sort of comfort and safety, needed all the friends they could get.

So, in the interests of survival, they trained themselves to be agreeing machines instead of thinking machines.[576]

In *Cat's Cradle*, the narrator and Mona have just performed the forbidden rite of boko-maru:

"I don't want you to do it with anybody but me from now on," I declared. . . .

"As your husband, I'll want all your love for myself." . . .

She was still on the floor, and I, now with my shoes and socks back on, was standing. I felt very tall, though I'm not very tall; and I felt very strong, though I'm not very strong; and I was a respectful stranger to my own voice. My voice had a metallic authority that was new.

As I went on talking in ball-peen tones, it dawned on me what was happening, what was happening already. I was already starting to rule.[577]

Marriage has been abolished since the year 23,011 in *Galápagos*, Vonnegut's next-to-last novel. The narrator reveals why the institution had been so problematic:

What made marriage so difficult back then was yet again that instigator of so many other sorts of heartbreak: the oversize brain. That cumbersome computer could hold so many contradictory opinions on so many different subjects all at once, and switch from one opinion or subject to another one so quickly, that a discussion between a husband and wife under stress could end up like a fight between blindfolded people wearing roller skates.[578]

If Mandarax [a translation machine] were still around, it would have had mostly unpleasant things to say about matrimony, such as:

Marriage: a community consisting of a master, a mistress and two slaves, making in all, two.

Ambrose Bierce (1842–?)[579]

Even blissful coupling can have a downside, Vonnegut shows. The double-agent narrator in *Mother Night* considers writing a play about that called *Das Reich der Zwei*—"Nation of Two."

It was going to be about the love my wife and I had for each other. It was going to show how a pair of lovers in a world gone mad could survive by being loyal only to a nation composed of themselves—a nation of two. . . .

. . . Good Lord—as youngsters play their parts in political tragedies with casts of billions, uncritical love is the only real treasure they can look for.

Das Reich der Zwei, the nation of two my Helga and I had . . . didn't go much beyond the bounds of our great double bed. . . .

Oh, how we clung, my Helga and I—how *mindlessly* we clung!

We didn't listen to each other's words. We heard only the melodies in our voices.[580]

Buried in each other's arms, they avoid responding to the world or even to the fuller reality of each other.

━━━∿━━━

Here's Vonnegut's wisdom on divorce, straight from the horse's mouth:

I'm to love my neighbor? How can I do that when I'm not even speaking to my wife and kids today? My wife [Jill] said to me the other day, after a knock-down-drag-out fight about interior decoration, "I don't love you anymore." And I said to her, "So what else is new?" She really didn't love me then, which was perfectly normal. She will love me some other time—I think, I hope. It's possible.

If she had wanted to terminate the marriage, to carry it past the point of no return, she would have had to say, "I don't *respect* you anymore." Now—that would be terminal.

One of the many unnecessary American catastrophes going on right now . . . is all the people who are getting divorced because they don't love each other anymore. That is like trading in a car when the ashtrays are full. When you don't *respect* your mate anymore—that's when the transmission is shot and there's a crack in the engine block. . . .

"Ye shall respect one another." Now there is something almost anybody in reasonable mental health can do day after day, year in and year out, come one, come all, to everyone's clear benefit.[581]

━━━∿━━━

But although they divorced, he and Jane never lost respect for each other.

Several weeks after giving birth for the first time at the age of thirty-nine, my stepdaughter remarked in her wonderfully understated way, "It gives a whole new meaning to full-time job."

In *Bluebeard*, the characters discuss art and family life.

> "I always wanted to be an artist," I said.
> "You never told me that," she said.
> "I didn't think it was possible," I said. "Now I do."
> "Too late—and much too risky for a family man. Wake up!" she said. "Why can't you just be happy with a nice family? Everybody else is."[582]

In *Palm Sunday*, Vonnegut says:

> I would actually like to have "The Class of '57" [a country hit about ordinary people's dreams and lives] become our national anthem for a little while. Many people have said that we [my generation] already have an anthem, which is my friend Allen Ginsberg's "Howl". . . . I like "Howl" a lot. Who wouldn't? It just doesn't have much to do with me or what happened to my friends. . . .
> Also, and again I intend no offense, the most meaningful and often harrowing adventures which I and many like me have experienced have had to do with the rearing of children. "Howl" does not deal with such adventures.[583]

"Meaningful" and "harrowing." Parenting is life changing. It's as demanding as anything can possibly be. Artists and writers are often notoriously poor parents. If you decide to parent, do so with your eyes wide open. Parenting, too, is an art.

"My mother and father," Mark Vonnegut wrote, "at the ripe old age of thirty-five, struggling financially (ten years prior to

Slaughterhouse-Five), took on four more children, two dogs, and a rabbit. Whatever else good or bad my parents did or didn't do with the rest of their lives, that was absolutely the right thing to do."[584]

As Vonnegut says, through his character Constant in *The Sirens of Titan*,

> A purpose of human life . . . is to love whoever is around to be loved.[585]

———

Doing the right thing can cost you.

A stew of factors led to the demise of Kurt and Jane's twenty-five-year-plus marriage. One, though, may have been the strain of loving, in practice, so many children over so many years.

———

What kind of a father was Kurt Vonnegut? A 1982 reminiscence from his eldest daughter, Edie, offers a glimpse:

> When I was sixteen and taking a lot of liberties, I decided to start calling my father "Junior." Just "Junior." "Uh, may I please have a ride to Hyannis, Junior?" I never got punished for this transgression; in fact, it was never even remarked on. He simply responded to the name as though nothing were different. I don't think he exactly thrilled to this new familiarity. It was not an appropriate name for a father, especially such a tall father. Junior had a diminutive ring to it. He never objected to it, though. I thought it was funny and meant it affectionately. It made him my size somehow. I think the reason I felt free to reduce him like this was because of something that happened when I was twelve. I remember being all confused about life and

God and all, and I asked him what was going on, thinking he'd know, being older and a father, and what he said was my first big revelation. He said that in the grand scheme of things we were scarcely older than each other. From our point of view there seemed to be a colossal difference, but in the bigger picture he was perhaps half a second ahead of me, if that . . . and that we were both experiencing the same things at the same time for the first time. Like our dog dying was a first for both of us. That he had no more of a handle on things than I did. This was really news to me. I thought it was just a matter of time before he let me in on what he knew. Ever since then I've seen him as a sort of peer and buddy, and a plain ordinary person trying to sort things out in the dark, just like me. I appreciate that, and admire that he didn't play the wise role. It's made me consider him a human being before a father. It also let me know full blast at a very early age that I was on my own as far as figuring things out went. I consider this all the Truth and am grateful for it. . . . Hence, Junior. . . . Since then he has formally dropped the Junior from his name, with a lot of philosophy behind it. I wonder if he wasn't just plain sick of his daughter calling him Junior all the time. I don't call him Junior anymore. I call him Dad. Though inside I'm mightily tempted to call him Junior, or Scooter or Butch or something very fond and funny and familiar. Maybe Fuzzy or Ducky.[586]

CHAPTER 37
BeTTeR TogeTHeR
oR COMMUNITy

Who cares more about writing than other writers? Your mates, family, and friends may care about you, but if writing is not their passion, you can't expect them to care about writing itself, or your particular writing, nearly as much as fellow writers will.

At lunch with Kurt and Jill soon after they returned from the Galápagos, where Kurt had been doing research for his novel of the same name, I asked how they enjoyed the trip. Kurt responded with enthusiasm, Jill not so much. Kurt remarked that it was nice of Jill to accompany him at all, since it wasn't her thing.

It's unfair to expect friends or your partner to always like what you like, let alone be your right hand as editor or coach. Therefore, your community of writers, however loose, may be the most valuable tool of all for buoying your writerly spirit and practice.

Communities are very comforting to human beings.[587]

Until recent times, you know, human beings usually had a permanent community of relatives. They had dozens of homes to go to. So when a married couple had a fight, one or the other could go to a house three doors down and stay with a close relative until he was feeling tender again. Or

> if a kid got fed up . . . he could march over to his uncle's for a while. And this is no longer possible. Each family is locked into its little box.[588]

> Artists of different kinds constitute a sort of extended family. . . . Artists usually understand one another fairly well, without anybody's having to explain much.[589]

———

Kurt Vonnegut learned the value of a communal extended family as a kid, in the summertime around a lake in northern Indiana, where his father and his father's sister and brother jointly owned a cottage.

> There were lots of Vonneguts in the phone book [in Indianapolis]. . . . And at Lake Maxinkuckee . . . I was surrounded by relatives all of the time. You know, cousins, uncles and aunts. It was heaven.[590]

If he got lost,

> The closed loop of the lakeshore was certain to bring me home not only to my own family's unheated frame cottage on a bluff overlooking the lake, but to four adjacent cottages teeming with close relatives. The heads of those neighboring households, moreover, my father's generation, had also spent their childhood summertimes at Lake Maxinkuckee.[591]

It was to that cottage he took his bride, just after being discharged from the army, on their honeymoon. By then, it had already been sold to a stranger.

Today, due to a man with a "love of local history" who, fittingly, gathered a community of like-minded investors to rescue the cottage from a developer's demolition in 2012, it stands, according to the rental website, as "a spiritual restoration of the cottage culture the Vonneguts enjoyed."[592] You can enjoy it yourself. Minus the relatives, of course.

———

Vonnegut's anthropological studies further influenced his ideas about communities, validated by his 1970 trip to war-torn Biafra. He reported:

> General Ojukwu gave us a clue, I think, as to why the Biafrans were able to endure so much so long without bitterness: They all had the emotional and spiritual strength that an enormous family can give. . . . [The general's family] was three thousand members strong. He knew every member of it by face, by name, and by reputation.
> A more typical Biafran family might consist of a few hundred souls. . . . The families took care of their own . . .
> The families were rooted in land. . . .
> Families met often, men and women alike, to vote on family matters.[593]

Vonnegut insinuates that such a survival mechanism, though in extremis for the Biafrans, should be adapted insofar as possible, simply for well-being.

The benefits of belonging and the sad lack of it pop up throughout Vonnegut's work. Minor characters often exhibit a longing for kinship, or show what a blessing even a fragile makeshift community can be. In *Breakfast of Champions*, for example, Kilgore Trout takes a ride with a truck driver.

> The driver . . . said it was hard for him to maintain friendships that meant anything because he was on the road most of the time. . . .

He suggested that Trout, since Trout was in the combination aluminum storm window and screen business, had opportunities to build many lasting friendships in the course of his work. "I mean," he said, "you get men working together day after day, putting up those windows, they get to know each other pretty well."

"I work alone," said Trout.

... "All the same," he insisted, "you've got buddies you see after work. You have a few beers. You play some cards. You have some laughs."

Trout shrugged.

"You walk down the same streets every day," the driver told him. "You know a lot of people, and they know you, because it's the same streets for you, day after day. You say, 'Hello,' and they say 'Hello,' back. You call them by name. They call you by name. If you're in a real jam, they'll help you, because you're one of 'em. You *belong*. They see you every day."[594]

Just out of prison, the narrator in *Jailbird* approaches a coffee shop his first morning, feeling so old and ugly that he's fearful everyone will be nauseated by him.

But I somehow found the courage to go in anyway—and imagine my surprise! It was as though I had died and gone to heaven! A waitress said to me, "Honeybunch, you sit right down, and I'll bring you your coffee right away." I hadn't said anything to her.

So I did sit down, and everywhere I looked I saw customers of every description being received with love. To the waitress everybody was "honeybunch" and "darling" and "dear." It was like an emergency ward after a great catastrophe. It did not matter what race or class the victims belonged to. They were all given the same miracle drug, which was coffee. The catastrophe in this case, of course, was that the sun had come up again.[595]

"Is there some way our country could encourage the growth of extended families?" a *Playboy* interviewer asked Vonnegut.

> By law. I'm writing a Kilgore Trout story about that right now. . . .
> . . . So the President happens to visit Nigeria, where extended families have been the style since the beginning of time. . . . So the President is going to have the computers of the Social Security Administration assign everybody thousands of relatives.[596]

The assigned-relatives conceit sprouted from a Trout story into a major framework for Vonnegut's novel *Slapstick*, subtitled *Lonesome No More*. In it, the would-be president campaigns on that platform:

> I spoke of American loneliness. It was the only subject I needed for victory, which was lucky. It was the only subject I had.
> It was a shame, I said, that I had not come along earlier in American history with my simple and workable anti-loneliness plan. I said that all the damaging excesses of Americans in the past were motivated by loneliness rather than a fondness for sin.
> An old man crawled up to me afterwards and told me how he used to buy life insurance and mutual funds and household appliances and automobiles and so on, not because he liked them or needed them, but because the salesman seemed to promise to be his relative, and so on.
> "I had no relatives and I needed relatives," he said.

"Everybody does," I said.

He told me he had been a drunk for a while, trying to make relatives out of people in bars. "The bartender would be kind of a father, you know—" he said. "And then all of a sudden it was closing time."

"I know," I said. I told him a half-truth about myself which had proved to be popular on the campaign trail. "I used to be so lonesome," I said, "that the only person I could share my innermost thoughts with was a horse named 'Budweiser.'"[597]

"If you get elected . . . what if I get some artificial relative I absolutely can't stand?"

"What is so novel about a person's having a relative he can't stand?" I asked him. . . .

. . . In all my years of public life, I had never said an off-color thing to the American people.

So it was terrifically effective when I at last spoke coarsely. . . .

"Mr. Grasso," I said, "I personally will be very disappointed, if you do not say to artificial relatives you hate, after I am elected, 'Brother or Sister or Cousin,' as the case may be, 'why don't you take a flying fuck at a rolling doughnut? Why don't you take a flying fuck at the moooooooooooooon?'"[598]

In *Jailbird* the character Cleveland Lawes—who has endured family ravages at the hands of the KKK—is befriended by a Chinese classmate at Harvard who "persuaded him to come to China instead of going back home to Georgia when the war was over."

And he worked for two years, as I say, as a deckhand on the Yellow Sea. He said that he fell in love several times, but that nobody would fall in love with him.

"So that was what brought you back?" I asked.

He said it was the church music more than anything else. "There wasn't anybody to sing with over there," he said. "And the food," he said.

"The food wasn't any good?" I said.

"Oh, it was good," he said. "It just wasn't the kind of food I like to talk about."

"Um," I said.

"You can't just eat food," he said. "You've got to talk about it, too. And you've got to talk about it to somebody who understands that kind of food."[599]

Whether by profession, personal history, purpose, or whatever, Vonnegut points out myriad ways in which we group ourselves so that, metaphorically, we're with "somebody who understands that kind of food."

There was nothing new about artificial extended families in America. Physicians felt themselves related to other physicians, lawyers to lawyers, writers to writers, athletes to athletes, politicians to politicians, and so on.[600]

"The people I am most eager to have news of, curiously enough," Vonnegut confided,

are those I worked with in the General News Bureau of the General Electric Company in Schenectady, New York—from 1948 to 1951, from the time I was twenty-six until I was twenty-nine....

I have heard other people say that they, too, remain irrationally fond of those who were with them when they were just starting out. It's a common thing.

In Charlottesville to give a speech at the University of Virginia one year, he got a note from a former Indianapolis next-door neighbor.

> But the best part of that visit was finding out what had happened to a childhood playmate of mine. . . .
> We refreshed our memories about neighborhood dogs we had known, dogs which had known us, too.[601]

A helpful thing to do, when you're feeling lonely and unsupported, is to list the groups in which you are both purposely and accidentally a part, from your biological relatives, neighbors, and friends to the people who go to your yoga class or get a coffee at the same time you do at your local Starbucks, and so on. And don't forget the pets you know.

> How did Americans beat the Great Depression? We banded together. In those days, members of unions called each other "brother" and "sister," and they meant it.[602]

After Donald Trump's inauguration, citizen calls to the Capitol switchboard surpassed any in US history for three days, from January 31 to February 2, jamming it.[603] An estimated 470,000 people showed up in Washington, DC, for the Women's March, one out of every one hundred Americans marched in towns all across America, and sister marches occurred worldwide.[604] His election galvanized people to join organizations to protect civil liberties, the environment, women's reproductive rights, immigrants' rights, and many others. Attendance at town hall meetings and citizens' groups soared, as did petitions and calls to Congress.

In crisis, people team up for a common cause. Whether personal or political.

But I am surely a great admirer of Alcoholics Anonymous, and Gamblers Anonymous, and Cocaine Freaks Anonymous, and Shoppers Anonymous, and Gluttons Anonymous, and on and on . . . since they give to Americans something as essential to health as vitamin C, something so many of us do not have in this particular civilization: an extended family.[605]

. . . [These groups are] very close to a blood brotherhood, because everybody has endured the same catastrophe. And one of the enchanting aspects . . . is that many people join who *aren't* drunks [or whatever the addiction is] . . . because the social and spiritual benefits are so large.[606]

Writers, too, have similar sob stories to offer one another, as well as ambitions, inspiration, tips, and chicken soup. They exchange work in progress to get feedback and help from their peers. They socialize. They organize, as in PEN, to ensure free speech and freedom of the press, and to assist threatened writers worldwide.

The military—a crisis-oriented, purposeful organization composed of people dislocated from their homes—utilizes the human need for association. This is how Kurt Vonnegut Jr. and Bernard O'Hare (mentioned in *Slaughterhouse-Five*) became friends:

The Army had instituted what it called the "Buddy System." Every Private or PFC was told to pick somebody else in his squad to know about and care about, since nobody else was going to do that. The show of concern had to be reciprocal, of course, and nobody was to be left a bachelor. . . . So O'Hare and I got hitched, so to speak.

It worked. He and O'Hare were selected to be battalion intelligence scouts. O'Hare had been trained how to sneak ahead of combat lines to check out the enemy. Vonnegut had not.

> I never told anybody but O'Hare about my lack of Infantry training, since somebody might have decided that I'd better have some. . . . Besides, *I didn't want to leave O'Hare* [italics mine].[607]

They endured combat, capture, and the bombing of Dresden together. They remained in touch for the rest of their lives.

Vonnegut's praise for communities as bastions of support is equaled by his criticism of their drawbacks. The human inclination to be part of a group can be poisonous, he warns.

> And here, according to Trout, was the reason human beings could not reject ideas because they were bad: "Ideas on Earth were badges of friendship or enmity. Their content did not matter. Friends agreed with friends, in order to express friendliness. Enemies disagreed with enemies, in order to express enmity.
>
> ". . . Agreements went on, not for the sake of common sense or decency or self-preservation, but for friendliness.
>
> "Earthlings went on being friendly, when they should have been thinking instead. . . . So they were doomed."[608]

Communities by definition are exclusive. Somebody or some class of person belongs, and somebody else doesn't. Taken to extremes, Vonnegut says through his fictional narrator in *Breakfast of Champions*, that can be lethal.

The Vietnam War couldn't have gone on as long as it did, certainly, if it hadn't been human nature to regard persons I didn't know and didn't care to know, even if they were in agony, as insignificant. A few human beings have struggled against this most natural of tendencies, and have expressed pity for unhappy strangers. But, as History shows, as History yells: "They have never been numerous!"[609]

Vonnegut's anthropology professors pointed out adverse aspects of the tight-knit societies they studied.

First of all, a Folk Society was isolated, and in an area it considered organically its own. It grew from that soil and no other. . . . There was such general agreement as to what life was all about and how people should behave in every conceivable situation that very little was debatable.

. . . Dr. Redfield denounced sentimentality about life in Folk Societies, saying they were hell for anyone with a lively imagination or an insatiable curiosity or a need to experiment and invent—or with an irrepressible sense of the ridiculous.[610]

Anyone like Kurt Vonnegut, for example.

A vitamin or mineral deficiency always has bad effects. A Folk Society deficiency (hereafter "FSD") quite often does. The trouble begins when a person suffering from FSD stops thinking, in order to become a member of an artificial extended family which happens to be crazy. The homicidal "family" of Charles Manson springs to mind. Or . . . the cult of the Reverend Jim Jones.[611]

In spite of what his big brain knew about the liabilities of folk societies, Vonnegut confessed:

> But I still find myself daydreaming of an isolated little gang of like-minded people in a temperate climate, in a clearing in a woodland near a lake.[612]

He sought communities all his life.

> Whenever I'm alone in a motel in a big city, I look up Vonneguts and Liebers [his mother's maiden name] in the telephone book.[613]

An eager young Kurt Vonnegut Jr. at Cornell University is depicted sitting on the floor next to his future wife, front row and center, in a fraternity portrait photograph.

When he and Jane moved to Iowa City, they joined the local country club, seeking to be part of the community. I waitressed, one year, at that country club. I can't imagine them feeling fulfilled as members there. And it didn't work out. People weren't very welcoming, he told me later, so they quit. They were to find a richer, more compatible community in the faculty and students at the Writers' Workshop.

Vonnegut loved the theater for its communal liveliness. On Cape Cod, he participated actively in local theater as well as the local library, and later, he delved in and out of playwriting. In one short story, a director invites a stranger to try out for a part, a beautiful woman who travels from place to place teaching employees how to use a new billing machine, who "seemed kind of numb, almost a machine herself."

> She looked surprised, and she warmed up a little. "You know," she said, "that's the first time anybody ever asked me to participate in any community thing."

"Well," I said, "there isn't any other way to get to know
a lot of nice people faster than to be in a play with 'em."[614]

———

Perhaps the most complex aim Vonnegut takes in crystallizing our
propensity for like-minded groups is this concoction in *Cat's Cradle*:

> Karass: "a team, one of many that humanity is organized
> into in order to do God's will (without ever discovering
> what they are doing)."[615]

The lack of *awareness* of being part of such a team separates the
members of a "karass" from those of all other groups. To emphasize
that vital distinction, Vonnegut conjured up another word:

> Hazel's obsession with Hoosiers around the world was
> a textbook example of a false *karass*, of a seeming team
> that was meaningless in terms of the ways God gets things
> done, a textbook example of what Bokonon calls a *gran-*
> *falloon*. Other examples of *granfalloons* are the Communist
> party, the Daughters of the American Revolution, the
> General Electric Company, the International Order of Odd
> Fellows—and any nation, anytime, anywhere.[616]

These "granfaloons" may be meaningless in terms of the way
"God gets things done," but as Vonnegut shows, however tongue-
in-cheek, they're meaningful to their members' sense of well-being.
Vonnegut's cockamamie-sounding concepts serve up the whole
platter of pros and cons of community.

———

Readers tend to misuse the word "karass," I've noticed when

teaching *Cat's Cradle*, perversely inverting it, as is the human penchant, into a recognizable, affinity-minded group: "You're in my karass!" someone might exclaim, meaning a fellow Vonnegut aficionado.

Google "karass" and you'll find several redefinitions. Some lean toward the fellow-traveler notion, others restate Vonnegut's original definition in other words. Some indicate that the word derives from similar-sounding words (alas, see chapter 21 again). All this is understandable, endearing. I've been told even Kurt misused it! We all so want to make sense of the world and be in community.

But identifying who is in your karass contradicts the definition. Teammates of a karass don't know that they are teammates. They are acting out *God's* mysterious, unfathomable will. Not their own.

Here's what the fictional guru and karass-creator Bokonon says about it:

> "If you find your life tangled up with somebody else's life for no very logical reasons," writes Bokonon, "that person may be a member of your *karass*."
>
> ... "Man created the checkerboard; God created the *karass*." ... A *karass* ignores national, institutional, occupational, familial, and class boundaries.
>
> It is as free-form as an amoeba.[617]

———

> Because of the sorts of minds we were given at birth, and in spite of their disorderliness, [my brother] Bernard and I belong to artificial extended families which allow us to claim relatives all over the world.[618]

Bernard belonged to the artificial extended family of scientists. Kurt belonged to the artificial extended family of writers.

If you're a writer, so do you. Vonnegut's advice? Make the most of it.

~

Vonnegut went to science fiction writers' conventions when he was starting out.[619]

He became a very active member of PEN, the international writers' organization, when he moved to New York. He first met his close friend Sidney Offit at a PEN seminar in 1970.

> I think [every writer] ought to join this group. I don't care if the person is a fascist or a member of the Klan—if the person's a writer, he belongs in PEN.[620]

It's doubtful that a fascist or a Klan member would want to join, given its mandate: "PEN America stands at the intersection of literature and human rights to protect open expression in the United States and worldwide."

In my inbox today appeared this subject line: "Dear Writers, You Are Not Alone" from *Poets & Writers Magazine*.

In this twenty-first century, ways for writers to connect abound—classes, magazines, websites, blogs, Facebook, conferences, residencies, workrooms, readings, organizations, and peer writing groups.

~

In 1951, slogging it out by himself, Vonnegut wrote to his friend Miller Harris:

> Dear Miller:
> Thought, rather fuzzily, about something I want to add to my recent letter to you. . . . At the instigation of a bright and neurotic instructor named Slotkin [in the anthropology

department at the University of Chicago], I got interested in the notion of the school. . . .

. . . What Slotkin said was this: no man who achieved greatness in the arts operated by himself; he was top man in a group of like-minded individuals. This works out fine for the cubists, and Slotkin had plenty of good evidence for its applying to Goethe, Thoreau, Hemingway, and just about anybody you care to name.

If it isn't 100% true, it's true enough to be interesting—and maybe helpful.

The school gives a man, Slotkin said, the fantastic amount of guts it takes to add to culture. It gives him morale, esprit de corps, the resources of many brains, and—maybe most important—one-sidedness with assurance. . . .

Slotkin also said a person in the arts can't help but belong to some school—good or bad. I don't know what school you belong to. My school is presently comprised of Littauer & Wilkinson (my agents), and Burger, and nobody else. . . .

. . . It isn't a question of finding a Messiah, but of a group's creating one—and it's hard work, and takes a while.

If this sort of thing is going on somewhere (not in Paris, says Tennessee Williams), I'd love to get in on it.[621]

Describing Jackson Pollock for *Esquire* years later, Vonnegut observed:

He was unique among founders of important art movements, in that his colleagues and followers did not lay on paint as he did. . . . Pollock did not animate a school of dribblers. He was the only one. . . . What bonded Pollock's particular family was not agreement as to what, generally, a picture should look like. Its members were unanimous, though, as to where inspiration should come from: the unconscious, that part of the mind which was lively, but which caught no likenesses, had no morals or politics, and had no tired old stories to tell yet again.[622]

The musician Brian Eno coined the word "scenius" to describe the kind of thing Kurt was getting at in his letter to Harris: "Scenius stands for the intelligence and the intuition of a whole cultural scene. It is the communal form of the concept of the genius." In other words, "Scenius is like genius, only embedded in a scene rather than in genes. . . . The extreme creativity that groups, places or 'scenes' can occasionally generate."[623]

Whether or not you have the good fortune to be part of a rarified school, like the Surrealists or the Beats, you can't help being part of a group as an artist or writer, as Vonnegut's professor said, delineated by similar sensibilities—such as the magical realists or the black humorists or the eco-fabulists, or broadly by genre, race, gender, region, nation, etc. Therefore, consider following the young Vonnegut's inclination: embrace the designations within which your work seems to fall, cleave to those with which you have an affinity, and thereby empower yourself.

> And anyone who has finished a book, whether the thing has been published or not, whether the thing is any good or not, is a colleague of ours.[624]

Vonnegut replied to a grateful first-time novelist, who had thanked him for being an inspiration:

> The fact that you have completed a work of fiction of which you are proud, which you made as good as you could, makes you as close a blood relative as my brother Bernard.[625]

Kurt was generous to other writers. He championed and encouraged. He was as good as a good relative.[626]

Go forth and be that, too.

And *thank* those who give you support. Acknowledgment is powerful.

———

Kurt told us once in class a definition of heaven and hell he'd heard somewhere that had charmed him:

In hell everyone is chained to a dining table laden with food, each trying but unable to eat. In heaven, it's exactly the same. Except in heaven, the people are feeding each other.

———

I invite you to join Kurt Vonnegut's awesome congregation.

WORSHIP

> I don't know about you,
> but I practice a disorganized religion.
> I belong to an unholy disorder.
> We call ourselves,
> "Our Lady of Perpetual Astonishment."
> You may have seen us praying
> for love
> on sidewalks outside the better
> eating establishments
> in all kinds of weather.
> Blow us a kiss
> upon arriving or departing
> and we will climax
> simultaneously.

It can be quite a scene,
especially if it is raining
cats and dogs.[627]

Consider practicing Vonnegut's holy and wholly fictional Bokonist ritual of boko-maru, two by two, while sole to sole, reciting its litany to one another. It begins:

"Gott mate mutt," crooned Dr. von Koenigswald.
"Dyot meet mat," echoed "Papa" Monzano.
"God made mud," was what they'd said, each in his own dialect. I will here abandon the dialects of the litany.
"God got lonesome," said Von Koenigswald.
"God got lonesome."
"So God said to some of the mud, 'Sit up!'"
"So God said to some of the mud, 'Sit up!'"
"'See all I've made,' said God, 'the hills, the sea, the sky, the stars.'"
"'See all I've made,' said God, 'the hills, the sea, the sky, the stars.'"
"And I was some of the mud that got to sit up and look around."
"And I was some of the mud that got to sit up and look around."
"Lucky me, lucky mud."
"Lucky me, lucky mud."[628]

ACKNOWLEDGMENTS

It takes a village.

First, I would like to thank Dan Wakefield for offering me the opportunity to compose this book and for his support whenever I've asked. I'm thankful to the late Don Farber, formerly head of the Vonnegut Trust, and Arthur Klebanoff of RosettaBooks for entrusting me by contract to do it, and Julia Whitehead of the Vonnegut Memorial Library for introducing me to Dan Simon, editorial director and publisher of Seven Stories Press.

I am grateful to both my publishers. I so appreciate the courtesy and ready communication of Arthur Klebanoff throughout the process and his immediate enthusiasm upon reading the completed manuscript. I am hugely thankful for Dan Simon's kind but firm editorial and publishing guidance, our lively exchanges, and his simpatico sensibility. I am grateful for the patience of both while I toiled far past the original deadline to realize an expanded vision of this book.

My thanks to the entire team at Seven Stories Press, particularly Lauren Hooker for her editorial and copyediting expertise, Victoria Nebolsin for contributing to those efforts, Ruth Weiner for informing me about and implementing the publicity process, Anastasia Damaskou for her assistance in that, and Stewart Cauley for his splendid design talent.

Next, my inexpressible gratitude to the members of my peer fiction writing group—Naomi Chase, Edith Konecky, Joan Leibowitz, Carole Rosenthal, NancyKay Shapiro, Diane Simmons, and Meredith Sue Willis—for their reliable community, unstinting enthusiasm, and frank feedback. Thank you for keeping me on target and buoyant as audience to my drafts during the four-year haul.

Special thanks to Carole Rosenthal, who insisted I drop everything else I was engaged in when Kurt Vonnegut died, in order to write about him while I was in mourning and overflowing with feeling. Thanks to Professor Gary Schmidgall for posting the resulting memoir on his Hunter Faculty website, Donald Breckenridge at the *Brooklyn Rail* for publishing it a few years later, and Zachary Petit for printing an excerpt in *Writer's Digest*: all turned out to be stepping-stones to this book.

Thanks to Mark Vonnegut, Edith Squibb Vonnegut, and Nanette Vonnegut, each of whom have generously allowed me reprint and reproduction permissions and have lent me their trust in this project. Thanks to Edie and Nanny for showing me their paintings, many of family members. I am forever indebted to Edie for including me in her father's memorial service, and for many summers of friendship, to Mark for graciously giving me a tour of his house that included personal treasures of and from his father and for his terrific book, *Just Like Someone Without Mental Illness Only More So*, which I called upon in this one, and to Nanny for her responsive communication and for preserving her father's artwork in *Kurt Vonnegut Drawings* and her memories of him in its foreword, from which I borrowed.

I am in debt to several librarians, notably Isabel Planton at the Lilly Library, Indiana University, for assisting me on my time-pressed visit to Vonnegut's archive, overseeing reproductions of his manuscripts, and for alerting me to the Granfalloon conference celebrating Vonnegut's work at Indiana University and introducing me to Ed Comantale, its director. Thanks to others at the Lilly who helped: Zachary Downey, Emily Grover, Jody Mitchell, Joe McManis, and especially Sarah McElroy Mitchell, whose determined search uncovered a much-needed original in the archive. Thanks to Squirrel C. Walsh at the Rare Books and Special Collections, Princeton University; to Franziska Schmor at the Stiftbibliothek in St. Gallen;

Eisha Neeley at the Carl A. Kroch Library, Cornell University; and Mike Perkins at the Indianapolis Public Library.

Thanks to experts on Vonnegut whose books and brains I've drawn upon, including Jerome Klinkowitz in conversation; Dan Wakefield's compilation of Vonnegut's letters and speeches in *Letters* and *If This Isn't Nice, What Is?*; Gregory Sumner's *Unstuck in Time*; Charles Shields's biography, *And So It Goes*, and his generosity in sharing quotes of Vonnegut's about writing and teaching that he hadn't used; and especially to Rodney Allen for his anthology *Conversations with Kurt Vonnegut*, which I replied upon heavily.

Thanks to fellow students of Vonnegut's whose invaluable recollections of him as a teacher enlarge my own portrayal, and often gave me a nostalgic laugh: Dick Cummins, John Casey, Dan Gleason, Gail Godwin, Barry Jay Kaplan, John Irving, Robert Lehrman, David Milch, Ronni Sandroff, and Jim Siegelman.

Thanks to Kurt's best friend Sidney Offit for a delightful afternoon, the gift of his book, and his marvelous tales about Kurt.

So many friends bestowed support in so many ways. Rhoda Waller counseled emphatically that the writing of this book was my unique political/humanitarian contribution, and not to bemoan greater activism post-Trump while buried in the writing of it, and sent me Gail Mazur's poem as comfort. Longtime friends Deborah McKay, Nicki Edson, and Skip Renker read early chapters and spurred me on. I am indebted to Leon Friedman for his singular contribution and generosity in providing legal expertise, and to his wife, Gail Marks, for conveying messages and encouragement. Marshall Smith offered his memoir of Kurt, and Charlie Rosarius provided translations from the German. Special thanks to Barry Jay Kaplan, whose phone number Kurt urged on me when I first arrived in the Big Apple in 1974, a close comrade in the writing trade ever since and the first reader of the complete manuscript, who sent comments and a magnanimous thumbs-up.

Thanks to acquaintances and friends who came my way with tips, information, insight, and support: Bob Atwan, Matt Bardin,

Rhonda Coulet, Arthur Diamond, Richard DiLallo, Susan DiLallo, Anita Feldman, Joy Fraser, Janis Graham, Nancy Green, John Hinant, David Hoppe, Axel Jablonsky, Sarah Jackson, Jeffery Laudenslager, John Laudenslager, John Luster, Ed McCann, Christiane Meyer-Stoll, Risa Mickenberg, Adam Murray, Scott Oglesby, Mo Ogrodnik, Carl Orstendorf, Richard Perry, Harriet Reisen, Debra Goldsmith Robb, Terrence Ross, Carolyn Steinhoff, Ann Stoney, Janet Sullivan, Marion St. Onge, Andrea Stappert, Patrick Strezlick, David Ulin, Steven Watson, Mimi Wheeler, Stephen White, Dorothea Zwirner, and Rudolf Zwirner.

I'm grateful to Julia Cameron for writing *The Artist's Way*, which I read long before writing this book, and which I believe helped lead me to it.

To my enormous sorrow, three people with whom I spent some remarkable hours talking about Vonnegut as I worked on this book have passed away and will not see their contributions: Ivan Chermayeff, Louise DeSalvo, and Frank Preuss.

My gratitude to Sam Strezlick and Christine Rousu for revealing their tattoos of Vonnegut's words and sharing the stories behind them, and also to Thais Miller, Joseph Shipley, Scott Sears, Joshua Weber, and the young employees at the Kurt Vonnegut Museum and Library, plus my dear grandson Conrad Wurzburg, all of whom jolted me into comprehending how much Vonnegut's work is cherished down the generations.

Thanks to loved ones for my three Vonnegut mugs, some notecards, and a "St. Vonnegut" candle, reminding me daily of the swag surrounding his legacy.

Special thanks to Charity Coleman, who assisted me early on in the daunting task of sorting the passages I'd marked in Vonnegut paperbacks into their digital equivalents and arranging them into the framework that would eventually become the chapters of this book; to Peter Tighe for his masterful massaging of pinched muscles and tissue from all my cutting, pasting, and indenting; to Joe Spallone for his superb physical therapy, which enabled me to go on; and to Cindy Hinant, my husband's studio manager, who, along with him, has been a sounding board throughout the writing of this book, and who came to my rescue in finalizing the endnotes, bibliography, and illustrations, with her eagle eye for precision and her incredible patience.

Thanks to my sister Judianne White, my loyal champion, for her ready support, only a dial away. Thanks to my longtime painter friend Karen Gunderson, my writing cheerleader supreme from the time we met at the University of Iowa, then pioneered Tribeca as roommates, to the present. Thanks to my stepdaughter, Nanette Kuehn, and son-in-law, Robert Wurzburg, for their constancy and affirmation, and to all the rest of my family—McConnells, Kuehns, Kanevskis, Schumakers, Chastains, Lauritsens, Frasers, Magics, and Cypherts—who have my back, especially my niece Angela, who shared special Vonnegut writing moments with me some years ago.

I am ever grateful to my husband, Gary Kuehn, consummate artist, for sumptuous meals, steadfast financial and artistic support, and for being my soul mate and teammate. I couldn't have done this without you.

And thanks most of all to Kurt Vonnegut, up in Heaven now, whose presence I've felt from the beginning of this project, for illuminating me.

PERMISSIONS

Permission for all quotes from Kurt Vonnegut's letters, books, articles, interviews and papers courtesy of the Trust u/w of Kurt Vonnegut, Jr.

Tim Youd, Kurt Vonnegut's *Breakfast of Champions*. Courtesy of the artist and Christin Tierney Gallery, New York.

Drafts of *Sirens of Titan*, drafts of *Slaughterhouse-Five*, diagrams from "Fluctuations Between Good and Ill Fortune in Simple Tales," drafts of *Cat's Cradle*, *Collier*'s rejection letter to Kurt Vonnegut, rejection letter from *Esquire* magazine to Kurt Vonnegut, letter from DeWitt Wallace to Kurt Vonnegut, doodle on draft of short story "Harrison Bergeron," and "How to Write with Style." Courtesy of the Lilly Library, Indiana University, Bloomington Indiana.

Letter from Kurt Vonnegut Sr. to Kurt Vonnegut Jr. Courtesy of the Vonnegut family.

Letter from Kurt Vonnegut to José Donoso. Courtesy of the Department of Rare Books and Special Collections, Princeton University, Princeton, New Jersey.

Gary Kuehn, *Practitioner's Delight*. Courtesy of the artist.

Kurt Vonnegut Jr. teaching a class in the Quonset huts at the Iowa Writers' Workshop, 1966. Courtesy of Robert Lehrman. Photo: John Zielinski.

Kurt Vonnegut, "There Is a Ceiling," June 8, 1980, from *Kurt Vonnegut Drawings*. Courtesy of Nanette Vonnegut.

BIBLIOGRAPHY

WORKS BY KURT VONNEGUT

Vonnegut, Kurt. *Armageddon in Retrospect*. New York: G. P. Putnam's Sons, 2008.

Vonnegut, Kurt. *Bagombo Snuff Box: Uncollected Short Fiction*. New York: G. P. Putnam's Sons, 1999.

Vonnegut, Kurt. *Between Time and Timbuktu: or, Prometheus-5, A Space Fantasy*. New York: Dell Publishing, 1972.

Vonnegut, Kurt. *Bluebeard*. New York: Delacorte Press, 1987.

Vonnegut, Kurt. *Breakfast of Champions*. New York: Delacorte Press, 1973.

Vonnegut, Kurt. *Cat's Cradle*. New York: Delacorte Press, 1963.

Vonnegut, Kurt. *Deadeye Dick*. New York: Delacorte Press, 1982.

Vonnegut, Kurt. "Despite Tough Guys, Life Is Not the Only School for Real Novelists." *New York Times*, May 24, 1999.

Vonnegut, Kurt. *Fates Worse than Death*. New York: G. P. Putnam's Sons, 1991.

Vonnegut, Kurt. *Galápagos*. New York: Delacorte Press, 1985.

Vonnegut, Kurt. *God Bless You, Mr. Rosewater or Pearls Before Swine*. New York: Delacorte Press, 1965.

Vonnegut, Kurt. *Hocus Pocus*. New York: G. P. Putnam's Sons, 1990.

Vonnegut, Kurt. *If This Isn't Nice, What Is?: Advice to the Young—The Graduation Speeches*. Edited by Dan Wakefield. New York: Seven Stories, 2014.

Vonnegut, Kurt. *Jailbird*. New York: Delacorte Press, 1979.

Vonnegut, Kurt. "Kurt Vonnegut at NYU." Radio broadcast of lecture, New York University. November 6, 1970. Pacifica Radio Archives, 1970. Copy of reel-to-reel tape, 40 minutes. https://www.pacificaradioarchives.org/recording/bc1568.

Vonnegut, Kurt. *The Last Interview and Other Conversations*. Edited by Tom McCartan. Brooklyn: Melville House Publishing, 2011.

Vonnegut, Kurt. *Letters*. Edited by Dan Wakefield. New York: Delacorte Press, 2012.

Vonnegut, Kurt, and Lee Stringer. *Like Shaking Hands with God: A Conversation About Writing*. New York: Seven Stories Press, 1999.

Vonnegut, Kurt. *Look At the Birdie: Unpublished Short Fiction*. New York: Delacorte Press, 2009.

Vonnegut, Kurt. *A Man without a Country*. New York: Seven Stories Press, 2005.

Vonnegut, Kurt. *Mother Night*. New York: Harper and Row, 1961.

Vonnegut, Kurt. "Mythologies of North American Indian Nativistic Cults." Master's thesis, University of Chicago, 1947.

Vonnegut, Kurt. *Palm Sunday*. New York: Delacorte Press, 1981.

Vonnegut, Kurt. Papers. Lilly Library, Indiana University, Bloomington.

Vonnegut, Kurt. *Player Piano*. New York: Delacorte Press, 1952.

Vonnegut, Kurt. "Poems Written During the First Five Months of 2005." Unpublished manuscript, 2005.

Vonnegut, Kurt. "The Salon Interview: Kurt Vonnegut." By Frank Houston. *Salon*, October 8, 1999. https://www.salon.com/1999/10/08/vonnegut_interview.

Vonnegut, Kurt. *The Sirens of Titan*. New York: Delacorte Press, 1959.

Vonnegut, Kurt. *Slapstick*. New York: Delacorte Press, 1976.

Vonnegut, Kurt. *Slaughterhouse-Five*. New York: Delacorte Press, 1969.

Vonnegut, Kurt, and Ivan Chermayeff. *Sun Moon Star*. London: Hutchinson, 1980.

Vonnegut, Kurt. *Timequake*. New York: G. P. Putnam's Sons, 1997.

Vonnegut, Kurt. *Wampeters, Foma & Granfalloons*. New York: Delacorte Press, 1974.

Vonnegut, Kurt. *We Are What We Pretend to Be*. New York: Vanguard Press, 2012.

Vonnegut, Kurt. *Welcome to the Monkey House*. New York: Delacorte Press, 1968.

OTHERS

Allen, William Rodney, ed. *Conversations with Kurt Vonnegut*. Jackson: University Press of Mississippi, 1988.

Andreasen, Nancy C. "Secrets of the Creative Brain." *Atlantic*, July/August 2014.

Arts Midwest. "NEA Big Read." https://www.artsmidwest.org/programs/neabigread.

Bambara, Toni Cade. "My Man Bovanne." In *Gorilla, My Love*. New York: Random House, 1972.

Bauby, Jean-Dominique. *The Diving Bell and the Butterfly*. New York: Knopf, 1997.

Becher, Jonathan. "Gladwell vs Vonnegut on Change Specialists." *Forbes*, October 14, 2014. https://www.forbes.com/sites/sap/2014/10/14/gladwell-vs-vonnegut-on-change-specialists/#c445b4d46f7d.

Belluck, Pam. "For Better Social Skills, Scientists Recommend a Little Chekhov." *New York Times*, October 3, 2013.

Benedict, Helen. *Sand Queen*. New York: Soho Press, 2012.

Blakeslee, Steve. "The Man from Slaughterhouse-Five: A Remembrance of Kurt Vonnegut." *Open Spaces: Views from the Northwest* 9, no. 3 (2007).

Blaser, Martin J. *Missing Microbes*. New York: Henry Holt and Company, 2014.

Bourjaily, Vance. "Dear Hualing." In *A Community of Writers: Paul Engle and the Iowa Writers' Workshop*, edited by Robert Dana. Iowa City: University of Iowa Press, 1999.

Bradshaw, Tom, and Bonnie Nichols. *Reading at Risk: A Survey of Literary Reading in America*. Washington: National Endowment for the Arts, June 2004. https://www.arts.gov/sites/default/files/ReadingAtRisk.pdf.

Buonarroti, Michelangelo. "To Giovanni da Pistoia When the Author Was Painting the Vault of the Sistine Chapel." Translated by Gail Mazur. In *Zeppo's First Wife: New and Selected Poems* by Gail Mazur. Chicago: University of Chicago Press, 2013.

Cadenhead, Rogers. "How to Join Kurt Vonnegut's Family." *Workbench* (blog). August 16, 2010. http://watchingthewatchers.org/read/3631.

Cameron, Julie. *The Artist's Way: A Spiritual Path to Higher Creativity.* New York: G. P. Putnam's Sons, 1992.

Céline, Louis-Ferdinand. *Journey to the End of the Night.* Translated by Ralph Manheim. New York: New Directions, 2006.

Cloud, John. "Inherit the Wind." *Time*, April 18, 2011.

Cottonwood Gulch Expeditions website, http://www.cottonwoodgulch.org.

Cunningham, M. Allen. "Rethinking Restriction: Creative Limitation as a Positive Force." *Poets & Writers*, January/February 2014.

Cunningham, Michael. "Found in Translation." *New York Times*, October 2, 2010. http://www.nytimes.com/2010/10/03/opinion/03cunningham.html.

Darrow, Barb. "Turns Out Attendance at Women's March Events Was Bigger Than Estimated." *Fortune*, July 23, 2017. http://fortune.com/2017/01/23/womens-march-crowd-estimates.

Davies, Alex. "I Rode 500 Miles in a Self-Driving Car and Saw the Future. It's Delightfully Dull." *Wired*, January 7, 2015. https://www.wired.com/2015/01/rode-500-miles-self-driving-car-saw-future-boring.

De Botton, Alain. "The True Hard Work of Love and Relationships." *On Being*, August 2, 2018. http://onbeing.org/programs/alain-de-botton-the-true-hard-work-of-love-and-relationships/#.WKOB5sF5Nvw.email.

DeSalvo, Louise. *Writing as a Way of Healing: How Telling Our Stories Transforms Our Lives.* Boston: Beacon Press, 2000.

Donoso, José. Papers. Department of Rare Books and Special Collections, Princeton University.

Elbow, Peter. *Writing Without Teachers.* New York: Oxford University Press, 1973.

Ely, Jeffrey, Alexander Frankel, and Emir Kamenia. "The Mathematics of Suspense." *New York Times*, April 26, 2015.

"Embattled: The Ramifications of War." Special issue, *Bellevue Literary Review* 15, no. 2 (Fall 2015).

Finch, Nigel, dir. *Kurt Vonnegut: So It Goes.* Aired 1983. Princeton: Films for the Humanities and Sciences, 2002. DVD, 63 minutes.

Godwin, Gail. "Waltzing with the Black Crayon." *Yale Review* 87, no. 1 (January 1999).

Goldberg, Natalie. *Writing Down the Bones: Freeing the Writer Within.* Boulder: Shambhala, 2016.

Goodstein, Laurie. "Serenity Prayer Stirs Up Doubt: Who Wrote It?" *New York Times*, July 11, 2008. https://www.nytimes.com/2008/07/11/us/11prayer.html.

Hemingway, Ernest. "The Art of Fiction No. 21." By George Plimpton. *Paris Review*, no. 18, Spring 1958.

Hemingway, Ernest. "The Killers." In *The Snows of Kilimanjaro and Other Stories.* New York: Charles Scribner's Sons, 1927.

Holsen, Laura. "Donald Trump Jr. Is His Own Kind of Trump." *New York Times*, March 18, 2017. https://www.nytimes.com/2017/03/18/stayle/ donald-trump-jr-business-politics-hunting-twitter-vanessa-haydon.html.

Hotchner, A. E. *Papa Hemingway*. New York: Random House, 1955.

Huber, Johannes, Ernst Tremp, and Karl Schmuki. *The Abbey Library of Saint Gall*. Translated by Jenifer Horlent. St. Gallen: Verlag am Klosterhof, 2007.

Humphreys, Josephine. Review of *The Collected Stories*, by John McGahern. *New York Times*, February 28, 1993.

"Indiana War Memorial Museum." Indiana State Official Government Website. Accessed November 20, 2018. https://www.in.gov/iwm.

Iowa Writers' Workshop. *Word by Word*. Iowa City: University of Iowa Printing and Mailing Services, 2011.

Jamison, Leslie. "Does Recovery Kill Great Writing?" *New York Times Magazine*, March 13, 2018.

Jung, C. G. "Christ, a Symbol of the Self." In *The Collected Works of C.G. Jung: Complete Digital Edition Vol. 9. Part II: Aion: Researches into the Phenomenology of Self*. Translated by R. F. C. Hull. Princeton: Princeton University Press, 1959. https://the-eye.eu/public/concen.org/Princeton%20Jung/9.2%20Aion_ Researches%20into%20the%20Phenomenology%20of%20the%20Self%20 %20(Collected%20Works%20of%20C.%20G.%20Jung%20Volume%209,%20 Part%202).pdf.

Kelly, Kevin. "Scenius, or Communal Genius." *The Technium* (blog). KK.org, June 10, 2008. https://kk.org/thetechnium/scenius-or-comm/.

Klinkowitz, Jerome. *Kurt Vonnegut's America*. Columbia: University of South Carolina Press, 2009.

Klinkowitz, Jerome. *The Vonnegut Statement*. New York: Doubleday, 1973.

Krementz, Jill, ed. *Happy Birthday, Kurt Vonnegut: A Festschrift for Kurt Vonnegut on His Sixtieth Birthday*. New York: Delacorte Press, 1982.

"Kurt Vonnegut: In His Own Words." *London Times*, April 12, 2007. https:// www.thetimes.co.uk/article/kurt-vonnegut-in-his-own-words-mccg7vog8cg.

Leegant, Joan. "Sisters of Mercy." *Bellevue Literary Review* 11, no. 2 (Spring 2011).

Lehrman, Robert. "The Political Speechwriter's Life." *New York Times*, November 3, 2012. https://opinionator.blogs.nytimes.com/2012/11/03/ the-political-speechwriters-life.

Levy, Ariel. "Catherine Opie, All-American Subversive." *New Yorker*, March 13, 2017. https://www.newyorker.com/magazine/2017/03/13/ catherine-opie-all-american-subversive.

"Literature and Medicine." Maine Humanities Council. Accessed November 20, 2018. http://mainehumanities.org/program/ literature-medicine-humanities-at-the-heart-of-healthcare/.

McConnell, Suzanne. "Book." *Per Contra*, no. 22 (Spring 2011), http://percontra. net/archive/22mcconnell.htm.

McConnell, Suzanne. "Do Lord." In *Fence of Earth*. *Hamilton Review*, no. 11 (Spring 2007). http://www.hamiltonstone.org/hsr11fiction.html#dolord.

McConnell, Suzanne. "Kurt Vonnegut at the Writers' Workshop." *Brooklyn Rail*, December 10, 2011. https://brooklynrail.org/2011/12/fiction/ kurt-vonnegut-at-the-writers-workshop.

McConnell, Suzanne. "Spirit, You Know the Way." *Cape Women Magazine*, 2002.

McConnell, Suzanne. "The Disposal." *Fiddlehead*, no. 110 (Summer 1976).

McPhee, Larkin, dir. *Depression: Out of the Shadows*. 2008; Twin Cities Public Television, Inc. and WGBH Boston for PBS. http://www.pbs.org/wgbh/ takeonestep/depression/.

Merleau-Ponty, Maurice. *Sense and Non-Sense*. Translated by Hubert L. Dreyfus and Patricia Allen Dreyfus. Evanston: Northwestern University Press, 1964.

Miller, Henry. "To Paint Is to Love Again." New York: Grossman, 1968.

Moore, Ed, dir. *Ride the Tiger: A Guide Through the Bipolar Brain*. 2016; Detroit: Detroit Public Television. http://www.pbs.org/ride-the-tiger/home/.

Neubauer, Alexander, ed. *Conversations on Writing Fiction: Interviews with 13 Distinguished Teaches of Fiction Writing in America*. New York: Harper Collins, 1994.

Morris, David J. "After PTSD, More Trauma." *New York Times*, January 17, 2015.

Offit, Sidney. "The Library of America Interviews Sidney Offit About Kurt Vonnegut." By Rich Kelley. *The Library of America e-Newsletter*. New York: Library of America, 2011. https://loa-shared.s3.amazonaws.com/static/pdf/ LOA_Offit_on_Vonnegut.pdf.

O'Neil, Chuck, dir. *The Daily Show with Jon Stewart*. Season 10, episode 115, "Kurt Vonnegut." Aired September 13, 2005, on Comedy Central.

Paley, Grace. "Distance." In *Enormous Changes at the Last Minute*. New York: Farrar, Straus and Giroux, 1985.

Paul, Annie Murphey. "Your Brain on Fiction." *New York Times*, March 17, 2012.

Perrin, Andrew. "Book Reading." Pew Research Center, September 2016. http:// www.pewinternet.org/2016/09/01/book-reading-2016.

Pinchefsky, Carol. "Wizard Oil." *Orson Scott Card's InterGalactic Medicine Show*, December 2006. http://www.intergalacticmedicineshow.com/cgi-bin/mag. cgi?do=columns&vol=carol_pinchefsky&article=015.

Popova, Maria. "To Paint Is to Love Again: Henry Miller on Art, How Hobbies Enrich Us, and Why Good Friends Are Essential for Creative Work." *Brain Pickings*. Accessed November 27, 2017. https://www.brainpickings. org/2015/01/21/to-paint-is-to-love-again-henry-miller.

Price, Reynolds. Review of *The Collected Stories*, by William Trevor. *New York Times*, February 28, 1993.

Rabb, Margo. "Fallen Idols." *New York Times*, July 25, 2013.

Reed, Peter, Nanette Vonnegut, and Kurt Vonnegut. *Kurt Vonnegut Drawings*. New York: Monacelli Press, 2014.

Reiner, Jon. "Live First, Write Later: The Case for Less Creative-Writing Schooling." *Atlantic*, April 9, 2013.

Rothman, Joshua. "Virginia's Woolf's Idea of Privacy." *New Yorker*, July 9, 2014. https://www.newyorker.com/books/joshua-rothman/ virginia-woolfs-idea-of-privacy.

Sandweiss, Lee. "Historic Vonnegut Cottage on Lake Maxinkuckee Saved from Demolition." *Herald-Times* (*Hoosier Times*), June 11, 2016. https://www.

hoosiertimes.com/herald_times_online/life/at_home/historic-vonnegut-cottage-on-lake-maxinkuckee-saved-from-demolition/article_714e551a-8b26-59aa-947d-f36a2761ab40.html.

Schnabel, Julian, dir. *The Diving Bell and the Butterfly*. 2007; Paris, France: Pathé Renn Productions, 2008. DVD.

Schultz, Kathryn. "Call and Response." *New Yorker*, March 6, 2017.

Schutz, Will. *Profound Simplicity*. New York: Bantam, 1979.

Schwartz, Barry, and Amy Wrzesniewski. "The Secret of Effective Motivation." *New York Times*, July 6, 2014.

Sheridan, Sara. "What Writers Earn: A Cultural Myth." *Huffington Post*. Updated June 24, 2016. https://www.huffingtonpost.co.uk/sara-sheridan/writers-earnings-cultural-myth_b_3136859.html?guccounter=1&guce_referrer_us=aHR0cHM6Ly93d3cuZ29vZ2xlLmNvbS8S8&guce_referrer_cs=fahUDQ-l9b4CWlwowtpjwA.

Shields, Charles. *And So It Goes*. New York: Holt and Company, 2011.

Snodgrass, Dana. "Outstanding Hoosier Women Honored by Theta Sigma Phi." *Indianapolis Star*, April 3, 1965.

Strand, Ginger. "How Jane Vonnegut Made Kurt Vonnegut a Writer." *New Yorker*, December 3, 2015.

Sullivan, James. "A Celebration of Kurt Vonnegut on Cape Cod." *Boston Globe*, October 7, 2014. https://www.bostonglobe.com/arts/2014/10/06/celebration-vonnegut-cape/RUegboNmUXBmi449E5TbJI/story.html.

Sumner, Gregory. *Unstuck in Time: A Journey Through Kurt Vonnegut's Life and Letters*. New York: Seven Stories Press, 2011.

Thomas, Dylan. "The Orchards." In *Adventures in the Skin Trade*. Cambridge: New Directions, 1969.

Tribune News Services. "Chicago Veterans Museum Acquires Kurt Vonnegut Art Prints." *Chicago Tribune*, January 11, 2017. https://www.chicagotribune.com/entertainment/ct-chicago-veterans-museum-kurt-vonne-gut-art-prints-20170111-story.html.

Truss, Lynne. *Eats, Shoots & Leaves: The Zero Tolerance Approach to Punctuation*. London: Profile Books, 2003.

"The U.S. Illiteracy Rate Hasn't Changed in 10 Years." *Huffington Post*. Last modified November 27, 2017. https://www.huffingtonpost.com/2013/09/06/illiteracy-rate_n_3880355.html.

Vonnegut, Mark. *Just Like Someone without Mental Illness Only More So*. New York: Delacorte Press, 2010.

Wakefield, Dan. "Kurt Vonnegut, Christ-Loving Atheist." *Image*, no. 82. https://imagejournal.org/article/kurt-vonnegut/.

Weber, Bruce. "Jack Leggett, Who Cultivated Writers in Iowa, Dies at 97." *New York Times*, January 30, 2015.

Wensink, Patrick. "My Amazon Best Seller Made Me Nothing." *Salon*, March 15, 2013. https://www.salon.com/2013/03/15/hey_amazon_wheres_my_money.

Winokur, Jon, ed. *W.O.W.: Writers on Writing*. Philadelphia: Running Press, 1986.

"Writing Is Easy; You Just Open a Vein and Bleed." Quote Investigator. Accessed April 9, 2019. https://quoteinvestigator.com/2011/09/14/ writing-bleed/.

Yarrow, Alder. "So You Wanna Be a Wine Writer." *Vinography* (blog). December 10, 2009. http://www.vinography.com/archives/2009/12/so_you_wanna_ be_a_wine_writer.html.

Yeats, William Butler. "The Circus Animals' Desertion." In *Selected Poems and Two Plays of William Butler Yeats.* New York: Collier, 1962.

NOTES

1   Wilfred Sheed, "The Now Generation Knew Him When," in *Conversations with Kurt Vonnegut*, ed. William Rodney Allen (Jackson: University Press of Mississippi, 1988), 13.
2   For a terrific piece about this in regard to writers, see Margo Rabb, "Fallen Idols," *New York Times Book Review*, July 25, 2013.
3   "Kurt Vonnegut: In His Own Words," *London Times*, April 12, 2007, https://www.thetimes.co.uk/article/kurt-vonnegut-in-his-own-words-mccg7vog8cg.
4   Kurt Vonnegut, *Palm Sunday* (New York: Delacorte Press, 1981), chap. 4.
5   Kurt Vonnegut, "How to Write with Style," International Paper Company Publicity Handout, May 1980, also appeared in the *New York Times*; collected in *Palm Sunday*.
6   Vonnegut, *Palm Sunday*, chap. 13.
7   Suzanne McConnell, "The Disposal," *Fiddlehead*, no. 110 (Summer 1976), 99–107.
8   In fact, one of my earliest glimpses of Kurt Vonnegut was at the Steak-Out restaurant in the basement of the Jefferson Hotel in Iowa City, with the order pad in my hand. He was with his wife Jane, Vance and Tina Bourjaily, José and Pilar Donoso, and, I think, Nelson Algren and his wife. It took quite a while for me to get the order. They were very interested in each other. It was early the first semester, and all the writers and their wives, except for the Bourjailys, were new to Iowa City. They were all just becoming acquainted.
9   Kurt Vonnegut, *Letters*, ed. Dan Wakefield (New York: Delacorte Press, 2012), 14–16.
10 Kurt Vonnegut, *Armageddon in Retrospect* (New York: G. P. Putnam's Sons, 2008), 11–13.
11 Vonnegut, *Palm Sunday*, chap. 4.
12 *The Daily Show With Jon Stewart*, season 10, episode 115, "Kurt Vonnegut," directed by Chuck O'Neil, aired September 13, 2005, on Comedy Central.
13 Vonnegut, "How to Write with Style."
14 Jill Krementz, ed., *Happy Birthday, Kurt Vonnegut: A Festschrift for Kurt Vonnegut on His Sixtieth Birthday* (New York, Delacorte Press, 1982), 49.
15 Kurt Vonnegut, "Fluctuations Between Good and Ill Fortune in Simple Tales (unpublished proposed master's thesis, University of Chicago, 1965)," 23, Kurt Vonnegut Papers, Lilly Library, Indiana University, Bloomington, IN.
16 Vonnegut, "How to Write with Style."
17 This began with a book called *Writing without Teachers* by Peter Elbow (New York: Oxford University Press, 1973). A simple book, it revolutionized the English department where I was teaching at the time. The title appealed to our '60s sensibilities.
18 Joe David Bellamy and John Casey, "Kurt Vonnegut Jr.," in *Conversations*, 158.
19 A declarative sentence is one that simply marches forward, by subject, verb, object, declaring something. It's free of dependent clauses that start with "if," "when," "although," and so on—those signifiers that that part of the sentence's thought will depend on the rest of the sentence's thought.
20 Vonnegut, "How to Write with Style."

21 Grace Paley, "Distance," in *Enormous Changes at the Last Minute* (New York: Farrar, Straus and Giroux, 1985), 13.

22 Ernest Hemingway, "The Killers," in *The Snows of Kilimanjaro and Other Stories* (New York: Charles Scribner's Sons, 1927), 71.

23 Toni Cade Bambara, "My Man Bovanne," in *Gorilla, My Love* (New York: Random House, 1972), 3.

24 Dylan Thomas, "The Orchards," in *Adventures in the Skin Trade* (Cambridge: New Directions, 1969), 137.

25 Kurt Vonnegut, *Jailbird* (New York: Delacorte Press, 1979), chap. 9.

26 Kurt Vonnegut, *The Sirens of Titan* (New York: Delacorte Press, 1959), chap. 10.

27 Kurt Vonnegut, *Breakfast of Champions* (New York: Delacorte Press, 1973), chap. 18.

28 Vonnegut, *Breakfast*, chap. 15.

29 Kurt Vonnegut, preface to *Wampeters, Foma & Granfalloons* (New York: Delacorte Press, 1974).

30 Vonnegut, "How to Write with Style."

31 Vonnegut, *Breakfast*, chap. 19.

32 Vonnegut, *Breakfast*, chap. 20–21.

33 Ernest Hemingway, "The Art of Fiction No. 21," interview by George Plimpton, *Paris Review*, no. 18 (Spring 1958).

34 Frank McLaughlin, "An Interview with Kurt Vonnegut, Jr.," in *Conversations*, 73.

35 Kurt Vonnegut, "Harrison Bergeron" (unpublished manuscript, ca. 1961), Kurt Vonnegut Papers, Lilly Library, Indiana University, Bloomington, IN.

36 Kurt Vonnegut, "Harrison Bergeron," in *Welcome to the Monkey House* (New York: Delacorte Press, 1968).

37 Vonnegut, "How to Write with Style."

38 Scholars quibble about the alphabet's origin, depending on whether "alphabet" is defined as the first representational marks for sound that the Phoenicians made, or the Semites' marks for consonants only, or the Greeks' more detailed symbol system for vowels as well as consonants, and whose "alpha" and "beta" came to form "alphabet."

39 Annie Murphey Paul, "Your Brain on Fiction," *New York Times*, March 17, 2012.

40 "The U.S. Illiteracy Rate Hasn't Changed in 10 Years," *Huffington Post*, last modified November 27, 2017, https://www.huffingtonpost.com/2013/09/06/illiteracy-rate _n_3880355.html.

41 Kurt Vonnegut, *Cat's Cradle* (New York: Delacorte Press, 1963), chap. 20.

42 Vonnegut, *Wampeters*, preface.

43 Vonnegut, Kurt, *Wampeters*, 281.

44 McLaughlin, "Interview," 73.

45 Kurt Vonnegut, *Player Piano* (New York: Delacorte Press, 1952).

46 Kurt Vonnegut, *Bluebeard* (New York: Delacorte Press, 1987), chap. 3.

47 Kurt Vonnegut, *Mother Night* (New York: New York: Harper and Row, 1961), chap. 37.

48 Kurt Vonnegut, *Hocus Pocus* (New York: G. P. Putnam's Sons, 1990), chap 6.

49 Vonnegut, *Mother Night*, chap. 25.

50 Kurt Vonnegut, *God Bless You, Mr. Rosewater* (New York: Delacorte Press, 1965), chap. 2.

51 Kurt Vonnegut, *Fates Worse than Death* (New York: G. P. Putnam's Sons, 1991), chap. 14.

52 Vonnegut, *Letters*, 316.

53 Vonnegut, *Letters*, 318–19.

54 *Kurt Vonnegut: So It Goes*, directed by Nigel Finch (1983; Princeton: Films for the Humanities and Sciences; 2002), DVD, 63 minutes.

55 Kurt Vonnegut, "Mythologies of North American Indian Nativistic Cults" (master's thesis, University of Chicago, 1947).
56 Vonnegut, "Mythologies."
57 Vonnegut, "Mythologies."
58 Vonnegut, *Player Piano*, chap. 17.
59 Finch, *Kurt Vonnegut*.
60 Kurt Vonnegut, introduction to *Bagombo Snuff Box* (New York: G. P. Putnam's Sons, 1999).
61 Vonnegut, *Player Piano*, chap. 1.
62 Bellamy and Casey, "Vonnegut," 157.
63 Vonnegut, *Palm Sunday*, chap. 5.
64 Kurt Vonnegut, *We Are What We Pretend to Be* (New York: Vanguard Press, 2012), chap. 4.
65 Vonnegut, *Player Piano*, chap. 33.
66 Vonnegut, *Sirens*, chap. 4.
67 Vonnegut, *Mother Night*, chap. 4.
68 Vonnegut, *Cat's Cradle*, chap. 120.
69 Vonnegut, *God Bless You*, chap. 13–14.
70 Kurt Vonnegut, "Kurt Vonnegut at NYU," lecture, New York University, November 6, 1970, New York, radio broadcast, KPFT, copy of a reel-to-reel tape, 40 minutes, Pacifica Radio Archives, https://www.pacificaradioarchives.org/recording/bc1568.
71 Suzanne McConnell, "Do Lord," in *Fence of Earth*, Hamilton Review, no. 11 (Spring 2007), http://www.hamiltonstone.org/hsr11fiction.html#dolord.
72 Edward Weeks to Kurt Vonnegut, 29 August 1949, Kurt Vonnegut Papers, Lilly Library, Indiana University, Bloomington, IN.
73 Vonnegut, *Palm Sunday*, chap. 6.
74 Vonnegut, *Player Piano*, chap. 14.
75 Robert Taylor, "Kurt Vonnegut," in *Conversations*, 9–10.
76 Kurt Vonnegut, *Slaughterhouse-Five* (New York: Delacorte Press, 1969), chap. 1.
77 Kurt Vonnegut, "There Must Be More to Love than Death," interview by Robert K. Musil, in *The Last Interview and Other Conversations*, ed. Tom McCartan (Brooklyn: Melville House Publishing, 2011), 67.
78 Kurt Vonnegut, *A Man without a Country* (New York: Seven Stories Press, 2005), 18.
79 Taylor, "Vonnegut," 9.
80 Vonnegut, *Cat's Cradle*, chap. 31.
81 Vonnegut, *Cat's Cradle*, chap. 1.
82 Jerome Klinkowitz, telephone conversation with Suzanne McConnell, October 2015.
    Coincidentally, perhaps eerily, the artwork resulting from Tim Youd's performance typing *Breakfast of Champions* echoes Vonnegut's impulse to render the destruction of Dresden in visual terms, using the typewriter. See introduction.
83 Kurt Vonnegut, "New Dictionary," in *Monkey House*.
84 For more about the power of commitment and synchronicity, check out *The Artist's Way: A Spiritual Path to Higher Creativity* by Julia Cameron (New York: G. P. Putnam's Sons, 1992).
85 Vonnegut, *Man Without*, 19.
86 Vonnegut, *Slaughterhouse-Five*, chap. 2.
87 For a brilliant essay on failure to realize one's writerly vision, see Michael Cunningham, "Found in Translation," New York Times, October 2, 2010, http://www.nytimes.com/2010/10/03/opinion/03cunningham.html.
88 Bellamy and Casey, "Vonnegut," 161–62.

89   Steve Blakeslee, "The Man from Slaughterhouse-Five: A Remembrance of Kurt Vonnegut," *Open Spaces: Views from the Northwest* 9, no. 3 (2007).

90   Vonnegut, *Man Without*, 20.

91   Vonnegut, *Slaughterhouse-Five*, chap. 3.

92   Vonnegut, *Mother Night*, chap. 22.

93   Kurt Vonnegut, "Poems Written During the First Five Months of 2005" (unpublished manuscript, 2005).

94   Vonnegut, *Palm Sunday*, chap. 5.

95   Vonnegut, *Palm Sunday*, chap. 2.

96   Kurt Vonnegut, *If This Isn't Nice, What Is?*, ed. Dan Wakefield (New York: Seven Stories Press, 2014), 9.

97   Vonnegut, *Palm Sunday*, chap. 5.

98   Vonnegut, *Fates*, chap 11.

99   Vonnegut, *Palm Sunday*, chap. 5.

100 Vonnegut, *Palm Sunday*, chap. 5.

101 Vonnegut, *Breakfast*, chap 16.

102 Barry Schwartz and Amy Wrzesniewski, "The Secret of Effective Motivation," *New York Times*, July 6, 2014.

103 Charles Shields, *And So It Goes* (New York: Holt and Company, 2011), 229.

104 Kurt Vonnegut, "Despite Tough Guys, Life Is Not the Only School for Real Novelists," *New York Times*, May 24, 1999.

105 Mark Vonnegut, introduction to *Armageddon in Retrospect*, 1.

106 Alder Yarrow, "So You Wanna Be a Wine Writer," *Vinography* (blog), December 10, 2009, http://www.vinography.com/archives/2009/12/so_you_wanna_be_a_wine_writer.html.

107 Vonnegut, *Man Without*, 56.

108 Vonnegut, *Man Without*, 24.

109 Vonnegut, *Breakfast*, chap. 19.

110 Vonnegut, *Wampeters*, preface.

111 Louise DeSalvo, *Writing as a Way of Healing* (Boston: Beacon Press, 2000), 25.

112 Josephine Humphreys, review of *The Collected Stories*, by John McGahern, *New York Times*, February 28, 1993.

113 Vonnegut, "More to Love," 74.

114 Vonnegut, "More to Love," 67–68.

115 Bellamy and Casey, "Vonnegut," 163.

116 Kurt Vonnegut, prologue to *Slapstick* (New York: Delacorte Press, 1976).

117 Kurt Vonnegut, *Deadeye Dick* (New York: Delacorte Press, 1982), chap. 13.

118 Vonnegut, *Wampeters*, 280–81.

119 Kurt Vonnegut and Lee Stringer, *Like Shaking Hands with God* (New York: Seven Stories Press, 1999), 29.

120 Reynolds Price, review of *The Collected Stories* by William Trevor, *New York Times*, February 28, 1993.

121 Vonnegut, *Fates*, chap. 2.

122 Vonnegut, *Wampeters*, 254.

123 Vonnegut, *Wampeters*, 254–55, 284.

124 David Standish, "Playboy Interview," in *Conversations*, 87, 108.

125 Vonnegut, *Breakfast*, chap. 18.

126 Vonnegut, *Palm Sunday*, chap. 18.

127 Vonnegut, *Wampeters*, 283.

128 Charles Reilly, "Two Conversations with Kurt Vonnegut," in *Conversations*, 202.

129 Richard Todd, "The Masks of Kurt Vonnegut, Jr.," in *Conversations*, 33.

130 Vonnegut, *Wampeters*, 283.

131 David J. Morris, "After PTSD, More Trauma," *New York Times*, January 17, 2015.

132 Vonnegut, *God Bless You*, chap. 6.

133 Vonnegut, *Sirens*, chap. 9.

134 Vonnegut, *Bluebeard*, chap. 37.

135 Vonnegut, *Palm Sunday*, chap. 19.

136 Vonnegut, *Sirens*, chap. 5.

137 William Butler Yeats, "The Circus Animals' Desertion," in *Selected Poems and Two Plays of William Butler Yeats* (New York: Collier, 1962), 184.

138 Vonnegut, *Breakfast*, chap. 19.

139 Vonnegut, *Bluebeard*, chap. 9.

140 Vonnegut, *Palm Sunday*, chap. 17.

141 Vonnegut, *Deadeye Dick*, chap. 24.

142 Vonnegut, *Wampeters*, 283.

143 Vonnegut, *Wampeters*, 237–38.

144 McLaughlin, "Interview," 72.

145 For more about Vonnegut's freethinker ancestors, see "Roots" and "Religion" in *Palm Sunday*.

146 "Indiana War Memorial Museum," Indiana State Official Government Website, accessed November 20, 2018, https://www.in.gov/iwm.

147 Bellamy and Casey, "Vonnegut," 166.

148 Standish, "Playboy," 76.

149 Vonnegut, introduction to *Bagombo*.

150 Vonnegut, *Player Piano*, chap. 1.

151 Vonnegut, *Player Piano*, chap. 1.

152 Alex Davies, "I Rode 500 Miles in a Self-Driving Car and Saw the Future. It's Delightfully Dull," *Wired*, January 7, 2015, https://www.wired.com/2015/01/rode-500-miles-self-driving-car-saw-future-boring.

153 Vonnegut, *Fates*, chap. 14.

154 Vonnegut, *Palm Sunday*, chap. 4.

155 Vonnegut, *Bluebeard*, chap. 24.

156 Jonathan Becher, "Gladwell vs Vonnegut on Change Specialists," *Forbes*, October 14, 2014, https://www.forbes.com/sites/sap/2014/10/14/gladwell-vs-vonnegut-on-change-specialists/#c445b4d46f7d.

157 Vonnegut, *Breakfast*, chap. 7.

158 Vonnegut, *Jailbird*, chap. 3.

159 Vonnegut, *Mother Night*, chap. 12.

160 Vonnegut, *God Bless You*, chap. 2.

161 Vonnegut, *Cat's Cradle*, chap. 103.

162 Vonnegut, *Slaughterhouse-Five*, chap. 3.

163 Carol Kramer, "Kurt's College Cult Adopts Him as Literary Guru at 48," in *Conversations*, 27.

164 Vonnegut, *Bluebeard*, chap. 30.

165 Vonnegut, *Mother Night*, chap 5.

166 Dan Wakefield, introduction to *If This Isn't Nice, What Is?*, by Kurt Vonnegut, ed. Dan Wakefield (New York: Seven Stories, 2014), xiv.

167 (My Fairy God Mama provided these at the time of this writing in the obituary of Jack Leggett, director of the Iowa workshop from 1970 to 1987):

Bruce Weber, "Jack Leggett, Who Cultivated Writers in Iowa, Dies at 97," *New York Times*, January 30, 2015.

168 Vonnegut, *If This Isn't Nice*, 29.

169 Vonnegut, *Cat's Cradle*, chap. 70.

170 Vonnegut, *Wampeters*, 274.

171 Vonnegut, *If This Isn't Nice*, 41–42.

172 Vonnegut, *Wampeters*, 259.

173 Vonnegut, *If This Isn't Nice*, 42.

174 See the brochure and more about these trips at Cottonwood Gulch's website, http:// www.cottonwoodgulch.org.

175 Standish, "Playboy," 104.

176 Vonnegut, *If This Isn't Nice*, 94.

177 Vonnegut, *Palm Sunday*, chap. 10.

178 Kurt Vonnegut, *Galápagos* (New York: Delacorte Press, 1985), book 1, chap. 6.

179 Vonnegut, *Galápagos*, book 1, chap. 19.

180 Vonnegut, *Galápagos*, book 1, chap. 20.

181 Vonnegut, *Hocus Pocus*, chap. 34.

182 Vonnegut, *Hocus Pocus*, chap. 21.

183 Vonnegut, *Hocus Pocus*, chap. 18.

184 Vonnegut, *Hocus Pocus*, chap. 37.

185 Vonnegut, *Jailbird*, chap. 18.

186 Kurt Vonnegut, *Timequake* (New York: G. P. Putnam's Sons, 1997), chap. 42.

187 Vance Bourjaily, "Dear Hualing," in *A Community of Writers: Paul Engle and the Iowa Writers' Workshop*, ed. Robert Dana (Iowa City: University of Iowa Press, 1999).

188 Hank Nuwer, "A Skull Session with Kurt Vonnegut," in *Conversations*, 242–43.

189 Vonnegut, *Palm Sunday*, chap. 5.

190 Suzanne McConnell, "Kurt Vonnegut and the Writers' Workshop," *Brooklyn Rail*, December 10, 2011, https://brooklynrail.org/2011/12/fiction/kurt-vonnegut-at-the-writers-workshop.

191 Vonnegut, *Letters*, 131.

192 Alexander Neubauer, ed., *Conversations on Writing Fiction* (New York: HarperCollins, 1994), 143.

193 Gail Godwin, "Waltzing with the Black Crayon," *Yale Review* 87, no. 1 (January 1999).

194 Godwin, "Waltzing."

195 Vonnegut, *Palm Sunday*, chap. 18.

196 Krementz, *Happy Birthday*, 71–75.

197 Godwin, "Waltzing," 52.

198 The scribbled "p. 114, Journey . . ." on the second assignment is a note to myself to attend that page in *Journey to the End of the Night* by Louis-Ferdinand Céline (a French doctor to the poor and WWI veteran), which Vonnegut had assigned. It's this novel that Kurt refers to in Rule #4 as being "so bloody depressing." Vonnegut read it and Theodore Roethke's poems on his first return trip to Dresden to do research for *Slaughterhouse-Five*.

199 Vonnegut, *Palm Sunday*, chap. 7.

200 From Kurt Vonnegut's letter to David Hoppe, Indiana journalist and friend of Kurt's. May 23, 2005.

201 Vonnegut, *Man Without*, 8–9.

202 Kurt Vonnegut, "God Bless You, Mr. Vonnegut," interview by J. Rentilly, in *The Last Interview*, 158.

203 Vonnegut, *Fates*, "On Literature by Karel Capek, From Toward the Radical Center."

204 Vonnegut, *Cat's Cradle*, chap. 70.

205 Vonnegut, *Timequake*, chap. 1.

206 Vonnegut, *Player Piano*, chap. 24.

207 Vonnegut, *Fates*, chap. 19.

208 Vonnegut, *If This Isn't Nice*, 29–30.

209 Pam Belluck, "For Better Social Skills, Scientists Recommend a Little Chekhov," *New York Times*, October 3, 2013.

210 Paul, "Your Brain."

211 "Literature and Medicine." Maine Humanities Council, accessed November 20, 2018, http://mainehumanities.org/program/literature-medicine-humanities-at-the-heart-of-health-care/.

212 Those assignments in order of citation were Helen Benedict, *The Sand Queen* (New York: Soho Press, 2011); Jean-Dominique Bauby, *The Diving Bell and the Butterfly* (New York: Alfred A. Knopf, 1997); *The Diving Bell and the Butterfly*, directed by Julian Schnabel (2007; Paris, France: Pathé Renn Productions, 2008), DVD; Joan Leegant, "Sisters of Mercy," in *Bellevue Literary Review* 11, no. 2 (Spring 2011); and *Bellevue Literary Review* 15, no. 2, "Embattled: The Ramifications of War" (Fall 2015).

213 Tom Bradshaw and Bonnie Nichols, *Reading at Risk: A Survey of Literary Reading in America* (Washington: National Endowment for the Arts, June 2004), https://www.arts.gov/sites/default/files/ReadingAtRisk.pdf.

214 For more information, see "NEA Big Read," Arts Midwest, https://www.artsmidwest.org/programs/neabigread/about.

215 Vonnegut, *Palm Sunday*, chap. 7.

216 Vonnegut, *If This Isn't Nice*, 1.

217 Vonnegut, *Palm Sunday*, chap. 5.

218 Vonnegut, *Wampeters*, 259.

219 Mark Vonnegut, introduction to *Armageddon*, 1.

220 Vonnegut, *Palm Sunday*, chap. 5.

221 Krementz, *Happy Birthday*, 72.

222 Vonnegut, *Palm Sunday*, chap. 4.

223 Vonnegut, "Despite Tough Guys."

224 Reilly, "Two Conversations," 196–97.

225 Sidney Offit, "The Library of America Interviews Sidney Offit About Kurt Vonnegut," interview by Rich Kelley, *The Library of America e-Newsletter* (New York: Library of America, 2011), 5, https://loa-shared.s3.amazonaws.com/static/pdf/LOA_Offit_on_Vonnegut.pdf.

226 Vonnegut, "Despite Tough Guys."

227 See Jon Reiner, "Live First, Write Later: The Case for Less Creative-Writing Schooling," *Atlantic*, April 9, 2013; or google "against writing programs" and you'll discover quite a discussion.

228 Reilly, "Two Conversations," 199.

229 Ronni Sandroff was an editor for thirty years: editor in chief of *Medica*, editor at *On the Issues*, and editorial director of Health and Family at *Consumer Reports*. She has published two books of fiction and many short stories.

230 McLaughlin, "Interview," 73.

231 Michelangelo Buonarroti, "To Giovanni da Pistoia When the Author Was Painting the Vault of the Sistine Chapel," trans. Gail Mazur, in *Zeppo's First Wife: New and Selected Poems* by Gail Mazur (Chicago: University of Chicago Press, 2013), 116.

232 For more information and wonderful photos, see Johannes Huber, Ernst Tremp, and Karl Schmuki, *The Abbey Library of Saint Gall*, trans. Jenifer Horlent (St Gallen: Verlag am Klosterhof St. Gall), 2007.

233 Vonnegut, *Fates*, chap. 3.

234 Dana Snodgrass, "Outstanding Hoosier Women Honored by Theta Sigma Phi," *Indianapolis Star*, April 3, 1965.

235 Vonnegut, *Fates*, chap. 3.

236 Thank you, Elizabeth Cook.

237 Vonnegut, *Timequake*, chap. 35.

238 Jon Winokur, ed., *W.O.W.: Writers on Writing* (Philadelphia: Running Press, 1986).

239 Vonnegut, introduction to *Bagombo*.

240 Shields, *And So It Goes*, 146.

241 Vonnegut, *Palm Sunday*, chap. 5.

242 Vonnegut, *Bluebeard*, chap. 7.

243 Vonnegut, *Deadeye Dick*, chap. 19.

244 Vonnegut, *Jailbird*, chap. 12.

245 Vonnegut, *Monkey House*.

246 Finch, *Kurt Vonnegut*.

247 Vonnegut, "More to Love," 81–82.

248 Vonnegut, *Fates*, chap. 3.

249 Bellamy and Casey, "Vonnegut," 160.

250 Vonnegut, *Wampeters*, 261.

251 Vonnegut, *Palm Sunday*, chap. 8.

252 Vonnegut, *Slaughterhouse-Five*, chap. 4.

253 Krementz, *Happy Birthday*, 35.

254 Vonnegut, *Slaughterhouse-Five*, chap. 3.

255 Attributed for years to theologian Reinhold Niebuhr (1892–1971), its source may go back much farther: see "Serenity Prayer Stirs up Doubt: Who Wrote It," *New York Times*, July 11, 2008.

256 Vonnegut, *Sirens*, chap. 7.

257 Vonnegut, *Cat's Cradle*, chap. 47.

258 Vonnegut, *Cat's Cradle*, chap. 61.

259 Todd, "Masks," 39.

260 Offit, "Library of America," 6.

261 Kurt Vonnegut to José Donoso, 26 May 1973, José Donoso Papers, Department of Rare Books and Special Collections, Princeton University.

262 Vonnegut, *Deadeye Dick*, chap. 24.

263 Vonnegut, *Deadeye Dick*, chap. 23.

264 Vonnegut, *Fates*, chap. 2.

265 Vonnegut, *Player Piano*, chap. 9.

266 Vonnegut, *Sirens*, chap. 10.

267 Vonnegut, *Sirens*, chap. 10.

268 Vonnegut, *Player Piano*, chap. 21.

269 Vonnegut, *Galápagos*, book 1, chap. 21.

270 Shields, *And So It Goes*, 85–86.

271 Kurt Vonnegut, "The Salon Interview: Kurt Vonnegut," interview by Frank Houston, *Salon*, October 8, 1999, https://www.salon.com/1999/10/08/vonnegut_interview.

272 Krementz, *Happy Birthday*, 39.

273 Bellamy and Casey, "Vonnegut," 158.

274 Vonnegut, *Fates*, chap. 4.

275 Vonnegut, introduction to *Bagombo*.
276 Reilly, "Two Conversations," 199.
277 Vonnegut, introduction to *Bagombo*.
278 Vonnegut, "Despite Tough Guys."
279 Vonnegut student Ronni Sandroff reports this as an admonishment Vonnegut gave Iowa students in class. I remember that too.
280 Vonnegut, introduction to *Bagombo*.
281 Vonnegut, introduction to *Bagombo*.
282 Offit, "Library of America," 6.
283 John Cloud, "Inherit the Wind," *Time*, April 18, 2011. After thirty-eight rejections, *Gone with the Wind* was published in the summer of 1936, and by Christmas it had sold a million copies. Margaret Mitchell received the Pulitzer for it the following year. To date, it's sold thirty million copies. A Harris Poll in 2014 found that Americans favored it second only to the Bible.
284 Vonnegut, *Player Piano*, chap. 1.
285 Vonnegut, *Sirens*, chap. 1.
286 Vonnegut, *God Bless You*, chap. 1.
287 Kurt Vonnegut, "Report on the Barnhouse Effect," in *Monkey House*.
288 Kurt Vonnegut, "Unready to Wear," in *Monkey House*.
289 Kurt Vonnegut, "Welcome to the Monkey House," in *Monkey House*.
290 Vonnegut, introduction to *Bagombo*.
291 Godwin, "Waltzing," 47.
292 Ronnie Sandroff, e-mail memoir to the author, unpublished, May 29, 2014.
293 Godwin, "Waltzing," 48.
294 Vonnegut, *Mother Night*, chap. 40.
295 Vonnegut, introduction to *Bagombo*.
296 Vonnegut, *Palm Sunday*, chap. 5.
297 Vonnegut, *Palm Sunday*, chap. 5.
298 Vonnegut, *Palm Sunday*, chap. 5.
299 Vonnegut, introduction to *Bagombo*.
300 Jeffrey Ely, Alexander Frankel, and Emir Kamenia, "The Economics of Suspense," *New York Times*, April 26, 2015.
301 Godwin, "Waltzing," 47.
302 Vonnegut, "Fluctuations."
303 Offit, "Library of America," 5.
304 Some of these graphs, minus the graph paper, are reproduced in *Palm Sunday* and *A Man without a Country*.
305 Shields, *And So It Goes*, 194.
306 Robert Lehrman, "The Political Speechwriter's Life," *New York Times*, November 3, 2012, https://opinionator.blogs.nytimes.com/2012/11/03/the-political-speechwriters-life.
307 Vonnegut, *God Bless You*, chap 13.
308 Vonnegut, *Player Piano*, chap. 31.
309 Vonnegut, *Player Piano*, chap. 31.
310 Vonnegut, *Palm Sunday*, chap. 10.
311 He commented on one of my Form of Fiction papers, "Full of life, Suzanne, and that's all I ever ask of anyone. (Believe me, most weren't.)" He scrawled a fat A, hailed me the next time I saw him.

      My paper wasn't brilliant. I'd responded fictionally to the assignment comparing the merits of the short story form versus that of the novel: narrated by a bubble-headed woman, the two opinions divided a town, created civil war. I suppose most papers were thoughtful essays. The fact that liveliness trumped erudition for my teacher, who had to grade eighty papers, impressed upon me the primo importance of keeping the reader awake.

312 Vonnegut, *Palm Sunday*, chap. 8.

313 Vonnegut, *What We Pretend*, chap. 7.

314 Vonnegut, "Fluctuations."

315 Vonnegut, *Cat's Cradle*, chap. 46.

316 Vonnegut, *Palm Sunday*, chap. 5.

317 Vonnegut, *Breakfast*, chap. 19.

318 Mel Gussow, "Vonnegut Is Having Fun Doing a Play," in *Conversations*, 24.

319 Vonnegut, *Breakfast*, chap. 20.

320 Vonnegut, *Timequake*, chap. 18.

321 Vonnegut, *Breakfast*, chap. 24.

322 Vonnegut, *Palm Sunday*, chap. 5.

323 Kurt Vonnegut, "Acceptance Speech" (speech, Eugene V. Debs Award ceremony, Terre Haute, IN, November 7, 1981), Kurt Vonnegut Papers, Lilly Library, Indiana University, Bloomington, IN.

324 Vonnegut, introduction to *Bagombo*.

325 Vonnegut, *Sirens*, epilogue.

326 Vonnegut, *Breakfast*, chap. 19.

327 Vonnegut, *Palm Sunday*, chap. 8.

328 Nuwer, "Skull Session," 244–45.

329 Vonnegut, *Slaughterhouse-Five*, chap. 2.

330 Vonnegut, *God Bless You*, chap. 7.

331 Maurice Merleau-Ponty, *Sense and Non-Sense*, trans. Hubert L. Dreyfus and Patricia Allen Dreyfus (Evanston: Northwestern University Press, 1964).

332 Kurt Vonnegut, "Adam," in *Monkey House*.

333 Vonnegut, *Galápagos*, book 1, chap. 2.

334 Kurt Vonnegut, "The Foster Portfolio," in *Monkey House*.

335 Vonnegut, "Fluctuations."

336 Vonnegut, *Deadeye Dick*, chap. 14.

337 Vonnegut, *Slaughterhouse-Five*, chap 8.

338 Vonnegut, "Adam."

339 Vonnegut, *Mother Night*, chap. 23.

340 A. E. Hotchner, *Papa Hemingway* (New York: Random House, 1955), 26.

341 Nanette Kuehn, foreword to *We Are What We Pretend to Be*, by Kurt Vonnegut (New York: Vanguard Press, 2012).

342 Bellamy and Casey, "Vonnegut," 159–60.

343 Vonnegut, *Sirens*, chap. 7.

344 Bellamy and Casey, "Vonnegut," 160.

345 Vonnegut, *Palm Sunday*, chap. 5.

346 Gifford Boies Doxsee to Ada Zouche German, #6311, 10 January 1981, Division of Rare and Manuscript Collections, Cornell University Library.

    This eighteen-page letter from Gifford Boies Doxsee to Ada Zouche German describes his memories of the Second World War, "especially during the months I was a prisoner of war . . . in Dresden." The letter was on display at an exhibit of Vonnegut's drawings and memorabilia at the Herbert F. Johnson Museum of Art at Cornell University in September 2015.

347 Nuwer, "Skull Session," 263.

348 Kurt Vonnegut, "Long Walk to Forever," in *Monkey House*.

349 Kurt Vonnegut, preface to *Between Time and Timbuktu* (New York: Dell Publishing, 1972).

350 Vonnegut, *Palm Sunday*, chap. 8.

351 Mark Vonnegut, introduction to *Armageddon*, 1.

352 Finch, *Kurt Vonnegut*.

353 Vonnegut, *Man Without*, 66.

354 Vonnegut, *Sirens*, chap. 8.

355 Vonnegut, *Mother Night*, chap. 2.

356 Vonnegut, *Galápagos*, book 2, chap. 6.

357 Vonnegut, *Man Without*, 67–68.

358 Vonnegut, *Hocus Pocus*, chap. 1.

359 Vonnegut, "Foster Portfolio."

360 Vonnegut, *Player Piano*, chap. 1.

361 Vonnegut, *Player Piano*, chap. 20.

362 Vonnegut, *Cat's Cradle*, chap. 42.

363 Vonnegut, *Jailbird*, chap. 20.

364 Vonnegut, *Cat's Cradle*, chap. 110.

365 Vonnegut, *Fates*, chap. 6. Vonnegut furnishes the original words in the book's appendix, so that you can "decide for yourself."

366 Vonnegut, *Fates*, appendix.

367 Vonnegut, *Fates*, chap. 6.

368 Vonnegut, *God Bless You*, chap. 13.

369 Vonnegut, *God Bless You*, chap. 4.

370 Vonnegut, *Slaughterhouse-Five*, chap. 3.

371 Vonnegut, *Slaughterhouse-Five*, chap. 2.

372 Vonnegut, *Player Piano*, chap. 3.

373 Vonnegut, *Galápagos*, book 2, chap. 4.

374 Vonnegut, *Mother Night*, chap. 9.

375 Vonnegut, *Galápagos*, book 1, chap. 25.

376 Vonnegut, *Galápagos*, book 1, chap. 30.

377 For a marvelous essay on that subject, see Dan Wakefield, "Kurt Vonnegut, Christ-Loving Atheist," *Image*, no. 82, https://imagejournal.org/article/kurt-vonnegut/.

378 Vonnegut, *Galápagos*, book 1, chap. 32.

379 Vonnegut, *Sirens*, chap. 9.

380 Bellamy and Casey, "Vonnegut," 160.

381 Vonnegut, *Slaughterhouse-Five*, chap. 3.

382 Vonnegut, *Slaughterhouse-Five*, chap. 2.

383 Vonnegut, *Sirens*, chap. 4.

384 Jerome Klinkowitz, *The Vonnegut Statement* (New York: Doubleday, 1973), 197.

385 Vonnegut, *Sirens*, chap. 8.

386 Vonnegut, *Breakfast*, chap. 12.

387 Vonnegut, *Slaughterhouse-Five*, chap. 5.

388 Reilly, "Two Conversations," 197.

389 Vonnegut, *Breakfast*, preface.

390 Vonnegut, *Slaughterhouse-Five*, chap. 5.

391 Vonnegut, *Slaughterhouse-Five*, chap. 2.

392 Vonnegut, *Slaughterhouse-Five*, chap. 2.

393 Finch, *Kurt Vonnegut*.

394 Finch, *Kurt Vonnegut*.

395 Finch, *Kurt Vonnegut*.

396 Vonnegut, *Hocus Pocus*, chap. 16.
397 Bellamy and Casey, "Vonnegut," 157–58.
398 Vonnegut, *Man Without*, 23.
399 Vonnegut, *Player Piano*, chap. 1.
400 Vonnegut, *Palm Sunday*, chap. 9.
401 Vonnegut, *Palm Sunday*, chap. 9.
402 Vonnegut, *Wampeters*, 258–59.
403 Vonnegut, *God Bless You*, chap. 12.
404 Vonnegut, *Player Piano*, chap. 6.
405 Vonnegut, *God Bless You*, chap. 9.
406 Vonnegut, *Fates*, chap. 6.
407 Vonnegut, *God Bless You*, chap. 5.
408 Vonnegut, *Breakfast*, chap. 4.
409 Vonnegut, *Breakfast*, chap. 21.
410 Vonnegut, *Palm Sunday*, chap. 5.
411 Vonnegut, *Jailbird*, chap. 12.
412 Vonnegut, *Jailbird*, chap. 20.
413 Vonnegut, *Jailbird*, chap. 20.
414 Vonnegut, *God Bless You*, chap. 12.
415 Vonnegut, *Palm Sunday*, chap. 9.
416 Vonnegut, *Fates*, chap. 8.
417 Vonnegut, *God Bless You*, chap. 13.
418 Vonnegut, *Slaughterhouse-Five*, chap. 5.
419 Vonnegut, *Timequake*, chap. 45.
420 Vonnegut, *Bluebeard*, chap. 31.
421 Vonnegut, *Wampeters*, 256.
422 Vonnegut, *Cat's Cradle*, chap. 73.
423 Bellamy and Casey, "Vonnegut," 156.
424 Vonnegut, *Wampeters*, 256–58.
425 Krementz, *Happy Birthday*, 72–73.
426 Vonnegut, *Cat's Cradle*, chap. 69.
427 Vonnegut, *If This Isn't Nice*, 57.
428 Vonnegut, *Timequake*, chap. 35.
429 Vonnegut, *Timequake*, chap. 38.
430 Vonnegut, *Jailbird*, chap. 11.
431 Vonnegut, *Man Without*, 39–40.
432 Vonnegut, *Wampeters*, 142.
433 Vonnegut, *Wampeters*, 144, 153.
434 Vonnegut, *Wampeters*, 145.
435 Vonnegut, *Wampeters*, 145–46.
436 Vonnegut, *Palm Sunday*, chap. 9.
437 Vonnegut, *Wampeters*, 259.
438 Vonnegut, *Palm Sunday*, chap. 9.
439 Vonnegut, *Fates*, chap. 19.
440 Vonnegut, *Palm Sunday*, chap. 8.
441 Vonnegut, *Hocus Pocus*, chap. 6.
442 Vonnegut, *Slapstick*, chap. 7.
443 Vonnegut, *Palm Sunday*, chap. 5.
444 Vonnegut, *Wampeters*, preface.

445 Kurt Vonnegut, "Kurt Vonnegut, The Art of Fiction," interview by David Hayman, David Michaelis, George Plimpton, and Richard Rhodes, in *The Last Interview*, 7.

446 Vonnegut, *Wampeters*, preface.

447 Vonnegut, *Armageddon*, chap. 2.

448 Offit, "Library of America," 8.

449 Todd, "Masks," 33.

450 Vonnegut, *Letters*, 168.

451 Vonnegut, *Wampeters*, 281.

452 Kurt Vonnegut, "Slaughterhouse-Five" (unpublished manuscript), Kurt Vonnegut Papers, Lilly Library, Indiana University, Bloomington, IN.

453 Vonnegut, *Slaughterhouse-Five*, chap. 3.

454 Vonnegut, introduction to *Bagombo*.

455 Vonnegut, *Letters*, 58.

456 Iowa Writers' Workshop, *Word by Word* (Iowa City: University of Iowa Printing and Mailing Services, 2011), 38.

457 Vonnegut, *Letters*, 88.

458 Bellamy and Casey, "Vonnegut," 166.

459 Kramer, "Kurt's College," 29.
    If you want to read a short-short story, written in a fit of pique, about revising fiction, which, coincidentally, features a similar plot, see my story "Book" in *Per Contra*, no. 22 (Spring 2011), http://percontra.net/archive/22mcconnell.htm.

460 Morgan Entrekin, editorial notes to Kurt Vonnegut, 1 March 1982, Kurt Vonnegut Papers, Lilly Library, Indiana University, Bloomington, IN.

461 Finch, *Kurt Vonnegut*.

462 Vonnegut, *Jailbird*, prologue.

463 Vonnegut, *Cat's Cradle*, chap. 70.

464 Vonnegut, *Palm Sunday*, chap. 5.

465 Vonnegut, *Slapstick*, chap. 14.

466 Vonnegut, *Palm Sunday*, chap. 5.

467 Vonnegut, *Fates*, chap. 3.

468 Vonnegut, *Player Piano*, chap. 32.

469 Vonnegut, *Breakfast*, chap. 8.

470 Krementz, *Happy Birthday*, 75.

471 Vonnegut, *Breakfast*, chap. 10.

472 Vonnegut, *Deadeye Dick*, chap. 24.

473 Rentilly, "God Bless," 157.

474 McLaughlin, "Interview," 70.

475 Carol Pinchefsky, "Wizard Oil," *Orson Scott Card's Intergalactic Medicine Show*, December 2006, http://www.intergalacticmedicineshow.com/cgi-bin/mag.cgi?do=columns&vol=-carol_pinchefsky&article=015.

476 Sara Sheridan, "What Writers Earn: A Cultural Myth," *Huffington Post*, updated June 24, 2016, https://www.huffingtonpost.co.uk/sara-sheridan/writers-earnings-cultural-myth_b_3136859.html?guccounter=1&guce_referrer_us=aHR0cHM6Ly93d3cuZ-29vZ2xlLmNvbS88&guce_referrer_cs=fahUDQ-l9b4CWlwowtpjwA.

477 Patrick Wensink, "My Amazon Best Seller Made Me Nothing," *Salon*, March 15, 2013, https://www.salon.com/2013/03/15/hey_amazon_wheres_my_money.

478 Vonnegut, *Palm Sunday*, chap. 5.

479 Andrew Perrin, "Book Reading," Pew Research Center, September 2016, http://www.pewinternet.org/2016/09/01/book-reading-2016.

480 Vonnegut and Stringer, *Like Shaking*, 19–20.

481 Finch, *Kurt Vonnegut.*
482 Vonnegut, *Letters*, 27.
483 Vonnegut, *Letters*, 32–34.
484 Finch, *Kurt Vonnegut.*
485 Mark Vonnegut, *Just Like Someone*, 15.
486 Vonnegut, *God Bless You*, chap. 2.
487 Finch, *Kurt Vonnegut.*
488 Vonnegut, *Fates*, chap. 20.
489 Lehrman, "Political Speechwriter's."
490 Vonnegut, *God Bless You*, chap. 8.
491 "I'm the dishwasher here," my first published story begins. See McConnell, "Disposal."
492 William Rodney Allen and Paul Smith, "Having Enough: A Talk with Kurt Vonnegut," in *Conversations*, 299.
493 Finch, *Kurt Vonnegut.*
494 For more on this, see M. Allen Cunningham, "Rethinking Restriction," *Poets & Writers*, January/February 2014.
495 Vonnegut, *Palm Sunday*, chap. 5.
496 C. D. B. Bryan, "Kurt Vonnegut, Head Bokononist," in *Conversations*, 4.
497 Shields, *And So It Goes*, 216.
498 Vonnegut, *Palm Sunday*, chap. 5.
499 Iowa Writers' Workshop, *Word by Word*, 36.
500 Shields, *And So It Goes*, 219.
    Unfortunately, when Knox Burger became a literary agent, Vonnegut reneged on a promise to go with his agency. He said in the *Paris Review* interview, "And let it be put on the record here that Knox Burger, who is about my age, discovered and encouraged more good young writers than any other editor of his time."
501 Shields, *And So It Goes*, 219.
502 Vonnegut, *Mother Night*, chap. 29.
503 Mark Vonnegut, *Just Like Someone without Mental Illness Only More So* (New York: Delacorte Press, 2010), 15.
504 *Publishers Weekly*, "The Conscience of the Writer," in *Conversations*, 45.
505 Mark Vonnegut, *Just Like Someone*, 15.
506 C. G. Jung, "Christ, a Symbol of the Self," in *The Collected Works of C. G. Jung: Complete Digital Edition Vol. 9 Part II: Aion: Researches into the Phenomenology of Self*, trans. R. F. C. Hull (Princeton: Princeton University Press, 1959), 101, https://the-eye.eu/public/concen.org/Princeton%20Jung/9.2%20Aion_Researches%20into%20the%20Phenomenology%20of%20the%20Self%20%20(Collected%20Works%20of%20C.%20G.%20Jung%20Volume%209,%20Part%202).pdf.
    Vonnegut fulfilled several of his mother's dreams, as he acknowledges. Whether intending to or not, according to Jung, it's a "psychological rule" that "When an inner situation is not made conscious, it happens outside, as fate. . . . That is to say, when the individual . . . does not become conscious of his inner opposite, the world must perforce act out the conflict." In simpler words, "What is not brought to consciousness, comes to us as fate."
507 Vonnegut, *Deadeye Dick*, chap. 1.
508 Bellamy and Casey, "Vonnegut," 161.
509 Shields, *And So It Goes*, 168. Shields notes that Vonnegut wrote a story about an epidemic of people killing themselves for their life insurance entitled "The Epizootic."
510 Bellamy and Casey, "Vonnegut," 161.
511 Vonnegut, *Hocus Pocus*, chap. 27.

512   Vonnegut, *If This Isn't Nice*, chap. 2.

513   Vonnegut, *Palm Sunday*, chap. 6.

514   Kurt Vonnegut, in a speech to Lehigh University. Quote sent from Charles Shields in an e-mail to Suzanne McConnell, July 19, 2014.

515   McLaughlin, "Interview," 73.

516   Vonnegut, "Unready to Wear," 249.

517   Kurt Vonnegut to José Donoso, 26 May 1973.

518   Vonnegut, *Letters*, 178.

519   Vonnegut, *Letters*, 40.

520   Vonnegut, *Letters*, 46.

521   Vonnegut, *Letters*, 47.

522   Vonnegut, *Fates*, chap. 2.

523   Vonnegut, *Wampeters*, 251–53.

524   Vonnegut, *Galápagos*, book 1, chap. 2.

525   Vonnegut, *Galápagos*, book 1, chap. 6.

526   Vonnegut, *Galápagos*, book 1, chap. 29.

527   Vonnegut, *Galápagos*, book 1, chap. 8.

528   Vonnegut, *Galápagos*, book 1, chap. 6.

529   Vonnegut, *Galápagos*, book 1, chap. 27.

530   Vonnegut, *Galápagos*, book 1, chap. 6.

531   Martin J. Blaser, *Missing Microbes* (New York: Henry Holt and Company, 2014), 25.

532   For more information, watch two excellent PBS documentaries on these topics: Ed Moore, dir., *Ride the Tiger: A Guide Through the Bipolar Brain* (2016; Detroit: Detroit Public Television), http://www.pbs.org/ride-the-tiger/home/; and Larkin McPhee, dir., *Depression: Out of the Shadows* (2008; Twin Cities Public Television, Inc. and WGBH Boston for PBS), http://www.pbs.org/wgbh/takeonestep/depression/.

533   Vonnegut, *Hocus Pocus*, chap. 4.

534   Vonnegut, *Wampeters*, 263.

535   Vonnegut, *Palm Sunday*, chap. 17.

536   Vonnegut, *Fates*, chap. 2.

537   Mark Leeds, "What Would Kurt Vonnegut Think of Donald Trump?," June 15, 2017, *Literary Hub*, https://lithub.com/what-would-kurt-vonnegut-think-of-donald-trump/.

538   Vonnegut, *Sirens*, chap. 9.

539   Vonnegut, *Timequake*, chap. 8.

540   Vonnegut, *Man Without*, chap. 4.

541   Vonnegut, *Fates*, chap. 14.

542   Vonnegut, *Fates*, chap. 2.

543   Vonnegut, *Fates*, chap. 2.

544   See Leslie Jamison, "Does Recovery Kill Great Writing?" *New York Times Magazine*, March 13, 2018, excerpted from her book *The Recovering: Intoxication and Its Aftermath* (New York: Little, Brown and Company, 2018).

545   Nancy C. Andreasen, "Secrets of the Creative Brain," *Atlantic*, July/August 2014.

546   This line or its variation is attributed to Red Smith, Hemingway, and others. See "Writing Is Easy; You Just Open a Vein and Bleed," Quote Investigator, http://quoteinvestigator.com/2011/09/14/writing-bleed/.

547   Andreasen, "Secrets."

548   Vonnegut, *Bluebeard*, chap. 32.

549   Vonnegut, *Jailbird*, chap. 12.

550   Vonnegut, *If This Isn't Nice*, 30–31.

551   Vonnegut, *Man Without*, chap. 6.

552 Allen and Smith, "Having Enough," 295.

553 Nanette Vonnegut, "My Father the Doodler," in *Kurt Vonnegut Drawings*, by Peter Reed, Nanette Vonnegut, and Kurt Vonnegut (New York: Monacelli Press, 2014), 9.

554 Vonnegut, *Mother Night*, chap. 11.

555 Peter Reed, "The Remarkable Artwork of Kurt Vonnegut," in *Kurt Vonnegut Drawings*, by Peter Reed, Nanette Vonnegut, and Kurt Vonnegut (New York: Monacelli Press, 2014), 13.

556 *At the Johnson: The Members' Newsletter of the Herbert F. Johnson Museum of Art*, Fall 2015.

557 Reed, "Remarkable Artwork," 15.

558 Tribune News Services, "Chicago Veterans Museum Acquires Kurt Vonnegut Art Prints," *Chicago Tribune*, January 11, 2017, https://www.chicagotribune.com/entertainment/ct-chicago-veterans-museum-kurt-vonnegut-art-prints-20170111-story.html.

559 Maria Popova, "To Paint Is to Love Again," *Brain Pickings*, accessed November 27, 2017, https://www.brainpickings.org/2015/01/21/to-paint-is-to-love-again-henry-miller.

560 Reed, "Remarkable Artwork," 19.

561 Vonnegut and Stringer, *Like Shaking*, 47.

562 James Sullivan, "A Celebration of Kurt Vonnegut on Cape Cod," *Boston Globe*, October 7, 2014, https://www.bostonglobe.com/arts/2014/10/06/celebration-vonnegut-cape/RUegboNmUXBmi449E5TbJI/story.html.

563 Mark Vonnegut, *Just Like Someone*, 172.

564 Iowa Writers' Workshop, *Word by Word*, 40–41.

565 Vonnegut, *Man Without*, 66.

566 Vonnegut, *Palm Sunday*, chap. 11.

567 For a thorough investigation of this subject, see Ginger Strand, "How Jane Vonnegut Made Kurt Vonnegut a Writer," *New Yorker*, December 3, 2015.

568 Vonnegut, preface to *Monkey House*.

569 Vonnegut, *Palm Sunday*, chap. 19.

570 For some gorgeous insight on privacy and relationship, see these two articles: Joshua Rothman, "Virginia Woolf's Idea of Privacy," July 9, 2014, http://www.newyorker.com/books/joshua-rothman/virginia-woolfs-idea-of-privacy; and Alain de Botton, "The True Hard Work of Love and Relationships," *On Being*, August 2, 2018, http://onbeing.org/programs/alain-de-botton-the-true-hard-work-of-love-and-relationships/#.WKOB5sF-5Nvw.email.

571 Kurt Vonnegut, "Basic Training," in *What We Pretend*, chap. 4, 46.

572 Vonnegut, *Bluebeard*, chap. 20.

573 Vonnegut, *Galápagos*, book 2, chap. 5.

574 Vonnegut, *Hocus Pocus*, chap. 1.

575 Vonnegut, *Player Piano*, chap. 4.

576 Vonnegut, *Breakfast*, chap. 15.

577 Vonnegut, *Cat's Cradle*, chap. 93.

578 Vonnegut, *Galápagos*, book 1, chap. 14. For a gloriously humorous example of a discussion between a husband and wife ending up "like a fight between blindfolded people wearing roller skates," read chapter 18 in *Player Piano*.

579 Vonnegut, *Gapápagos*, book 1, chap. 14.

580 Vonnegut, *Mother Night*, chap. 9–10.

581 Vonnegut, *Fates*, chap. 16.

582 Vonnegut, *Bluebeard*, chap. 31.

583 Vonnegut, *Palm Sunday*, chap. 7.

584 Mark Vonnegut, *Just Like Someone*, 21.

585 Vonnegut, *Sirens*, epilogue.

586 Krementz, *Happy Birthday*, 156.

587 Vonnegut, *Wampeters*, 241.

588 Vonnegut, *Wampeters*, 242.

589 Vonnegut, *Wampeters*, 244.

590 Kurt Vonnegut, "The Last Interview," interview by Heather Augustyn, in *The Last Interview*, 166–67.

591 Vonnegut, *Fates*, chap. 4.

592 Lee Sandweiss, "Historic Vonnegut Cottage on Lake Maxinkuckee Saved from Demolition," *Herald-Times* (*Hoosier Times*), June 11, 2016, https://www.hoosiertimes.com/herald_times_online/life/at_home/historic-vonnegut-cottage-on-lake-maxinkuckee-saved-from-demolition/article_714e551a-8b26-59aa-947d-f36a2761ab40.html.

593 Vonnegut, *Wampeters*, 147–48.

594 Vonnegut, *Breakfast*, chap. 12.

595 Vonnegut, *Jailbird*, chap. 12.

596 Vonnegut, *Wampeters*, 247–48.

597 Vonnegut, *Slapstick*, chap. 33.

598 Vonnegut, *Slapstick*, chap. 33.

599 Vonnegut, *Jailbird*, chap. 8.

600 Vonnegut, *Slapstick*, chap. 32.

601 Vonnegut, *Palm Sunday*, chap. 7.

602 Vonnegut, *Wampeters*, 274.

603 Kathryn Schulz, "Call and Response," *New Yorker*, March 6, 2017.

604 Barb Darrow, "Turns Out Attendance at Women's March Events Was Bigger than Estimated," *Fortune*, July 23, 2017, http://fortune.com/2017/01/23/womens-march-crowd-estimates.

605 Vonnegut, *Fates*, chap. 2.

606 Vonnegut, *Wampeters*, 241.

607 Vonnegut, *Fates*, chap. 10.

608 Vonnegut, *Breakfast*, chap. 2.
      Check out these two quotes regarding community, one from Donald Trump Jr. about hunting and one from photographer Catherine Opie about belonging to an S/M group. Each acknowledges that the main value of the activity had or has to do primarily with the sense of being in a community.
      "What is lost on nonhunters, he [Donald Trump Jr.] said, is the sense of community that is part of hunting trips. 'Too much of hunting has turned into the notion of the kill,' he said. 'It's a component, the meat. But so much is experiential, so much is relationships. It is sitting in a duck blind with seven people, cooking breakfast. For me, it's been a great way to see the world. The least interesting part is the three seconds it takes to pull the trigger.'" Laura Holsen, "Donald Trump Jr. Is His Own Kind Of Trump, *New York Times*, March 18, 2017, https://www.nytimes.com/2017/03/18/style/donald-trump-jr-business-politics-hunting-twitter-vanessa-haydon.html.
      "Really, what Opie liked best about transgressive sex was the way it created a feeling of family. 'S/M was all about community for me,' she said one afternoon, sitting in her sunny kitchen in Los Angeles." Ariel Levy, "Catherine Opie, All-American Subversive," *New Yorker*, March 13, 2017, https://www.newyorker.com/magazine/2017/03/13/catherine-opie-all-american-subversive.

609 Vonnegut, *Hocus Pocus*, chap. 32.

610 Vonnegut, *Fates*, chap. 13.

611 Vonnegut, *Fates*, chap. 13.

612 Vonnegut, *Fates*, chap. 13.

613 Vonnegut, *Wampeters*, 248.

614 Vonnegut, "Who Am I This Time?," in *Monkey House*.

615 Vonnegut, *Cat's Cradle*, chap. 1.

616 Vonnegut, *Cat's Cradle*, chap. 42.

617 Vonnegut, *Cat's Cradle*, chap. 2.

618 Vonnegut, prologue to *Slapstick*.

619 Mark Vonnegut, *Just Like Someone*, 14.

620 Allen and Smith, "Having Enough," 279.

621 Vonnegut, *Letters*, 38–40.

622 Vonnegut, *Fates*, chap. 3.

623 See this article for more explanation: Kevin Kelly, "Scenius, or Communal Genius," *Technium* (blog), KK.org, June 10, 2008, http://kk.org/thetechnium/scenius-or-comm/.

624 Vonnegut and Stringer, *Like Shaking*, 48.

625 Rogers Cadenhead, "How to Join Kurt Vonnegut's Family," *Workbench* (blog), August 16, 2010, http://watchingthewatchers.org/read/3631.

626 The most heartening words I've ever received as a writer were from him. See letter in chap. 31.

627 Vonnegut, "Poems."

628 Vonnegut, *Cat's Cradle*, chap. 99.

KURT VONNEGUT was one of the few grandmasters of American literature, whose novels continue to influence new generations about the ways in which our imaginations can help us to live. Few aspects of his contribution have not been plumbed—fourteen novels, a collection of his speeches, essays, letters, a play—so this fresh self-portrait, written with the aid of a former student, is a bonanza for writers and readers everywhere.

Author, editor, and writing teacher SUZANNE MCCONNELL was a student of Kurt Vonnegut's at the Iowa Writers' Workshop from 1965 to 1967, when Vonnegut—along with Nelson Algren and other notable authors—was in residence and finishing his masterpiece, *Slaughterhouse-Five*. Vonnegut and McConnell became friends, and stayed so for the rest of his life. She has published short memoirs of him in the *Brooklyn Rail* and the *Writer's Digest*, and led a panel at the 2014 AWP conference titled "Vonnegut's Legacy: Writing About War and Other Debacles of the Human Condition." McConnell taught writing at Hunter College for thirty years, and she serves as the fiction editor of the *Bellevue Literary Review*. Twice nominated for the Pushcart Prize, her fiction also won first prize in the *New Ohio Review*'s 2015 Fiction Contest, first prize in *Prime Number Magazine*'s 2014 Awards for Flash Fiction, and second prize in *So to Speak*'s 2008 Fiction Contest. She lives in New York City and Wellfleet, Massachusetts, with her husband, the artist Gary Kuehn.

"Be merciless on yourself. If a sentence does not illuminate your subject in some new and useful way, scratch it out."

meant them to say. My teachers wished me to write accurately, always selecting the most effective words, and relating the words to one another unambiguously, rigidly, like parts of a machine. The teachers did not want to turn me into an Englishman after all. They hoped that I would become understandable – and therefore understood. And there went my dream of doing with words what Pablo Picasso did with paint or what any number of jazz idols did with music. If I broke all the rules of punctuation, had words mean whatever I wanted them to mean, and strung them together higgledy-piggledy, I would simply not be understood. So you, too, had better avoid Picasso-style or jazz-style writing, if you have something worth saying and wish to be understood.

Readers want our pages to look very much like pages they have seen before. Why? This is because

and employs a vocabulary as unornamental as a monkey wrench.

In some of the more remote hollows of Appalachia, children still grow up hearing songs and locutions of Elizabethan times. Yes, and many Americans grow up hearing a language other than English, or an English dialect a majority of Americans cannot understand.

So this discussion must finally acknowledge that our stylistic options as writers are neither numerous nor glamorous, since our readers are bound to be such imperfect artists. Our audience requires us to be sympathetic and patient teachers, ever willing to simplify and clarify – whereas we would rather soar high above the crowd, singing like nightingales.

That is the bad news. The good news is that we Americans are governed under a unique Constitution, which allows us to write whatever we please without fear of punishment. So the most meaningful aspect of our styles, which is what we choose to write about, is utterly unlimited.

8. For really detailed advice

For a discussion of literary style in a narrower sense, in a more technical sense, I commend to your attention *The Elements of Style*, by William Strunk, Jr., and E.B. White (Macmillan, 1979). — E.B. White's, of